Diversity in AMERICA

SECOND EDITION

TITLES OF RELATED INTEREST FROM PINE FORGE PRESS

Key Ideas in Sociology, Second Edition, by Peter Kivisto

Sociological Theory in the Classical Era: Text and Readings, by Laura D. Edles and Scott A. Appelrouth

The Social Theory of W. E. B. Du Bois, edited by Phil Zuckerman

Sociological Theory, by Bert N. Adams and R. A. Sydie

Classical Sociological Theory, by Bert N. Adams and R. A. Sydie

Contemporary Sociological Theory, by Bert N. Adams and R. A. Sydie

The Globalization of Nothing, by George Ritzer

Enchanting a Disenchanted World, Second Edition, by George Ritzer

McDonaldization: The Reader, edited by George Ritzer

Second Thoughts: Seeing Conventional Wisdom Through the Sociological Eye, Third Edition, by Janet M. Ruane and Karen A. Cerulo

Development and Social Change, Third Edition, by Philip McMichael

Investigating the Social World, Fourth Edition, by Russell K. Schutt

Race, Ethnicity, Gender, and Class: The Sociology of Group Conflict and Change, Third Edition, by Joseph F. Healey

Diversity and Society: Race, Ethnicity, and Gender, by Joseph F. Healey

Race, Ethnicity, and Gender: Selected Readings, edited by Joseph F. Healey and Eileen O'Brien

The Production of Reality: Essays and Readings on Social Interaction, Third Edition, by Jodi O'Brien and Peter Kollock

Sociology: Exploring The Architecture of Everyday Life, Fifth Edition, by David M. Newman

Sociology: Exploring the Architecture of Everyday Life, Readings, Fifth Edition, edited by David M. Newman and Jodi O'Brien

Diversity in
AMERICA
SECOND EDITION

Vincent N. Parrillo
William Paterson University

PINE FORGE PRESS
An Imprint of Sage Publications, Inc.
Thousand Oaks • London • New Delhi

For information:

Pine Forge Press
A Sage Publications Company
2455 Teller Road
Thousand Oaks, California 91320
E-mail: order@sagepub.com

Sage Publications Ltd.
1 Oliver's Yard
55 City Road
London EC1Y 1SP
United Kingdom

Sage Publications India Pvt. Ltd.
B-42, Panchsheel Enclave
Post Box 4109
New Delhi 110 017 India

Printed in the United States of America.

Library of Congress Cataloging-in-Publication Data

Parrillo, Vincent N.
Diversity in America / Vincent N. Parrillo.— 2nd ed.
    p. cm.
Includes bibliographical references and index.
ISBN 1-4129-1516-3 (pbk.)
    1. Pluralism (Social sciences)—United States—History. 2. United States—Race relations. 3. United States—Ethnic relations. I. Title.
E184.A1P329 2005
305.8'00973—dc22

                                                2004027614

This book is printed on acid-free paper.

05   06   07   08   09   10   9   8   7   6   5   4   3   2   1

Acquisitions Editor:	Jerry Westby
Editorial Assistant:	Laura K. Shigemitsu
Production Editor:	Tracy Alpern
Copy Editor:	Liann Lech
Typesetter:	C&M Digitals (P) Ltd.
Indexer:	Michael Ferreira
Cover Designer:	Michelle Lee Kenny

To my friends and acquaintances, both in the United States and abroad, for the enrichment their diversity has brought into my life.

Contents

About the Author xiii

Preface xv

1. Perception and Reality 1
  What This Book Is All About 3
  Seeing Is Believing, But Is It Knowing? 4
  The Cultural Homogeneity Myth 5
  The Rise, Fall, and Rise of Pluralism 6
    Early Advocates 6
    Assimilationists Prevail 7
    The Reassertion of Pluralism 7
    The Multiculturalist Challenge 8
  The Melting Pot 8
    Overstating Ethnic Intermarriages 9
    No Racial Minorities 9
    Emerson's Vision 10
    Turner's Frontier 10
    Zangwill's White Fusion 11
    Recent Studies on Intermarriage 12
  The Dillingham Flaw 12
    The Dillingham Commission 12
    The Concept of the Dillingham Flaw 14
    The Dillingham Flaw Chain Reaction 15
  Believing Is Seeing 16
  The Boundary Flaw 16
  Understanding Today by Knowing About Yesterday 17

2. Diversity in Aboriginal America 21
  Diversity in Language 22
    The Interdependence of Language and Culture 23
    Language and Social Reality 24
  Diversity in Gender Roles 24
    Division of Labor 24
    Status and Influence 25

Diversity in Clothing   26
   Northwestern Native Americans   27
   Southwestern Native Americans   27
   Northern Plains Native Americans   27
   Southeastern Native Americans   28
   Northeastern Native Americans   28
Diversity in Housing   29
   Large Communal Structures   29
   Single-Family Dwellings   32
Diversity in Social Organization   32
   Social Status Variations   33
   Northwestern Slavery   33
   Southeastern Caste Systems   34
   Iroquois Consensus-Building   34
   Diversity in Social Organization   35
Diversity in Values   35
The Next Horizon   36

3.   **Diversity in Colonial Times**   39
Colonial Beginnings   43
   A Patchwork Quilt of Ethnic Settlements   43
   Diversity in the Early Settlements   44
Geographic Variances in Diversity   45
   The New England Colonies   45
   The Middle Colonies   45
   The Southern Colonies   48
   African Diversity on the Plantations   48
   Three Regional Cultures   50
Religious Diversity   51
   Religious Intolerance   52
   The Great Awakening   53
   The Legacy of Religious Pluralism   54
A Kaleidoscope Society   54
   Minority Separatism   55
   The Multicultural Revolutionary Army   55
The Next Horizon   56

4.   **Diversity in the Early National Period** 59
Building a National Identity   61
   Arts and Letters   61
   Linguistic Independence   62
   Religious Independence   62
Social Structure and Social Class   63
Religion, Power, and Group Consciousness   64

Religion and Politics 64

Parallel Religious Institutions 65

The Nation's First Census 66

The Other Side of the Coin 67

Eurocentric Use of Census Data 68

Expanding Territory and Diversity 69

The Drop in Immigration 70

The Significance of Natural Population Growth 71

Emergence of a Common Culture 71

Decline of Foreign Languages 72

Antiforeign Responses 73

The False Horizon 74

5. **Diversity in the Age of Expansion** 77

Travelers Discover the Ethnic Mosaic 78

Tocqueville's Dismay at Racial Suffering 78

Martineau's Defense of Immigrants 79

Olmsted's Reaction to Isolated

Ethnic Communities 80

The French 80

America's "Flanders" 80

America's "Little Paris" 81

French Immigration 81

The Irish 82

America's First Ghetto People 82

Labor, Religion, and Politics 82

The Germans 83

The "German Athens" 84

German Diversity 84

Native Americans 85

Assimilation Efforts 85

"As Long as Grass Grows and Water Runs" 86

The End of Forever 87

The Africans 88

Southern Blacks 88

Northern Blacks 89

The Chinese 90

The Mexicans 91

Intergroup Conflicts 92

The Next Horizon 92

6. **Diversity in the Industrial Age** 95

Minority Family Economies 96

Population Diversity 97

African Americans 98
Asian Americans and Pacific Islanders 100
Hispanic Americans 101
Native Americans 102
Middle Eastern Americans 103
Northern and Western European Americans 104
Southern, Central, and Eastern European Americans 105
Intergroup Conflicts 107
The Next Horizon 108

7. **Diversity in the Information Age** **111**
The Human Element 112
 Unexpected Consequences 113
 A Different America 113
Institutionalizing Minority Rights 114
The Europeans 116
Asians and Pacific Islanders 116
Black Americans 119
Hispanic Americans 121
North Africans and Middle Easterners 124
Native Americans 124
Religious Diversity 125
The Next Horizon 126

8. **Intergenerational Comparisons** **129**
Why Are Voices Raised Against Immigration? 130
 Religious, Racial, and Cultural Biases 130
 Economic Competition 131
 The "Tipping Point" 131
 Today Isn't Yesterday, or Is It? 131
Immigration Rate 133
 Immigration Rate Caveats 134
Foreign-Born Population 135
Race in America 137
Mainstream Americans 139
 Mainstream American Caveats 141
 The "Wall" 143
Perception and Reality 144
Today's Patterns in Perspective 144

9. **Is Multiculturalism a Threat?** **147**
The Umbrellas of Multiculturalism 148
 The Inclusionists 149
 The Separatists 149
 The Integrative Pluralists 150

Roses and Thorns   152
The "Thorns" of Multiculturalism   152
    The "Immigrant Thorns"   153
    The "Language Thorns"   154
    The "Cultural Thorns"   155
    The "Racial Thorns"   156
The Roses of Multiculturalism   158
    The "Immigrant Roses"   158
    The "Language Roses"   158
    The "Cultural Roses"   161
    The "Racial Roses"   162
Is Multiculturalism the Enemy?   163

10. **Multiculturalism After 9/11**   **167**
Government Response   168
Public Response   169
Measuring Social Distance After 9/11   171
Have Attitudes Changed About Immigration?   173
What About Tomorrow?   174

11. **The Next Horizon**   **177**
The Dawning of a New Century   178
World Population Growth   179
U.S. Population Predictions   180
    The Alarm Bells Ring   182
    Resetting the Alarm   182
The Dillingham Flaw in Reverse   184
Factors Influencing Change   185
    Interethnic Marriages and
        Children of Mixed Ancestry   185
    Interracial Marriages and Biracial Children   186
The Challenge of Racial Diversity   187
Increased Religious Diversity   188
The Mainstreaming of Women   190
The Ever-Changing Mosaic   191

Index   **195**

About the Author

Vincent N. Parrillo is an internationally recognized expert in the field of immigration and multiculturalism. He has spoken on these subjects on numerous occasions throughout Canada, Europe, and the United States to government officials and to public and university audiences under the sponsorship of the U.S. Information Agency. A Fulbright scholar in 2000 in the Czech Republic, he was a scholar-in-residence at the University of Pisa in 1998. Listed in the *International Who's Who in Education* and a past recipient of the Outstanding Educator of America Award, Dr. Parrillo is Professor and Chair of the Department of Sociology at William Paterson University in Wayne, New Jersey. In 2004, his University honored him with its "Excellence in Scholarship Award." His writings have been translated into eight languages. Some of his recent books include *Strangers to These Shores* (7th ed.), *Cities and Urban Life* (3rd ed.), *Contemporary Social Problems* (6th ed.), and *Rethinking Today's Minorities*. He is also the writer and producer of the award-winning PBS documentary *Ellis Island: Gateway to America*.

Preface

This book is about race and ethnicity in the United States and the inter-action of gender relations within that context. Because of this special focus, my use of such terms as *diversity* and *multiculturalism* does not include sexual preference, the aged, or the physically challenged, as in other books on diversity with a wider perspective. Although this book examines the subject of multiculturalism, it is not a paean to either antiassimilationists or antipluralists. It is instead a moderate approach to a volatile subject with the goal of demonstrating that multiculturalism is neither a new social phenomenon nor a threat to U.S. society.

All of us know something about diversity in this country. We probably learned a little about it in our past, continue to bear witness to it in our pre-sent, and may hold expectations about it for the future. Yet although many extol the legacy of our immigrant heritage and/or lament the injustices of our race relations history, to many we seem to be on the brink of a societal unraveling. As in generations past, voices rise up against immigration, foreign language retention, "nonproductive" or "nonassimilating" racial/ethnic groups, and racial/ethnic leaders espousing separatist policies or actions. Similar concerns find expression in Australia, Canada, and Europe, where unprecedented migrations of diverse racial/cultural groups have also made an impact.

These responses were the catalyst for my originally writing this book. All of my discussions on the subjects of multiculturalism or diversity—with students and colleagues, government officials, the general public during my various lecture tours abroad for the U.S. Information Agency, or listeners and viewers when I appeared on numerous Canadian or U.S. radio/television call-in shows—played a role that impelled me to write this book. Between the arguments of voices advocating policies that challenge the dominant culture and those denouncing multiculturalism as a threat to society are, I believe, the ambivalent but concerned feelings of the vast majority.

As a sociologist aware of the patterns of dominant-minority relations, I wanted to dispel misconceptions about our past, misunderstandings about our present, and anxieties about our future that appear to be so prevalent. This book is written for the general reader, but rooted in the sociological perspective. It is thus an effort to look at U.S. diversity objectively, not with a revisionist or a special advocacy position.

Both pluralism and assimilation have been dual realities throughout the often-raucous history of intergroup relations in the United States. This book is an effort to show that, in many ways, what we witness today is a continuation of those dual processes, that the social dynamics we observe are not new, including the efforts of minority separatists and the outcries of alarmists. In fact, most Americans can find examples of the duality of pluralism and assimilation in their own family histories.

When my mother's Irish forebears came to the United States, for example, many native-born Americans looked on them and their compatriots with scorn and dismay. By then, the large presence of Irish Catholics had been a reality for a couple of generations, but other Americans remained convinced that this "inferior" group tainted the "purity" of the American character. Undaunted, the Irish persevered, overcoming religious bigotry and flagrant discrimination to become an integral part of American society.

Andrew Kohns, my maternal grandfather, typified the immigrant saga. The son of German immigrants who lived in Paterson, New Jersey, in the mid-19th century, he and thousands of other first- and second-generation Americans worked in the city's textile mills, and he eventually opened his own business. He became a political leader, and one of his greatest satisfactions as an American was personally escorting presidential candidate Woodrow Wilson to a major political rally in Paterson in 1912.

Andrew and Mary Kerr Kohns had 14 children, several of whom died young, and they also adopted three newly orphaned kin. Betty, my mother, was their second-youngest child and, as a beautiful woman, had many Irish American suitors. All of her older sisters married Irish Americans, each a successful middle-class businessman. But Betty, resisting family pressures to do likewise, broke the endogamy pattern when she married my father, Vince, a second-generation Italian American who was the second of three sons born to Nicola and Giovanna Infante Parrillo.

Like Betty's mother, his mother died when he was a youth. Nicola had been a highly respected Italian community leader and publisher of an Italian weekly newspaper before his death, but Vince's family background hardly impressed Betty's family. They were aghast at her even dating Vince, let alone marrying him, convinced that he and his family—in fact, all Italians—were beneath them. Although restrictive immigration laws a decade earlier had drastically reduced the flow of new arrivals from southern, central, and eastern Europe, these groups—particularly Italians and Jews—remained stigmatized as personifying all that was wrong with America. They had replaced the Irish as the subculture deemed "unassimilable." Betty, though, was an independent and open-minded person who rejected such prejudices.

Her job as school secretary in Paterson's North Ward brought her into daily contact with youngsters and parents from all backgrounds, so possibly this interaction helped break down some barriers. I think, though, that her acceptance of others was heavily augmented by a vacation in Cuba before she met my father. Her fascination with the Hispanic culture began there and was furthered by later visits with my father to the Caribbean, South America, and Spain.

The oldest of five children, I grew up exposed to more than just my dual cultural heritage. We lived on the northern edge of Paterson in a neighborhood that straddled a tightly knit Dutch community on one side and a mixed second-generation German/Italian/Polish neighborhood on the other. Not surprising, my boyhood pals were of all four backgrounds, as were my first dates.

My family lived nine blocks from the black neighborhood down the hill that, in my boyhood, I would often walk through, without incident, on my way to or from the movies downtown. When I reached Paterson Central High School—through classes, sports, and other extracurricular activities—my social world expanded to include many African American and Jewish students, along with many other second-generation White ethnic students.

As the years passed, this mixture of race and ethnicity among my closest companions continued and expanded as I moved through high school, college, and graduate school, and into academia. On my wedding day, my closest friend, an African American, served as best man in my marriage to Beth, a Scots-English Presbyterian. Dennis remains one of my best friends among others who are Czech, English, German, Greek, Irish, Italian, and Saudi Arabian; their religions are Christian, Greek Orthodox, Islamic, and Jewish. What is important here is not just that I have such diversity within my social circle, but that each of these persons has also welcomed me into his or her social circle as well.

In my lifetime, I first witnessed the influx of African Americans and Puerto Ricans into nearby urban areas, then the arrival of Korean, Cuban, and Vietnamese refugees, and thereafter the immigration of millions of Asians, Latinos, and Middle Easterners. Their difficulties in acculturating, their determination to succeed, and their struggles to gain acceptance are, in many ways, similar to those on both sides of my family in years long past. So, too, are the criticisms, social ostracism, and discrimination today's newcomers all too frequently encounter, although no one in my family suffered from the racism that many people of color still encounter today.

As an American of mixed ethnic heritage, my biography is far more representative than it is unique. Hundreds of millions of American biographies contain homogenizing/integrating elements across racial, religious, and ethnic lines. Often, these did not come about quickly or easily, but, taken together, they form an interwoven tapestry that is forever a tribute to the American spirit. Despite the isolationists and separatists, despite the radicals and reactionaries, despite the skeptics and pessimists, assimilation continues as a powerful social force, keeping alive the country's motto of *e pluribus unum* (from the many, one).

Witnessing the millions of Americans living in poverty, in cultural isolation, or out of the mainstream, one might reasonably argue that the preceding statement is too sweeping and ignores harsh reality. Yet the imperfections of U.S. society do not negate the social forces within it, nor the means its members have to accelerate the process. This book offers both a sociohistorical perspective and a sociological analysis to provide insights into U.S. diversity and into how the forces of pluralism are a necessary counterpart to the forces of assimilation.

This book is an updated, revised, and expanded version of the first edition, which was published in 1996. New to this edition are (a) a chapter on multiculturalism after 9/11; (b) commentary on the location of the United States within the world's geoculture in each era; (c) expanded discussion about Arabs, Asians, Hispanics, and Native Americans; and (d) expanded discussion on race relations and gender in our multicultural world.

I am especially grateful for the valuable comments and critiques from the reviewers, who helped shape this book into its final form. For the second edition, my thanks go to Kevin Delaney, Temple University; Lynn Hempel, Mississippi State University; Gonzalo Santos, California State Bakersfield; and Leigh A. Willis, University of Georgia. For the first edition, I thank Kevin Delaney again, as well as Ellen Rosengarten, Sinclair Community College; Susan Hoerbelt, University of South Florida; Peter Rose, Smith College; Raul Fernandez, University of California, Irvine; and Maura Toro-Morn, Illinois State University. Also providing some helpful suggestions for the first edition were Richard D. Alba, State University of New York–Albany; Charley Flint, Ronald Glassman, Geoffrey Pope, and Peter Stein, William Paterson University; and I thank them for their input.

I hope this book provides the reader with a greater understanding about our multicultural past and present. If so, perhaps more of us can break down the barriers of social distance that separate us, becoming more aware that diversity is not the problem. Intolerance by anyone—assimilationist, multiculturalist, or undeclared—is the problem we must fight.

Vincent N. Parrillo
William Paterson University
Wayne, NJ 07470
parrillov@wpunj.edu

Chapter Opening
Photo Credits

Chapter 1: Two Children Seated. National Photo Company Collection, Library of Congress photo ID: LC-USZ62-106966.

Chapter 2: Hopi Angel. Courtesy of the Edward S. Curtis Collection (Library of Congress). Library of Congress photo ID: LC-USZ62-41459.

Chapter 3: Portrait of a boy. Photographer: Frank W. Benson, 1896. Library of Congress photo ID: LC-D429-48225

Chapter 4: Cohit Songwi (Tewa girl). Courtesy of the Edward S. Curtis Collection (Library of Congress). Library of Congress photo ID: LC-USZ62-112220.

Chapter 5: Black boy near Cincinnati, Ohio. Photographer: John Vachon, 1914-1975. Library of Congress photo ID: LC-USF35-276.

Chapter 6: Children wearing velvet suits inspired by Little Lord Fauntleroy style. Library of Congress photo ID: LC-USZ62-67632.

Chapter 7: Louise Tami Nakamura, Manzanar Relocation Center, California. Photograph by Ansel Adams. Library of Congress photo ID: LC-A35-T01-4-M-20.

Chapter 8: Chinese woman with four children. C.M. Bell Studio Collection. Library of Congress photo ID: LC-USZ62-111879.

Chapter 9: Mexican girl who picks peas for the eastern market. Imperial Valley, California. Photographer: Dorothea Lange. Library of Congress photo ID: LC-USF34-019171-E.

Chapter 10: Daughter of Mexican field laborer. Near Chandler, Arizona. Photographer: Dorothea Lange. Library of Congress photo ID: LC-USF34-016792-C.

Chapter 11: Qahatika child. Edward S. Curtis Collection. Library of Congress photo ID: LC-USZ62-112213.

1

Perception and Reality

Emblazoned in virtually every individual's mind is the knowledge that the United States is a nation of immigrants. That realization—taught in our schools and reinforced in political speeches, particularly on the Fourth of July—serves as a source of nationalistic pride for all Americans, even those who trace their ancestry back to 17th-century colonists. The American Dream—that promise of freedom of choice, education, economic opportunity, upward mobility, and a better quality of life—inspires many to come here. It also serves as the underpinning for basic value orientations that are the foundation of American beliefs, behaviors, definitions of social goals, and life expectations.

Today, immigrants continue to arrive in pursuit of that dream, just as others have done for more than 200 years. Yet these newcomers frequently generate negative reactions among native-born Americans despite their common pride in belonging to a nation of immigrants. In all parts of the United States, we often find frequent expressions of fear, suspicion, anxiety, resentment, hostility, and even violence in response to the immigrant presence. Immigrants are not the only group triggering a backlash. African American and Native American assertiveness often provokes resistance. Challenges to the status quo by feminists and gay rights activists regularly induce adverse responses as well.

Why this contradiction? If Americans value their nation's immigrant heritage and ideals of equality and opportunity, why do they begrudge those traveling the same path to the same destination? Answers come readily from the critics. It's different now. When earlier immigrants came, they learned the language, worked hard, and became Americanized. We're getting too many immigrants now. They take away jobs from Americans. They drain our tax dollars through health and welfare benefits and schooling for their children. They don't want to assimilate or even learn English, and therefore present a threat of unraveling the fabric of our society. Too many people today are just lazy and want a handout. Too many want undeserved privileges at the expense of everyone else. They want the rewards without earning them.

Complaints by the citizenry in everyday conversations are partially fueled by the media or by public pronouncements from reactionaries and immigrant-bashers. Sometimes, though, even respected scholars are in the forefront. Noted historian Arthur M. Schlesinger, Jr., for example, denounced "the cult of ethnicity" (an insistence on maintaining vibrant ethnic subcultures) as a forerunner to the imminent "balkanization" of U.S. society.[1] His reference to the hostility that led to intense violence among Bosnians, Croats, and Serbs in the Balkan Peninsula is a scary one. No one wants U.S. society disintegrating into a collectivity of groups hostile to one another. Nor do they want the "snuffing out" or "shipwreck" of the American republic by new immigrants that English immigrant Peter Brimelow ironically warned us about with apocalyptic rhetoric in *Alien Nation*.[2]

Minority actions also reinforce nativist perceptions. The rhetoric of leaders from the National Council of *La Raza* and from the League of United Latin American Citizens (LULAC) for the maintenance of Spanish language and culture at public expense, in both the schools and the workplace, demonstrates to native-born Americans an unwillingness to assimilate.[3] The insistence of some African American leaders for slavery reparation payments to all Blacks enrages many Whites as an unreasonable demand. The "clannish" retail shopping patterns of Asian Americans and their noninvolvement in community activities annoy many local residents and merchants. News reports about militant actions, public mayhem, street crimes, and mob violence all trigger other negative reactions against minorities.

Once we talked about the United States as a melting pot. Now there is something called multiculturalism, which Schlesinger and others fear is undermining the cohesiveness of U.S. society.

What is happening? Are such instances illustrations of a different pattern emerging than in previous generations? Are we witnesses to a new social phenomenon? Is a flood of immigrants who do not wish to integrate overwhelming us? Are they and the people of color born in the United States pursuing separatist paths that will lead to the disuniting of our society? Is the land of *e pluribus unum* therefore disintegrating into *e pluribus plures* right before our very eyes, as Diane Ravitch warned?[4]

What This Book Is All About

These questions and issues reflect real concerns. They require responses that are more than subjective impressions of the current scene, for what people may think is happening is not necessarily what is actually occurring. This book is an attempt to provide those responses.

The famed Roman orator Cicero once remarked, "Not to know what happened before we were born is to remain perpetually a child." Just as children gaze with wonderment on new sights, so, too, can adults react to social phenomena as new and different unless they recognize these phenomena as variations of past patterns. It is my contention that the perception of many Americans is tainted because (a) they lack an accurate understanding of past American diversity, and (b) they fail to view contemporary events in a larger context.

A central thesis of this book is that multiculturalism has always been part of the American scene and is no more a threat to the cohesiveness of society today than at any time in the past. Rejecting claims that modern circumstances create a different situation than in the past, this book will show parallels, similarities, and continuities. It will also show instances when U.S. society was actually more multicultural than today.

Another central tenet of the book is that assimilation and pluralism are not mutually exclusive entities, nor are they necessarily enemies of one another. They have always existed simultaneously among different groups, at different levels. Whether they are persistent or multigenerational convergent subcultures, culturally distinct groups have always existed. Even when their numbers have been great, they never threatened the core culture. Assimilation remains a powerful force affecting most ethnic groups even though it has been less effective with racial minorities. While proponents of one position may decry the other, both pluralism and assimilation have always been dual realities within U.S. society.

The idea behind this book, then, is to place the current debate on immigration and multiculturalism in a proper sociohistorical perspective. Within a sociological context of social patterns and social change, the historical record of America's past and present cultural diversity will be presented. Included will be the factors of economic conditions, elitism, nativism, racism, social class biases, and the struggle for power that mitigate against harmonious intergroup relations.

The first half of this book contains a brief portrait of U.S. diversity through five eras: Colonial, Early National, Growth and Change, Industrial, and Information Ages. These chapters outline how cultural diversity has always been characteristic of U.S. society. They also show the continuity of various social patterns from one era to the next, down to the present.

Women, of course, have constantly been an integral part of the American experience, although their efforts often received little public attention until recent decades. Partly to compensate for that neglect, the period portraits in the following chapters will include information about women during these times. My intent is to emphasize more fully their gender experiences of status, power, and influence within a sociohistorical framework as a prelude to understanding today's feminism.

In these discussions of women, you will learn how their experiences varied greatly depending on their locale, social class, and length of residency in the United States. Indicators of how they fared compared to men will delineate gender diversity in terms of rights and power. Explanations about their social activism will also show a parallel to the militancy of other minority groups seeking equal treatment.

Seeing Is Believing, But Is It Knowing?

Some people believe what they see, but appearances can be deceptive, as are optical illusions or mirages. Magicians are human illusionists, and the good ones can stupefy us with their artful tricks on a grand scale. We know they tricked us, but we don't know how.

In everyday life, we think we know what we see, but here, too, we may be deceived. As Peter Berger once observed, "The first wisdom of sociology is this—things are not what they seem."[5] He was suggesting that social reality has many layers of meaning, and as you discover one layer, your perspective of the whole changes. So, perceptions, about diversity or anything else, change with increased knowledge. Seeing is not enough. You need to know what it is that you are seeing.

Complementary to Berger's statement is the aphorism "You can't see the forest for the trees." Its message is clear. When you are too close to the situation, you can't see the entire picture. You can't get a sense of the whole because you are caught up in small details. It is necessary to find a detached viewpoint if you are to comprehend what you see. (Later in this chapter, we will discuss the reverse problem of perception and reality, that believing is seeing.)

That detached viewpoint can be found in the sociological perspective, which provides, says Berger, "a special form of consciousness" (p. 23). It enables us to focus objectively on aspects of our social environment that may have previously escaped our notice, allowing us to interpret them in a different, meaningful way. If we add a historical frame of reference along with a sociological analysis to our study of diversity, we gain a valuable dimension to observe what continuities and changes are occurring.

The Cultural Homogeneity Myth

Diversity in America has been an ongoing social reality in the United States, not just since its inception as a nation, but even in its primeval colonial cradle. This viewpoint is not the prevalent one. The prevailing belief that this nation was essentially a culturally homogeneous launching pad for the new nation is steeped in the historic myth that the 13 colonies were almost entirely populated by English immigrants and their descendants. Such was not quite the case. As we shall see shortly, this "historic reality"—this fallacy of cultural homogeneity—changes under careful sociohistorical analysis.

That we are a nation of immigrants is an undeniable fact, but often not connected to the current multicultural picture. Contemporary public views on multiculturalism often assume erroneously that what occurred in the past were fleeting moments of heterogeneity that yielded to fairly rapid assimilation. Today's cultural diversity is misperceived as different, more widespread, and resistant to assimilation—something to be celebrated, respected, and maintained, say its proponents—thus making it, in the eyes of alarmed others, not only a new construction but somehow also a threat to the cohesiveness of society.

Only an objective analysis that peels away layers of myths, assumptions, presumptions, and misconceptions can provide an accurate assessment. To do so, we must take a sociohistorical perspective, moving beyond only present-day realities and noting instead long-term patterns throughout the nation's history. In this way, we can put the current scene in a wider context and determine more precisely how unique or not our situation is.

Before we can embark on this examination of our past and present, however, we must first address three areas that affect judgments about diversity in the United States. The first of these is the changing views about minority adaptation to U.S. society. Second is the melting pot concept and its limitations of application. Last, but extremely important, is the Dillingham Flaw, in which perceptions about immigrants can be misdirected through faulty comparisons.

The Rise, Fall, and Rise of Pluralism

Because the term is of recent vintage, many incorrectly conclude that multiculturalism is therefore a fairly new social phenomenon, the product of a changing world and of changing government policies. But as Nathan Glazer (1993) and Peter Rose (1993) correctly assert, "multiculturalism" is actually a refashioning of an older concept of cultural pluralism.[6]

Early Advocates

In the early 20th century, educator John Dewey and social worker Jane Addams both spoke out against assimilation destroying the cultural values of immigrants. In 1915, Horace Kallen, an immigrant from Eastern Europe, advocated this ideology in an essay in *Nation*; by citing the persistence of cultural identity among the Irish in Massachusetts, Norwegians in Minnesota, and Germans in Wisconsin, he promoted a multicultural society, a confederation of national cultures.[7] As Peter Rose puts it:

> To Kallen . . . the United States was not a fondue of amalgamation but a symphony of accommodation. Pushing his own metaphor, Kallen saw the orchestra—that is, the Society—as consisting of groups of instruments—nationalities—playing their separate parts while together making beautiful music resonant with harmony and good feeling.[8]

Kallen's ideas, expanded in his seminal work on cultural pluralism, *Culture and Democracy in the United States* (1924), contained only incidental references to racial groups.[9] Foreshadowing today's opponents to multiculturalism, part of Kallen's focus was on public concern that the recent arrivals of his time might not integrate fully into society.

Assimilationists Prevail

Despite the pluralist advocates, a chain of events encouraged assimilation over ethnic persistence. Patriotic hysteria following U.S. entrance into World War I effectively ended the German subculture. Restrictive immigration laws in the 1920s, a world depression in the 1930s, and World War II dramatically reduced immigration. With little new blood to keep everyday ethnicity viable, with the second generation growing up as Americans, and with the housing and education entitlements offered to GIs, White ethnics by midcentury had moved closer to the center, loosening their ethnic ties as they did.

As the old idea of America as a melting pot seemed to reaffirm itself, major books by sociologists Robert E. Park[10] and Milton M. Gordon[11] influenced social scientists to think more about assimilation than pluralism.

In *Race and Culture* (1950), Park offered a universal cycle theory suggesting that all groups go through a progressive, irreversible process of contact, competition, accommodation, and eventual assimilation. Park acknowledged that the process might take centuries, possibly even including a semipermanent racial caste system, but ultimately even racially subordinate groups would assimilate.

Gordon delineated, in *Assimilation in American Life* (1964), seven processes of group adaptation to the host society. Most important was his distinction between cultural and structural assimilation, showing how a group can change its cultural patterns but not yet mainstream into primary relationships in the cliques and associations of the society.

The Reassertion of Pluralism

Just as a series of social changes enabled assimilationists to prevail over the pluralists, a new set of circumstances reversed the situation. The civil rights movement of the 1960s and the White ethnic revival of the 1970s were precipitating factors. However, a major element was the third wave of immigration that began after the 1965 immigration law removed national quota restrictions, opening the door to millions of developing world immigrants.

Pluralism flourished at a time of peak immigration to the United States and ebbed when immigration declined. With a new influx of culturally distinct immigrants, it flowered again. Renamed multiculturalism, its advocacy of the preservation and appreciation of ethnic cultures and identities, as well as peaceful coexistence between groups, echoed the sentiments of Kallen, Addams, Dewey, and other cultural pluralists.

This time, however, the movement included people of color, not just White ethnics. Some arrived with a strong background that empowered them economically, allowing them to organize more effectively and assert themselves more so than past immigrants. Their ranks include educated, articulate spokespersons who used television and computerized direct mailings to reach millions of potential members whom their predecessors could not.

Yet even as pluralism gained new advocates, another influential sociological voice reaffirmed assimilationist patterns. In *The Ethnic Myth* (1981), Stephen Steinberg argued that pluralism only appeals to groups that benefit from maintaining ethnic boundaries.[12] Disadvantaged groups, he maintained, willingly compromise their ethnicity to gain economic security and social acceptance. Moreover, he claimed, the United States was closer than ever before to welding a national identity out of its mélange of ethnic groups.

The Multiculturalist Challenge

Nevertheless, with minority group assertiveness, massive immigration, and bilingual/pluralist government policies, the change in popular usage from "cultural pluralism" to "multiculturalism" helped suggest to some that a new era for social consciousness of diversity had arrived. To others, it signaled that the disuniting of America through "ethnic tribalism" was upon us. The battle was joined and still continues.

Multiculturalism is especially strong on college campuses, where the ranks of multiculturalists include many college professors whose advocacy in their teaching and publications has spread the doctrine far and wide to millions of others. They have challenged the once-prevailing idea of the United States as a melting pot, a concept many social scientists now regard as an idealized myth.

The Melting Pot

In an oft-quoted passage in *Letters from an American Farmer* (1782), Michel Guillaume Jean de Crèvecoeur, an immigrant to the United States from France, defined an American and popularized the concept of America as a melting pot:

> What is an American? He is either a European, or the descendant of a European; hence that strange mixture of blood which you will find in no other country. I could point out to you a man whose grandfather was an Englishman, whose wife was Dutch, whose son married a French woman, and whose present four sons have now four wives of different nations. . . . Here individuals of all nations are melted into a new race of men, whose labors and posterity will one day cause great changes in the world.[13]

Overstating Ethnic Intermarriages

Even if Crèvecoeur actually knew of such an exogamous family and did not invent it to illustrate his idealized concept of a melting pot, he was not accurately portraying the reality of his times. His would have been an atypical family in the late 18th century, because most White ethnics then did not intermarry. Ingroup solidarity—based on nationality, clustering, geographic separatism, and most especially religion—mitigated against personal social interaction among the distinct groups, let alone intermarriage.

When Crèvecoeur spoke of those English, Dutch, and French intermarriages, he was covering a considerable span of the 18th century and most likely including several religious faiths in a time when religious ecumenism was unknown. Religious tolerance may have slowly evolved out of a period of bigotry, close-mindedness, and intolerance just a few generations before, but that hardly meant that the ethnocentric barriers had vanished and amalgamation was flourishing.

No Racial Minorities

The greatest problem with Crèvecoeur's melting pot model is his omission of African and Native Americans.[14] Was this a reflection of his ethnocentrism, or a deliberate choice to augment his concept? Surely he was aware of their presence in significant numbers throughout the colonies. Perhaps he thought they were not relevant to the destiny of a nation struggling to be born.

Many shared this attitude. The framers of the Constitution, in Article I, Section 2, excluded "Indians" and counted each slave as three-fifths of a person to determine a state's representatives. In 1790, the First Congress passed the Naturalization Law, which limited citizenship only to free

White aliens. Until passage of the Fourteenth Amendment in 1868, people of color born in the United States were not citizens.

Crèvecoeur's melting pot model was not accurate for several reasons. By restricting its application only to those with political power (Whites), it excluded a sizable segment of the population (people of color). Thus, it did not describe a society that had "melted." Moreover, even in its narrow focus on Whites, the model ignored the existing cultural diversity and social distance existing among the diverse White groups.

Emerson's Vision

Crèvecoeur influenced others who helped popularize the image of the United States as a melting pot. Ralph Waldo Emerson, for example, struck a similar theme in 1845:

> Well, as in the old burning of the Temple at Corinth, by the melting and intermixture of silver and gold and other metals, a new compound more precious than any, called Corinthian brass, was formed; so in this continent—asylum of all nations—the energy of Irish, Swedes, Poles, and Cossacks, and all the European tribes—of the Africans, and of the Polynesians, will construct a new race, a new religion, a new state, a new literature, which will be as vigorous as the new Europe which came out of the smelting-pot of the Dark Ages, or that which earlier emerged from Pelasgic and Etruscan barbarism.[15]

Emerson's private journal entry is interesting for several reasons. He "hated" the "narrowness" of nativist reactions against immigrants as "precisely the opposite of true wisdom." Significantly, he included people of color (but not Native Americans!) in his vision of an amalgamated society, and it was a vision of the future, not a pretense about his times or of Crèvecoeur's time 63 years earlier. For Emerson, America as a melting or smelting pot was a tomorrow to come, not a reality that was.

Turner's Frontier

On the other hand, Frederick Jackson Turner saw the American frontier as the catalyst that had already fused the immigrants into a composite new national stock. His frontier thesis of 1893 followed the 1890 declaration of the Census Bureau that the "unsettled area has been so broken into . . . that there can hardly be said to be a frontier line."[16] Unlike Emerson's private musings known only to a few, Turner's update of Crèvecoeur's melting pot greatly influenced historical scholarship for more than 40 years.

Thus the Middle West was teaching the lesson of national cross-fertilization instead of national enmities, the possibility of a newer and richer civilization, not by preserving unmodified or isolated the old component elements, but by breaking down the line-fences, by merging the individual life in the common product—a new product, which held the promise of world brotherhood.[17]

The above quotation is taken from Turner's 1920 book, *The Frontier in American History,* where he expanded on his 1893 essay. He argued that, because pioneers confronted many problems and harsh conditions, their adaptation necessitated innovative solutions that they shared with others. Out of this mutual assistance evolved a new and distinct culture, a blend of shared cultural contributions but noticeably different from any of their source cultures.

Turner's argument popularized further the romanticized notion of a melting pot, but it also did not accurately reflect frontier reality any more than Crèvecoeur had depicted his times. The pioneers did adapt to their new environment, but the culture remained Anglo-American in form and content. Furthermore, in many areas of the Middle West that Turner speaks about, culturally homogeneous settlements of Germans or Scandinavians, for example, often maintained distinct ethnic subcultures for generations.

Zangwill's White Fusion

Another voice raised in support of the melting pot was Israel Zangwill in a 1908 play appropriately called *The Melting Pot.* Some of its oft-quoted lines are these:

Ah, what a stirring and a seething—Celt and Latin, Slav and Teuton, Greek and Syrian. America is God's Crucible, the Great Melting Pot where all the races of Europe are melting and reforming!

. . . Germans and Frenchmen, Irishmen and English, Jews and Russians, into the Crucible with you all! God is making the American!

. . . the Real American has not yet arrived. . . . He will be the fusion of all races, perhaps the coming superman.[18]

The term *race* once referred more loosely to either racial or ethnic groups. So, Zangwill appears to mean only White ethnic groups in the melting or fusion of all races when he speaks of the "races of Europe" and excludes any specific example of people of color. Even though he curiously includes Syrians as Europeans, Zangwill's words nonetheless echo those of Crèvecoeur in describing the melting pot as a White ethnic phenomenon, thereby implying that an "American" is a White person.

Recent Studies on Intermarriage

The White ethnic intermarriage that Crèvecoeur prematurely asserted as evidence of his melting pot is now a reality. Alba (1991) reported that only half as many third-generation Italians of unmixed ancestry born after 1949 had spouses of unmixed Italian ancestry compared to third-generation Italian males born before 1920.[19] Lieberson and Waters (1988) found significant declines in endogamous marriages among virtually all White groups.[20]

Although such intermarriage patterns provide support for melting pot proponents, they do not necessarily indicate assimilation. As Lisa Neidert and Reynolds Farley (1985) reported, third-generation members of second-wave ethnic groups were not indistinguishable from the core English group, although they had been successful in their occupational achievements.[21] That is, they remained distinct, and a considerable social distance existed between them and mainstream society. Furthermore, within-group marriages are still fairly common among people of unmixed ethnic ancestry.

When race and culture are similar, marital assimilation is more likely. If the past patterns of 19th- and 20th-century White Americans are an indicator, however, this process may require three or more generations to blend together the post-1965 ethnic groups.

The Dillingham Flaw

The continuing debate between assimilationists and pluralists revolves around the issue of cultural homogeneity. Part of those polemics often contain what I identify as the *Dillingham Flaw,* an erroneous way of comparing people from one time period with people living in the present. As a consequence, one group usually suffers in the comparison and is judged negatively.

The Dillingham Commission

Sen. William P. Dillingham of Vermont chaired the House-Senate Commission on Immigration (1907–1911), which listened to the testimony of civic leaders, educators, social scientists, and social workers. It even made on-site visits to Ellis Island and New York's Lower East Side, where hundreds of thousands of impoverished immigrants lived. When its investigation was completed, the Commission issued a 41-volume report, part of which was based on social science research and statistics.

Unfortunately, the report was flawed in its application and interpretation of the data. It was more than the fact that the Commission members, however well-intentioned they may have been, reflected the perceptions and biases of their times. The Dillingham Commission committed several errors of judgment that led them to conclude that the immigration from southern, central, and eastern Europe was detrimental to U.S. society. Their conclusion led them to recommend the enactment of immigration restrictions.

The Commission erred in its use of simplistic categories and unfair comparisons of the "old" and "new" immigrants, thus ignoring differences of technological evolution in their countries of origin. It also erred in overlooking the longer time interval that immigrants from northern and western Europe had to adjust, as well as the changed structural conditions wrought by industrialization and urbanization.

No doubt influencing the Commission members were the highly reported intelligence test findings. By 1908, Alfred Binet and Thomas Simon had developed the intelligence quotient (IQ) measurement scale. Using an alpha test (for those literate in English) and a beta test (for those illiterate or non-English-speaking), the low scores of newly arriving southern, central, and eastern Europeans, in contrast to higher scores by native-born Black and White Americans, seemingly gave scientific evidence that mentally deficient ethnic groups were entering the United States.

Although many social scientists today recognize that cultural biases affected those outcomes, controversy continues about whether intelligence measures reveal genetic or environmental differences. This "nature versus nurture" issue boiled over in the 1960s with the writings of Arthur Jensen and William Shockley, and again in 1994 with the publication of *The Bell Curve* by Richard Herrnstein and Charles Murray. Each of these writers argued that genetic differences existed between Black and White Americans, a point fiercely contested by many others.

Back in 1911, however, these test results were unquestioned and were just one more aspect to convince Commission members about the rightness of their views. The social conditions in 1911 help explain how such flawed conclusions were accepted so easily. President Theodore Roosevelt had called for the Commission to address the "immigrant problem," thereby creating a mind-set about the situation in the first place. Both he and the Commission reflected the biases and perceptions of most native-born Americans witnessing the unprecedented mass influx of immigrants who were culturally, and often physically, different. The Commission's findings reinforced public opinion and were therefore readily accepted.

The Concept of the Dillingham Flaw

In our society, similar errors of thinking also influence people's perceptions of outgroup members. An outgroup is any group with which an individual does not identify or belong. In our discussion, we are referring to the foreign born as the outgroup to native-born Americans of different backgrounds.

Because some of today's negative judgments flow from the same faulty logic as that of the Dillingham Commission, I call this weakness the *Dillingham Flaw*. Quite simply, this term refers to inaccurate comparisons based on simplistic categorizations and anachronistic observations. We make these comparisons when we apply modern classifications or sensibilities to a time when they did not exist, or, if they did, they had a different form or meaning. To avoid the Dillingham Flaw, we must avoid the use of modern perceptions to explain a past that its contemporaries viewed quite differently.

One example of an inappropriate modern classification would be the term *British* to describe colonial Americans from the British Isles. Today, this word refers collectively to the people of Great Britain (the English, Welsh, Scots, and Scots-Irish). However, in the 18th century, *British* had the much narrower meaning of only the English, and for good reason. The English, Scots, and Scots-Irish may have been English-speaking, but significant cultural and religious differences existed among them. Moreover, the geographic segregation, social distance, and even hostility that existed between English Anglicans and Scots-Irish Presbyterians created a wide cultural gulf between them. They did not view each other as "similar."

Among the English themselves, divergent religious beliefs created various subcultures whose shared sense of identity, social insulation, and endogamy resulted in limited social interaction. *Ecumenicism,* the tendency toward greater Christian unity that is occurring in our times, is a far cry from the antipathy among the Protestant sects of colonial America. A meaningful component of everyday life in the 18th century, religion was cause for outgroup prejudice and avoidance, and we must not overlook its significant impact on intergroup relations. It would be a mistake to presume the English were a single, cohesive entity.

It is also misleading to speak broadly of either African slaves or Native Americans as single entities. In a period of White dominance and racial exploitation, ethnocentric generalizations such as these failed to pay heed to the fact that these groups consisted of diverse peoples with distinctive cultures. Similarly, European immigrants were not alike, despite their collective grouping by mainstream society. Instead, all of these groups—African American, Native American, and immigrant—were diverse peoples with linguistic and cultural distinctions that set them apart from one another.

The Dillingham Flaw Chain Reaction

Once someone falls victim to the Dillingham Flaw, other misconceptions usually follow about one's own time. This is to be expected. Such victims falsely believe that they understand their nation's past and so confidently assess their own world in what they presume is a wider context. Certain they have a knowledgeable, objective frame of reference, they tend to be highly critical of the present scene because they perceive it as different from the past.

However, because their observations and reactions are predicated on a reference point rendered inaccurate by the Dillingham Flaw, they will be more likely to reach incorrect conclusions. Like that old congressional commission, they will be susceptible to mistaken impressions about a "threat" posed by recent immigrants whose presence and behavior they view as different from past immigrants.

For instance, some people suggest that today's steadily increasing ranks of Asians, Hispanics, and Muslims present an unprecedented challenge to an integrative society. The undercurrent of this thinking includes the continuing large numbers of new arrivals, their racial group membership and/or non-Judeo-Christian background, and their alleged nonassimilationist patterns.

Such concerns and fears are echoes of those raised about earlier groups, such as the racist responses to the physical appearance of southern Europeans or the anti-Semitic reactions to eastern European Jews. Or, consider the petition to Congress by 19th-century Germans in the Northwest Territory to create a German state with German as the official language; it easily matches the fear of some nativists that Florida may become "America's Quebec."

Believing Is Seeing

In writing about the improper use of biology as ideology to justify the "naturalness" of gendered behavior and social statuses, Judith Lorber (1993) informed us that the way we think about a particular social phenomenon affects what we actually see, or at least think we see.[22] The actions of the Dillingham Commission and the politics of those times are another illustration of this concept. When we feel most threatened by outsiders who are different because of their religion, skin color, or social class, we may see different things in the current immigration (they are a threat because there are too many of them and/or they "fail" to assimilate) rather than see other things (ourselves, our ancestors, past generations of immigrants, new workers, new consumers, new taxpayers, human capital to fuel our economic growth).

In other words, the two major themes of this book are interconnected. The political controversies swirling around the assimilation/pluralism debates affect how people think about and react to diversity in society at any given time. Thus, the influence of beliefs on perceptions and reactions is an important element in understanding why some groups or issues become problematic and others do not.

The Boundary Flaw

With the oldest democratic constitution among all nations, and its centuries-old experience of accepting tens of millions of immigrants from all parts of this planet, the United States certainly offers a rich reservoir of history, social change, and patterns of intergroup relations. Furthermore, it was the first to offer the promise of freedom and opportunity to one and all, while showing the rest of the world its willingness to accept and include foreigners within its societal mainstream. Yet however special many of these elements may have been, they did not occur in a global vacuum. A second flaw we must thus avoid is the *boundary flaw,* the assumption that we can explain everything solely in the context of internal social dynamics unique to American culture.[23]

Virtually nothing has ever occurred in the United States that was self-contained or universal within its borders. In the early stages of its sociocultural evolution, when it was a minor player on the world stage and there was no such entity yet as a global community, regional—even local—cultural differences abounded. In the sociocultural epochs described in the next six chapters, the United States went through changing positions in the world order even as it was buffeted by external social forces that affected its citizens' sense of self and perceptions of demographic and technological changes.

This interplay of regional, national, and global forces often generated tensions as cultural and social changes occurred and new migration patterns emerged. Part of the explanation for the dualities of, and conflicts between, assimilation and pluralism trends lies in recognizing this process. In each of the following chapters, then, we will attempt to identify the place of the United States in the world system as a key referent to understanding more fully the developing themes of this book.

Understanding Today by Knowing About Yesterday

Understanding the sociohistorical reality of the diversity of America's past allows for a more accurate comparison with today's multicultural society without falling victim to either the Dillingham Flaw or the Boundary Flaw. In this way, we can avoid those flaws and debunk the cultural homogeneity myth. It is essential to know truly what we were if we are to comprehend what we are now and what we are becoming.

Telecommunications today enable each of us to bear witness to many aspects of our multicultural society, but our knowledge about our nation's past comes to us chiefly through the words of others whose ethnocentric perceptions often hid from us what truly was that reality. Although rarely presented in the comprehensive form found in this book, enough data exist to peel away the layers of nationalist myth-building to get at the sociocultural actualities about our multicultural past.

What follows is not an exercise in revisionist thought, but a sociohistorical analysis of the past and present. Hopefully, this book provides the perspective that diversity is America's strength, not its weakness.

Notes

1. Arthur M. Schlesinger, Jr., *The Disuniting of America: Reflections on a Multicultural Society* (Knoxville, TN: Whittle Communications, 1991).

2. Peter Brimelow, *Alien Nation: Common Sense About America's Immigration Disaster* (New York: Random House, 1995).

3. Hispanic leaders' views on language maintenance appear in Linda Chavez, "Hispanics vs. Their Leaders," *Commentary* (October 1991): 47–9.

4. Diane Ravitch's much-discussed views appeared in her article "Multiculturalism: E Pluribus Plures," *American Scholar,* 59 (1990): 337–54.

5. Peter Berger's thoughts are expressed in his wonderful sociological primer, *Invitation to Sociology* (Garden City, NY: Doubleday, 1963), 23. Another classic on perception and reality is Peter L. Berger and Thomas Luckmann, *The Social Construction of Reality* (New York: Doubleday, 1966).

6. The comparison of multiculturalism and cultural pluralism by Nathan Glazer and Peter Rose appeared in the special issue edited by Peter I. Rose, "Interminority Affairs in the U.S.: Pluralism at the Crossroads," *The Annals of the American Academy of Political and Social Science,* 530 (1993). The two articles are Nathan Glazer, "Is Assimilation Dead?" 122–36; Peter I. Rose, "Of Every Hue and Caste," 187–202.

7. Horace Kallen, "Democracy versus the Melting Pot," *Nation,* February 18, 1915, pp. 190–4, and February 25, 1915, pp. 217–20.

8. Peter Rose, "Of Every Hue and Caste," *The Annals of the American Academy of Political and Social Science,* 530 (1993): 193.

9. Horace Kallen, *Culture and Democracy in the United States* (New York: Boni and Liveright, 1924).

10. The posthumous publication of Robert E. Park's writings is *Race and Culture: Essays in the Sociology of Contemporary Man* (New York: Free Press, 1950).

11. Milton Gordon's seminal work on assimilation is *Assimilation in American Life* (New York: Oxford University Press, 1964).

12. Stephen Steinberg, *The Ethnic Myth* (New York: Atheneum, 1981).

13. Crèvecoeur's famous statement appears in *Letters from an American Farmer* (1782; reprint, New York: Alert and Charles Boni, 1925), 54–5.

14. Observations about Crèvecoeur's omission of racial minorities first appeared in Vincent N. Parrillo, *Strangers to These Shores* (Boston: Houghton Mifflin, 1980), 98, and then in all subsequent editions; Nathan Glazer's "Is Assimilation Dead?" *The Annals of the American Academy of Political and Social Science,* 530 (1993): 124.

15. Emerson's recorded thoughts appear in *The Journals and Miscellaneous Notebooks of Ralph Waldo Emerson,* ed. Ralph H. Orth and Alfred K. Ferguson (Cambridge, MA: Belknap, 1971), 9:299–300.

16. James A. Henretta et al., *America's History Since 1865* (Homewood, IL: Dorsey Press, 1987), 588.

17. Frederick Jackson Turner, *The Frontier in American History* (New York: Henry Holt, 1920), chap. xiii.

18. Israel Zangwill, *The Melting Pot: Drama in Four Acts* (New York: Macmillan, 1921), 33.

19. The intermarriage findings of Richard D. Alba are reported in "The Twilight of Ethnicity Among Americans of European Ancestry: The Case of the Italians," *Rethinking Today's Minorities,* ed. Vincent N. Parrillo (Westport, CT: Greenwood Press, 1991), 29–62.

20. The study by Stanley Lieberson and Mary C. Waters is *From Many Strands* (New York: Russell Sage Foundation, 1988).

21. Lisa Neidert and Reynolds Farley, "Assimilation in the United States: An Analysis of Ethnic and Generation Differences in Status and Achievement," *American Sociological Review,* 50 (1985): 840–50.

22. Judith Lorber, "Believing is Seeing: Biology as Ideology," *Gender & Society*, 7 (1993): 568–81.

23. I am indebted to Gonzalo Santos for suggesting this concept.

2

Diversity in Aboriginal America

Multiculturalism flourished in the land for centuries before Europeans ever set foot on its soil. Although students in an anthropology course on Native Americans learn that fact quickly, most Americans are typically caught in the Dillingham Flaw when thinking about these diverse peoples. For many, the image of Native Americans is a stereotypical generalization of tipis, buffalo, warriors on horseback, warpaint, feathers, moccasins, and either brutish savages depicted in countless Westerns or romanticized noble primitives, as depicted in the film *Dances With Wolves* (1990).

Such a simplistic misconception is easy to understand. Those early explorers, missionaries, traders, soldiers, colonial officials, and settlers were untrained observers who generalized about the various tribes as if they were a single entity. Reflecting both ethnocentric judgments and racial prejudice, most Whites saw little value in learning about the cultural differences among the tribes. Their concerns rested primarily on conquest, expansion, profit, survival, and their own welfare. Whites tended to view "Indians" more as an obstacle to their own goals than as a people of equal importance worthy of understanding, not exploitation.

In modern times, most films have also offered simplistic portrayals, stamping in the average moviegoer's mind a picture of the nomadic Plains Indians on horseback as representative of all tribes. However, the indigenous peoples have always been far more diversified than these simplistic portrayals. Cultural pluralism was the ongoing reality before the Europeans arrived, although those who became members of other tribes— usually through capture by raiding parties—typically assimilated into the culture of their new tribe.

Yet even as the many tribes experienced differentiated sociocultural evolutions for centuries before European contact, they also encountered certain outside influences through contact with other aboriginal societies. Migrations and trade led to a gradual cultural diffusion that altered certain ways of life, most significantly through domestication of the plant, but also in adaptation of other values and practices that intrigued the tribes. Thus, even as local and regional cultures retained unique characteristics because of their relative isolation and adaptation to their environment, they were not immune to certain hegemonic trends on the continent.

To offer a detailed account of the many aspects of Native American diversity would require an entire book much larger than this one.[1] In the pages that follow, then, is only a brief overview to provide the reader with at least some sense of the multiculturalism present in precolonial America.[2]

Diversity in Language

Before European colonization, somewhere between 2 and possibly 10 million aboriginals, divided into about 200 or more distinct societies, spoke approximately 200 mutually unintelligible languages, along with hundreds of dialects. The reasons these languages were so incomprehensible among the tribes were the many variances in phonetics, speech sounds, and grammatical structure.

In their expedition to chart the northern section of the Louisiana territory (1804–1806), Capt. Meriwether Lewis and Lt. William Clark repeatedly commented in their journals about the phonetic differences among the languages of the various Native American peoples they met. As the explorers traveled from tribe to tribe across the North American continent, they observed how some of the tongues sounded harsh and guttural, whereas others were liquid and melodious.[3]

The Interdependence of Language and Culture

The significance of these many Native American languages is the mutual interdependence of language and culture. Whereas a culture's language expresses how that society perceives and understands the world, the language itself influences that society's perceptions and understandings. This concept was effectively argued two generations ago by Edward Sapir and Benjamin Whorf, pioneers in American linguistics. They contended that human beings live in a social reality that is at the mercy of their language. The so-called real world is, to a large extent, subconsciously built up on the group's language habits. Because no two languages are ever sufficiently similar to represent the same social reality, they reasoned, the worlds in which different societies live are distinct worlds, and not merely the same world with different labels attached.

For example, in 1929, Sapir explained that the Hopi in the Southwest use verbs that have no tense—no past, present, or future.[4] Instead, their verbs differ depending on such factors as the relative length of time an event lasts, its completion or expected occurrence, and its regularity or predictability of occurrence. The Hopi focus on the recurring cycles of life, rather than viewing their reality as a segmented series of events locked into a time frame.

Another example is the Yana of California, who have both masculine and feminine forms of most words, the former used only in all-male conversations and the latter in male-female or all-female conversations. The language of another tribe, the Navajo, does not distinguish among such third-person pronouns as "his," "her," "its," or "their," and instead uses a compound word of adjectives and nouns such as "one-wife-of-one-man" to indicate "his wife."

These examples are just small indicators of the significant differences in grammatical structures among Native American languages. The many languages of the indigenous people are not a single entity with 200 minor variations. Their differences are far too complex and reflect the different worlds of the many diverse tribes.

Language and Social Reality

The prevalence of 200 distinct languages is one dimension of the multicultural reality of pre-Columbian America. Just as we view White ethnic groups speaking different languages as distinct from one another, so, too, must we look upon the many Native American tribes as diverse entities. Speaking in different tongues, they constituted a mosaic of separate worlds, each aware of neighboring tribes but nonetheless dissimilar in language.

We begin to overcome any Dillingham Flaw simplistic judgments by recognizing further that the interdependent relationship of language with culture results in a social reality for tribal members that sets them culturally apart from another tribe that is linguistically different. Although it may take a skilled linguist to understand the diversity among these 200-plus languages, social observers can distinguish other cultural attributes more easily, as we shall now discuss.

Diversity in Gender Roles

In matrilineal and matrilocal societies, women had considerable power because property (housing, land, and tools) belonged to them. Because property usually passed from mother to daughter, and the husband joined his wife's family, he was more the stranger and yielded authority to his wife's eldest brother. As a result, the husband was unlikely to become an authoritative, domineering figure. Moreover, among such peoples as the Cherokee, Iroquois, Pueblo, and Navajo, a disgruntled wife, secure in her possessions, could simply divorce her husband by tossing his belongings out of their residence.

Women's role in tribal governance was often influential in matrilineal societies, as among the Iroquois, where the principal civil and religious offices were kept within maternal lineages. The tribal matriarch or a group of tribal matrons nominated each delegate, briefed him before each session, monitored his legislative record, and removed him from office if his conduct displeased the women. Despite the feminine checks and balances, the actual business of government was a masculine affair.

Division of Labor

In the Northeastern Woodlands and on the Plains, where hunting and warfare demanded strenuous activity away from home, the men often returned exhausted and required a few days to recover. Wearied by both these arduous actions and the religious fasting that usually accompanied them, the men relaxed in the village while the women went about their many tasks. Seeing only female busyness in these native encampments, White observers misinterpreted what they saw and wrote inaccurate stereotypical portrayals of lazy braves and industrious squaws. Such was not the case.

In the Southeast and Southwest, men and women performed their daily labors with observable equality because the men did not go out on grueling expeditions as did the men in the Northeast and Plains. In California, the Great Basin, and the Northwest Coast, the sexual division of labor fell somewhere between these two variations.

Women had certain common tasks in each of the U.S. culture areas: cleaning and maintaining the living quarters, tending to children, gathering edible plants, pounding corn into meal, extracting oil from acorns and nuts, cooking, sewing, packing, and unpacking. Certain crafts were also usually their responsibility: weaving such items as cloth, baskets, and mats; brewing dyes; and making pottery. In the Southwest, however, men sometimes made baskets and pottery, and even wove cloth.

In regions where hunting provided the main food supply, the women were also responsible for house building, processing carcasses of game, preparing hides or furs, and whatever food gathering or farming that could be done. In the mostly agricultural societies in the East, the women primarily worked in the fields and the men built the frame houses, as both shared duties for preparing hides or furs. Similarly, in the fishing communities of the Northwest, the men built the plank houses and helped with the processing of animal skins. In California and the Great Basin, most aspects of labor, except the defined female tasks of weaving and basket and pottery making, were fairly evenly shared. In the Southwest, the men did most of the field work, house building, weaving, cloth manufacture, and animal skin processing.

Status and Influence

Female prestige among the Iroquois grew greater after the Revolutionary War, as male prestige ebbed as a result of continual defeats and the men's inability to do much hunting because of scarcity of game. By the 19th century, mothers played a greater role in approving marriage partners for their children and more consistently got custody of their children in a divorce, unlike the uncertainty of custody in earlier times.

Among many southeastern tribes, the women were influential in tribal councils, and in some places, they cast the deciding vote for war or peace. The Cherokee designated a female as "Beloved Woman," through whom they believed the Great Spirit spoke. Consequently, her words were always heard, but not necessarily heeded. However, she headed the influential Woman's Council, made up of a representative from each clan, and sat as a voting member of the Council of Chiefs, where she exercised considerable influence. She also held absolute authority over prisoners, and when she died, a successor would be chosen.

The Cheyenne also held women in particularly high regard. They played an influential role in determining warfare and sometimes even fought alongside the men. A woman's display of grief over a slain son was an effective arousal for a punitive expedition. On a war party's successful return, the women danced about while waving the scalps, exhibited their men's shields and weapons, and derived honors from their husbands' deeds.

The statuses and roles for men and women thus varied considerably among Native Americans, depending on each tribe's cultural orientations. Property possession, inheritance, power, and influence rested on whether a tribe's structure was matrilineal or patrilineal. Although a few universal female-designated work tasks existed (cleaning, nurturing, edible plant gathering, food preparation, cooking, packing, and unpacking), others varied by region, means of food production, and social organization. Such variances in gender roles further exemplify the diversity that existed among Native Americans.

Diversity in Clothing

Choice of clothing was in large measure dependent on geographical environment and the materials available from which to make them. Although all tribes fashioned clothing from hides and fur, these were less available to tribes primarily dependent on agriculture or seafood products, so they tended to make more clothing from plant materials, unlike the tribes who mainly hunted. Yet even among tribes using similar materials, a wide variety of styles could be found.

Generally speaking, the men plucked their facial and body hair, typically using shells as tweezers. Both women and men wore necklaces and earrings made of shells, claws, teeth, beads, or precious stones. Otherwise, great variance in clothing and bodily adornment could be found.

Northwestern Native Americans

Because cedar trees abound along the Pacific Northwest coast, tribes twisted strips of inner bark into string and wove this into clothing. In summer, the men usually went naked, but sometimes wore tunics; in winter and on ceremonial occasions, they wore a knee-length robe made of animal skins (especially otter) or of woven plant fiber. If traveling to the interior, they wore leggings and moccasins.

Women were always clothed, usually with a plant fiber skirt and a woven robe over both shoulders covering the upper body. Frequent rainy weather occasioned the wearing of conical hats of woven plant fiber and waterproof ponchos of the same material. Both men and women wore tattooed family crests and other designs on their face, chest, back of arms, or front of legs. On festive occasions both sexes applied red, white, and black paints to their bodies.

Southwestern Native Americans

The Pueblo of Arizona and New Mexico and their Anasazi ancestors were unique in wearing mostly cotton garments. Women's dresses were rectangular cloths worn under the left arm and tied above the right shoulder, the open right side of the dress kept fastened by a belt of the same material. Buckskin leggings were wrapped around lower legs, and the buckskin moccasins had buffalo hide soles.

Men wore a cotton loincloth, its ends held in place by a belt. Over this, they wore a kilt that came to midthigh, set off by a sash of braided cotton cords around the top of the kilt and hanging down one side. Sometimes, they wore shirts tied at the sides, with flaps for sleeves. Moccasins also had the stiff buffalo hide for soles sewn to buckskin that covered the ankle or else went halfway to the knee. Cold weather prompted the wearing of woven rabbit fur blankets or a cape of feathers fastened to a netted base. Interestingly, the men wore more jewelry than the women. Both sexes styled their hair the same: bangs just above the eyes, below the ears on the sides, and full length in back.

Northern Plains Native Americans

As elsewhere, the women of the Northern Plains wore more clothing than the men. Their dresses, midcalf in length and fringed at the bottom, were made of two deer or elk hides sewn together. Below-knee leggings and moccasins completed their outfit. The men often wore only moccasins and a breechcloth, adding leggings tied to a belt when they traveled. A buckskin shirt with sleeve flaps was worn only on special occasions or in cold weather, as was a buffalo robe. Women sometimes wore such robes also, and they could be pulled over the head in bitter weather. Otherwise, a fur cap might be worn.

Plains natives often made their clothing more elaborate by ornamenting the material with quills and/or beads. Both sexes seldom tattooed their bodies. They wore their hair in two braids hanging in front, and the men typically wore one or more feathers in their hair, depending on tribal custom.

Southeastern Native Americans

In the Southeast, both sexes covered the upper part of their bodies only in cold weather or on special occasions, at which time they wore robes made of animal hide or of feathers thatched on a netted base. Otherwise, the men wore a buckskin breechcloth and the women a wraparound skirt from the waist to the knees. These skirts could be made of buckskin or woven from such materials as grass, inner bark, or bison hair. When traveling, the men wore moccasins and full-length leggings fastened at the belt; women seldom wore moccasins and only half-length leggings, fastened with a garter just below the knee.

Both sexes had tattoos of elaborate design on their faces, trunks, arms, and legs. Women grew their hair full length, sometimes wearing it upswept and other times parted and braided. Men grew a scalp lock from the crown of their heads; the remainder of the scalp was either completely shaved or else partially shaved except for a crewcut-style border running from front to back around the scalp lock.[5]

Northeastern Native Americans

Native Americans living in the Northeast woodlands wore little clothing in the summer. Children were usually naked, whereas the men wore only deerskin breechcloths and the women knee-length skirts and wampum headbands. In southern New England, both men and women might wear light capes or shawls of woven textiles. Colder weather throughout the Northeast required robes of fur or woven downy, waterproof turkey feathers, along with leather leggings and moccasins made of moose or deer skin.

Boys' hair was kept short until they turned 16, whereas girls and women wore full-length hair. Hairstyles, some very elaborate and decorated with porcupine quills, varied from tribe to tribe. Males from the Lenni Lenape and several Algonquian tribes would pluck their hair with mussel-shell tweezers except for a central cock's crest, but other tribes did not follow this practice. Among all Northeast tribes, ornamental jewelry included necklaces of beads or pearls with copper tubing; jeweled earrings; and bracelets, pendants, and belts of brightly colored or shining stones, shells, and beads.[6]

Clothing and body adornment, varying so greatly both among and within the 10 culture areas (see Figure 2.1), were cultural attributes that attested to Native American diversity. As the tribes made cultural contact with one another, style fashions spread from one to the other. European contact also brought changes in materials and styles as trade brought in more furs, hides, and needles to sew better garments, often in imitation of European full-length sleeves and trouser legs. When game became scarce, use of the Whites' clothing fabrics and styles became more common among Native Americans.[7]

Diversity in Housing

Climate, terrain, and available building materials all influence housing construction, of course, but so, too, does the culture of a people. And because extensive cultural diversity existed among Native Americans, their housing styles varied significantly.

John White's exquisite 16th-century watercolor of a typical Algonquian village of the Secotan tribe in North Carolina depicts the layout of one type of a permanent Native American settlement. Along a thoroughfare stands a series of barrel-roofed, multifamily houses made of arched saplings covered with bark and woven mats that are easily removable to let in light. Nearby are newly planted and ripening corn fields, an open ceremonial center with a circle of elaborately carved posts, a place of solemn prayer, and a tomb for departed chiefs.

Large Communal Structures

Although all tribes lived within a tribal enclave, some did so within larger communal structures. Perhaps the greatest of these was in Chaco Canyon, New Mexico. There, the ruins of Pueblo Bonito reveal a gigantic,

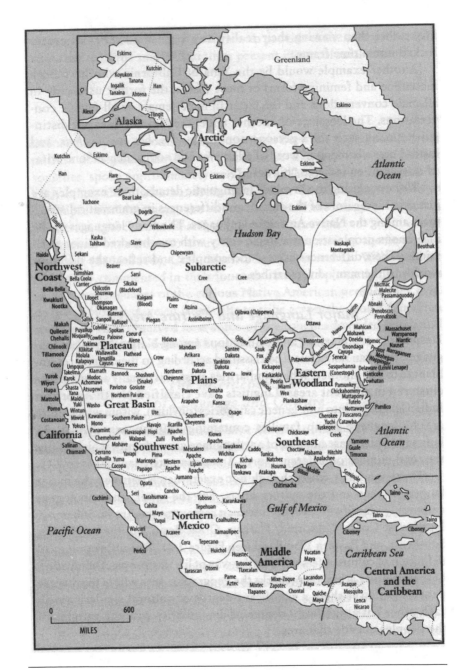

Figure 2.1   Culture Areas and Tribal Locations in North America

SOURCE: Alvin M. Josephy, Jr., *The Indian Heritage of America* (New York: Knopf, 1968).

crescent-shaped, single-structure housing project covering more than three acres. It rose to a height of four or five stories around its outer rim and was enclosed along the front by a long wall. In the central plaza, around which the Pueblo Bonito arched, were two great *kivas*—enormous subterranean ceremonial chambers, each able to accommodate hundreds of people for the sacred rites performed there.

This edifice housed 1,000 people and thrived for 400 years until a sustained drought ended its existence in the late 13th century. At its peak, this monolithic dwelling place contained 660 rooms, the adjoining units interconnected by doorways and built on a series of graduated terraces that served as streets. Built of stone set in mud mortar, the ceilings were supported by wooden beams and made of sticks, grass, and several inches of mud.

In New York State, the five nations of the Iroquois Confederation—the Cayuga, Mohawk, Oneida, Onondaga, and Seneca (later, a sixth nation, the remnants of the Tuscarora, were admitted in 1722)—lived in rectangular-shaped longhouses. These ranged in size from 50 to 150 feet in length, and 18 to 25 feet in width, depending on the number of families living inside. A barrel-shaped roof, made from seasoned elm bark sewn in overlapped layers, hung like shingles over a framework of elm-wood poles lashed together. Smaller versions existed among many eastern tribes.

A similar multifamily concept can be found in the rectangular plank houses in the Pacific Northwest. Built of wide planks including the floor, they measured anywhere from 30 by 45 feet to 50 by 60 feet. Roofs were two-pitched with a gable end facing the sea. Inside, families each had their own allocated sleeping quarters that, like those of the Iroquois, had drop screens for privacy. These areas were typically on platforms, or else the center of the house was excavated to achieve the same effect. Fire smoke went out through an opening in the roof with a sliding panel that was closed during inclement weather. Outside the house, a totem pole—native only to the Northwest peoples and bearing accumulated family crests and honors—indicated a clan's history and rank.

The Pueblo lived in rectangular, flat-roofed rooms directly adjoining one another in multistoried complexes that are comparable to modern low-rise apartment buildings. The Hopi and Navajo lived in mud-and-stone dwellings with heavy wooden roof beams, the scarcity of wood in the Southwest prompting them to salvage beams from old housing for any new construction. The Mojave-type multifamily structure of the Colorado River Yumans was almost square-shaped, its side dimensions about 20 or

25 feet and covered outside on three sides by sand. The dwelling had a low, four-pitched roof without a smoke hole, requiring the fire to be placed near the door.

Single-Family Dwellings

Elsewhere, most housing units held single families, although extended family units within the tribal village usually clustered in adjacent dwellings. Southeastern tribes lived in small houses almost square-shaped, the mud-plastered-over-wooden-pole walls about 15 feet long on each side, covered by a 6-foot high, two-pitched, thatched roof. In contrast, the Seminole in Florida lived in an open-sided, thatched-roof *chickee.*

The Lenni Lenape mostly lived in round, domed bark wigwams, whereas the same style housing among the tribes around the western Great Lakes was made of other materials. The Menominee typically covered theirs with mats of reeds and cattails, whereas other tribes used pieces of bark and hide, in addition to woven or sewn mats. Nearby, the Kickapoo lived in picturesque reed-woven lodges.

Among the nomadic tribes of the Plains, their pursuit of the roaming buffalo led to portable housing, well-constructed conical tipis made of long wooden poles covered with tailored buffalo hides. These tipis often stood 10 to 12 feet high and were 12 to 15 feet in diameter. As in most Native American structures, the fire was in the center and the beds were around the sides. In the Southwest, the Apache resided in a *wick-iup,* a small, domed hut made of slender poles, brush, and grass that stood about 6 feet high. In the same region, the impoverished Ute lived in primitive lean-tos.

These differences in housing style were much more than architectural variations. They were another cultural mark that reflected the diversity among the tribes. Their differing value orientations about family life, communal living, social hierarchy, and tribal welfare affected their housing designs.

Diversity in Social Organization

Most Native American tribes maintained a more democratic structure than that found among the indigenous peoples in Africa and Oceania. In America, they usually had a tribal structure of equal clans, although some societies were organized into small bands. These bands could be a loosely organized number of extended families with no central tribal government, such as the Apache, or they could be like the Plains natives, who remained in separate groups most of the year but came together as a composite tribe for the annual summer encampment.

Social Status Variations

Among the tribes in the Great Basin culture area (Nevada, Utah, parts of California, Oregon, Idaho, Wyoming, and Colorado), differences in social class, status, and rank, other than those based on age and sex, were minimal. This arid region—home to the Paiute, Shoshoni, and Ute—offered only a meager, harsh livelihood to the sparse native population. Leadership was not hereditary, but rested in the most competent man until he proved otherwise in his skills and judgment and was then replaced by someone better.

Other indigenous peoples had some ranking system to determine social standing, usually determined by an office held, wealth, or war deeds. After introduction of the horse and trade with the Whites, Plains culture changed. Accumulation of wealth—such as medicine bundles, horses, guns, and kitchenware—became important, and a class structure based on wealth arose out of previously egalitarian societies.

Northwestern Slavery

A notable exception to democratic structure was the peoples of the Northwest Coast, where two distinct social classes—freemen and slaves—existed. Usually obtained as prisoners in raids, slaves could thereafter be bought or sold in an institutionalized slave trade. Normally, they could marry one another, but their children then typically became slaves also. Captive slaves could be ransomed by relatives, but the stigma of a slave status was so great that some refused to do so.

Slaves could be freed on such occasions as the death of the slave's owner, or when the owner's child had ears pierced for earrings, or at a potlatch to demonstrate the owner's wealth in giving up such property. However, "freed" often meant killing slaves at these occasions and was, in fact, mandatory for foundation sacrifices when building a new home. At this time, the slaves' bodies were thrown into the holes dug by the front door to hold the carved totems. In their lifetimes, slaves performed only menial tasks and served primarily as prestige items, offering visible evidence of their owners' wealth and high rank.

Southeastern Caste Systems

A caste system apparently existed among the Chitimacha in Louisiana, where endogamous marriages maintained a dichotomy between nobles and commoners. However, the most stratified social order existed among the Natchez people of Mississippi, headed by a chief known as the Great Sun, who claimed descent from the sun. Natchez society consisted of three levels of nobility: Suns, Nobles, and Honored People, and a single group of commoners called Stinkards. The Great Sun held unlimited power over his subjects, but a council of elders limited his authority on matters of general concern to the entire society. Curiously, the three upper ranks could only marry Stinkards, although the latter group could also marry within their own social group. The potential depletion of the Stinkards through their upward mobility marriages was offset through replenishment by peoples from nearby conquered tribes.

Both the Chitimacha and Natchez are thought to be remnants of a Mississippian culture that peaked from about 1200 to 1500 A.D. From Ohio to Louisiana, from Arkansas to Tennessee, these mound builders constructed pyramidal or conical mounds as foundations for temples or chiefs' houses. These earthworks, still standing today, were built by tens of thousands of people who, without benefit of wheeled vehicles or beasts of burden, carried all the dirt in baskets to the sites. Most impressive is Monk's Mound at Cahokia, Illinois, across the Mississippi River from St. Louis. It is a massive earthwork 1,000 feet long, 700 feet wide, and 100 feet high, upon which stood either a temple or the residence of Cahokia's ruler.

Iroquois Consensus-Building

The Iroquois confederacy, or League of the Five Nations, was an alliance apparently formed to end warfare among the Cayuga, Mohawk, Oneida, Onondaga, and Seneca. It permitted each tribe to govern itself, with larger issues such as relations with other tribes decided at the annual meeting of the Great Council. At this meeting the 49 councillors, with apportioned representation from the five tribes, acted only after unanimous agreement was reached on an issue.[8]

Oratorical skills were important in persuading other members and resulted in some historians identifying this primitive democracy form as a prototype for such provisions of the U.S. Constitution as reconciliation of differing House-Senate legislation, impeachment, and expansion. Just as the Iroquois admitted the Tuscarora in 1722 as a Sixth Nation, so did the new U.S. government admit new states.

This Iroquois model of a collective political institution resembled the form of authority within almost all North American tribes. The chief held an honorary status and primarily played ceremonial and religious roles. Real authority rested not in an individual but in a group, the tribal council.

Diversity in Social Organization

In this section, we have discussed social structures that ranged from the southeastern caste system and northwestern slave system to mostly democratic structures elsewhere. Leadership could be hereditary or not, and social class could be nonexistent (Great Basin) or significant (Plains). There could be loose bands with no central tribal government (Apache), tribes who merged once a year (Sioux), or a formal confederacy (Iroquois). The plurality of tribal organizations offers us yet another instance of Native American diversity and further ammunition against the Dillingham Flaw of simplistic categorizations of the past based on present-day sensibilities.[9]

Diversity in Values

Among the tribes throughout the land, value orientations about wealth varied. The Hupa, Karok, and Yurok of northern California were obsessed by personal wealth; it was to be accumulated, ostentatiously displayed, guarded, and bestowed intact on one's children. In contrast, the people of the Northwest Coast accumulated quality possessions only to have enough to give away at a potlatch. They did so to gain honor among their people, humiliate enemies, or legitimize hereditary claims. In contrast, the Shoshoni measured wealth by the kin upon whose aid one could depend, and the Zuni considered wealth as determined by the time and resources one had to participate in religious ceremonies and host the ceremonial dancers.

Religious values and beliefs permeated every aspect of Native American life in thought, word, and deed, but once again, differences existed among the tribes. Their religiosity ranged from the simple social organization of the Iroquois, who believed in the Great Spirit as a supreme being, to the complexity of interrelated religious groupings among the Zuni, who were possibly the most religious indigenous people on the continent. The Pueblo acknowledged numerous spiritual entities as equally ranked gods, and the peoples of the Plateau and Great Basin culture areas also believed in large numbers of spirits.

Full-time priests existed within the Mississippian culture and the derivative cultures such as the Natchez, whereas part-time priests, who also earned their livelihood in some other economic activity, functioned among the Pueblo. Shamans operated only in the Plateau and Great Basin regions, but religious leaders in most of the East and Southwest, on the Plains and prairies, in California and on the Northwest Coast displayed attributes of both priests and shamans. For example, Northwest Coast shamans typically came from certain families specializing in shamanism, virtually creating a permanent priesthood. They performed ceremonial rites that also had strong social functions, unlike the Sanpoil in the Plateau area of eastern Washington. The Sanpoil had no standardized rituals and drew their shamans—who held little distinction from others—from anyone in the tribe whose vision quests resulted in unusual good fortune.

Perhaps the most important aspect of Native American cultural values was the ubiquitous idea that humans were "embedded" in nature. This concept was very different from the Europeans' view of nature as something meant to serve them. These contrasting values would generate controversies with Whites virtually from first contact to the present.

The Next Horizon

As culturally distinct as the hundreds of tribes were from one another, the arrival of Whites would have a single effect on all of them: catastrophe. All the tribes would find their self-reliant way of life changed forever by disease, conquest, and loss of their ancestral lands.

Far more deadly than all warfare would be European diseases, against which the Native Americans had no immunity because they had been isolated from that continent's sicknesses for thousands of years. Carried by European explorers, fishermen, and fur traders, these diseases would spread like wildfire among the indigenous tribes. Smallpox, measles, typhus, tuberculosis, chicken pox, influenza, cholera, and diphtheria would weaken and kill them by the thousands, wiping out whole villages, even decimating entire tribes.

Tribal disintegration would further result from other causes. In return for axes, blankets, cloth, kettles, knives, and rum, many tribes would deplete their environment of beaver and deer to meet European demand for their hides, or else raid neighboring communities to procure slaves for local colonists or slave traders. Westward expansion would lead to continual land thefts, warfare, further decimation, subjugation, segregation on reservations, and dependency.

The rich, vibrant multiculturalism that predated European contact would yield to this relentless onslaught of settlement and expansion. Any violent resistance would reaffirm the European and Euro-American stereotype of Native Americans as "cruel, bloodthirsty savages." They would lose their lands and independence and become a colonized, exploited people.

Although their conquerors would continue to view them as a single entity, the Native Americans were never that. Some tribes would internalize others' views of themselves and try to act "White." Other tribes would attempt to negotiate a path of marginality, taking what they considered to be the best of both worlds. Many others would struggle, as best they could, to preserve both their culture and their identity.

Notes

1. An excellent, highly readable overview of Native American civilizations is Peter Farb, *Man's Rise to Civilization as Shown by the Indians of North America From Primeval Times to the Coming of the Industrial State* (New York: E. P. Dutton, 1968).

2. Much of the material about Native American cultural attributes is drawn from James A. Maxwell (ed.), *America's Fascinating Indian Heritage* (Pleasantville, NY: Reader's Digest, 1978); Alvin M. Josephy, Jr., *The Indian Heritage of North America* (New York: Knopf, 1968); Harold E. Driver, *Indians of North America*, 2nd ed. (Chicago: University of Chicago Press, 1969).

3. A good source for information about Whites' perceptions of Native Americans is Robert F. Berkhofer, Jr., *The White Man's Indian: Images of the American Indian from Columbus to the Present* (New York: Knopf, 1978).

4. The original source of Edward Sapir's observations is "The Status of Linguistics as a Science," *Language*, 5 (1929): 207–14. Other references include the "Selected Writings of Edward Sapir," in *Language, Culture and Personality*, ed. David G. Mandelbaum (Berkeley: University of California Press, 1949); J. B. Carroll, *Language, Thought, and Reality: Selected Readings of Benjamin Lee Whorf* (Cambridge: MIT Press, 1961).

5. Helpful information about Southeastern Native Americans can be found in Jesse Burt and Robert B. Ferguson, *Indians of the Southeast: Then and Now* (New York: Abingdon, 1973).

6. A good source for further information about Northeastern Native Americans is Howard S. Russell, *Indian New England Before the Mayflower* (Hanover, NH: University Press of New England, 1980).

7. Native American response to culture contact is detailed in Nancy O. Lurie, "Indian Cultural Adjustment to European Civilization," in *Seventeenth-Century America*, ed. James M. Smith (Chapel Hill: University of North Carolina Press, 1959).

8. The Iroquois political consensus model is fully examined in Jack Weatherford, *Indian Givers: How the Indians of the Americas Transformed the World* (New York: Crown, 1988).

9. Wilcomb F. Washburn offers succinct insights into Native American social structures in *The Indian in America* (New York: Harper & Row, 1975), 25–65.

3

Diversity in Colonial Times

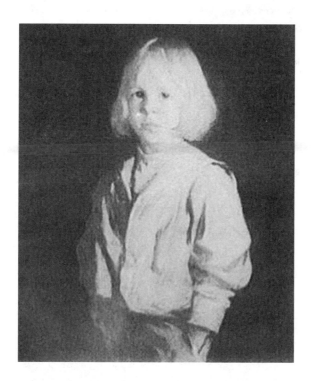

What most people remember about early U.S. history is that the 13 English colonies fought for their independence from the "Mother Country" of England. Because the English held cultural and political preeminence in the colonial and early national periods, this myth of cultural homogeneity arose. The actions and/or writings of contemporary English American leaders, historians, and literary figures enhanced the myth, and their dominance and influence cast a long shadow across subsequent generations.

Colonial America existed on the periphery of the "civilized world." Although England was dominant in its cultural, economic, and political influence, Europe also exerted a profound impact. For example, the Age of Enlightenment—an 18th-century philosophical movement that embraced rationalism, emphasized learning, and encouraged a spirit of skepticism and practicality in social and political thought—guided the founding fathers in their thinking and eventual formulation of a new nation. Before the new republic became a reality, however, what occurred in colonial thoughts, words, and actions reflected, for the most part, the dominance of European culture, both abstract (values, ideas) and material (fashions, manufactured goods).

Colonial cultural norms reflected European patriarchal values, which became embedded in English law. For example, a woman's marriage automatically transferred the legal ownership of the bride's personal property—money, land, household goods, and clothing—to her husband. If he died, the property went to the children, not her, with male heirs receiving larger inheritances than their sisters. Even children could become the wards of the father's male relatives and not of his widow. In the rare instance of a divorce, the father indisputably retained custody of the children.

As to the composition of the colonial population under English rule, the presence of non-English colonial Americans at first was not a significant factor. In commenting about the population composition of the 17th century, historian Mildred Campbell remarked,

> For despite the Dutch on the Hudson, and small groups of Swiss, Swedes, Finns, and French Huguenots pocketed along the coast, the small vessels which set out on the American voyage were chiefly English built and English manned. Their cargoes, moreover, consisted largely of Englishmen and, later and in smaller numbers, Englishwomen. Even the Scots and Irish, who in the next century would crowd the harbors of the New World, were a minority in the first century.[1]

By the early 18th century, however, an important change in immigration dramatically altered the population mix. As Stephen Steinberg observed,

> The simple truth is that [the] English were not coming in sufficient numbers to populate the colonies. . . .
> If there were no compelling "pull" factors luring Englishmen to America, neither were there potent "push" factors. In fact, after 1718 labor shortages at home induced the British government to place

restrictions on emigration, especially of skilled artisans and other
laborers needed in Britain's nascent industries. It was this scarcity of
emigrants from Britain that induced colonial authorities to permit the
immigration of non-English nationalities.[2]

Historians Bruce Catton and William B. Catton described the new
colonial immigration as continually increasing:

> Homogeneity was altered in a different way by the increasing infusion of
> non-English elements into the colonial bloodstream. This did not become
> noticeable until late in the seventeenth century and assumed its largest
> proportions in the eighteenth, when the seaboard colonies entered upon
> their great period of sustained growth. Of greatest significance was the
> large-scale influx of men and women of African descent. Next in impor-
> tance were those from the Rhine Valley and the north of Ireland. (p. 165)[3]

The Cattons also provide some insight into differences among the
so-called British immigrants, a theme introduced in the first chapter with
reference to the Dillingham Flaw that will be further developed in this chapter:

> The Scotch-Irish added something special to the colonial brew. They
> tended to be hard cases politically—unyielding Presbyterians, schooled
> and scarred by generations of turmoil in Ireland, caught in the middle
> between oppressed Irish Catholics and the Anglican establishment, hated
> from both sides, returning the hatred at compound interest. (p. 166)

One of their other observations relates to the social distance the ethnic
groups deliberately set between themselves:

> These people did not all want the same things, beyond the elemental
> notions of escape and a fresh start. If, for a determined handful, this
> meant social engineering and creating communities, for untold larger
> numbers it meant simply a vague but compelling desire to go where they
> could be left alone. "Get off my back" is a piece of twentieth-century
> slang, distinctively American, which well summarized the prime motiva-
> tion and prevailing mood among immigrants to Britain's mainland
> colonies. (p. 168)

Some social scientists, while admitting the continued presence of cultural pluralism up to the Revolutionary War, suggest that it was minimal
and that assimilation was virtually complete, even among non-English-
speaking ethnic groups. Lawrence Fuchs, for example, asserted that

by the time of the Revolution, most of the children and grandchildren of Dutch, French, German, and Swedish immigrants in the colonies spoke English and were otherwise indistinguishable from the children and grandchildren of English settlers, although in Albany, where the Dutch predominated, it was difficult to assemble an English-speaking jury, and several counties in Pennsylvania were overwhelmingly German-speaking. Hostility toward speakers of Dutch and German and toward the English-speaking Scotch-Irish, the newest large immigrant group, was widespread.[4]

Fuchs's claim of indistinguishable characteristics among these four groups is questionable for reasons beyond his own inclusion of contradictory examples illustrating both cultural pluralism and intergroup tensions. Many Dutch, French, and Germans continued to live in social, sometimes even geographic, isolation within culturally distinct ethnic communities apart from English-American society. Moreover, Fuchs cites the source of his Dutch and German "exceptions" as *To Seek America* (1977) by Maxine Sellers. Yet in the very chapter upon which Fuchs draws, Sellers argues that although by the outbreak of the Revolution, "The Swedes . . . had become indistinguishable in language and life style from the dominant English . . . [o]thers—including some Jews, some French Huguenots, many Dutch, and many more Germans, had not."[5]

This minimization of ethnic diversity that overstresses English-American cultural and political hegemony illustrates the Dillingham Flaw. So, too, do claims that English numerical superiority reflects cultural homogeneity. Stephen Steinberg, for example, pre-sets this view by stating, "Three-fourths of the white population in 1790 had their origins in the English-speaking states of the British Isles." (This statement ignores the different cultures, religions, and Gaelic and Scotch languages.) Then, after saying the other immigrants were mostly from northern or western Europe with "important cultural affinities to the English majority" (a claim many Scandinavians, Germans, and French might question), he adds,

> At its inception, the United States had a population that was remarkably homogeneous in terms of both ethnicity and religion [Protestant]. Devoid of its invidious implications, the claim that the nation was founded by white Anglo-Saxon Protestants is reasonably accurate.
>
> To be sure, there was some ethnic differentiation in terms of both population and patterns of settlement. New York still reflected its Dutch origins, and had a far greater ethnic mix than did New England. Pennsylvania had sizable concentrations of Germans and Scotch-Irish,

and the Southern states, which a century later would become the last bastion of "ethnic purity," were characterized by a high degree of ethnic heterogeneity, at least in comparison to New England. But it would be a mistake to construe this as evidence of a rudimentary pluralism, at least in a political sense. Not only were the English predominant numerically, but they enjoyed a political and cultural hegemony over the life of the fledgling nation.

Non-English colonials were typically regarded as aliens who were obliged to adapt to English rule in terms of both politics and culture.[6]

Steinberg is correct in saying that political pluralism did not exist. However, cultural pluralism did exist in a very real sense. Non-English colonials, often clustered in their own ethnic communities, did not necessarily feel any compulsion to forego their language and culture, nor did officials force them. Furthermore, the English were not as cohesive a group as one might think, as the following pages will show.

The colonies were not a culturally homogeneous launching pad for the new nation, which only later received several waves of "different" immigrants. Colonial America was a rich mixture of racial and ethnic heterogeneity right up to the Revolutionary War. As Gary B. Nash states, "Any attempt to portray the colonies as unified and homogeneous would be misguided."[7]

Colonial Beginnings

Coming in the 17th century to a land already populated by indigenous people of many cultures was a steady stream of adventurers, debtors, opportunists, social outcasts, and desperate people, all risking a perilous 3-month journey across an often-stormy ocean to forge a better life for themselves in the New World. Sickness, disease, and death were common traveling companions on those voyages, and many never completed their journey, their lives ending with burial at sea.

A Patchwork Quilt of Ethnic Settlements

Those who successfully completed their journey came from many parts of the European continent, speaking different tongues and varying in their religious beliefs, customs, skills, and talents. And when they settled in this new land, they sometimes intermingled but more often clustered together with their own kind, creating a mosaic of subcultural enclaves, at first on or near the coast, and later inland.

The names given to areas by early settlers reflected this ethnic mix by colony (New Belgium, New England, New France, New Netherland, New Spain, New Sweden). Settlement names were either new versions of their homeland—New Amsterdam (Holland), New Orleans (France), and New Smyrna, Florida (Greece)—or simply the same as in their native land—Cambridge (England /Massachusetts), Guttenberg (Germany/New Jersey), Haarlem (Holland/New York), Hamburg (Germany/New Jersey), and Plymouth (England/Massachusetts). At first fairly self-contained and separate from one another, most were culturally homogeneous within their boundaries, but together they constituted a patchwork quilt of ethnic diversity. Two early settlements, however, attracted a variety of peoples almost from their inception.

Diversity in the Early Settlements

Philadelphia, and its adjoining area offered one example of cultural pluralism. Still a small village in 1700, its population was mostly English and Welsh, but this area also included Danes, Dutch, Finns, French, Germans, Irish, Scots, and Swedes. Even within these individual groups, further diversity could be found.[8] The 300 or so Germans, for example, were a mixture of Lutherans, Mennonites, and Quakers, each group remaining separate from the others.

The greatest concentration of cultural diversity, however, was in New Amsterdam, where 18 languages were spoken on Manhattan Island as early as 1646. The Dutch, Flemish, Walloons, French, Danes, Norwegians, Swedes, English, Scots, Irish, Germans, Poles, Bohemians, Portuguese, and Italians were among the settlement's early inhabitants. After the English takeover in 1664, New York's slave population became the largest north of the Chesapeake region. In 1720, the city's Black population numbered 20,000, one third of the total; by 1741, slaves were still a substantial proportion, one sixth of the population.

Elsewhere in the colonies, some European ethnic mix could be found in most small cities. For the most part, however, the various groups clustered together, at first on the outskirts of the municipality and then more and more to the west along the edge of the frontier.

By the late 17th century, the English dominated all 13 colonies. By 1689, the population of colonial America had reached an estimated 210,000 Europeans, about 80% of them "transplanted Englishmen."

After that, however, the proportion of English Americans declined. Between 1689 and 1775, the population increased twelvefold to about 2.6 million, with only a small portion due to natural increase. Rather, the rapid growth of African slavery and the influx of hundreds of thousands of non-English immigrants in the mid-18th century significantly changed the character of the colonial population.

Geographical Variances in Diversity

Three geographic regions developed distinct population mixtures and cultures. The following data are based on information from the U.S. Bureau of the Census, as well as 1790 census data extrapolations and anthropological estimates about the Native American population at that time made by me.[9]

The New England Colonies

The greatest degree of cultural homogeneity was in the New England colonies, with English Americans representing about 70% of all inhabitants (see Figure 3.1). In Massachusetts, home to two out of every five New Englanders, lived the greatest concentration of English Americans of all 13 colonies, with 82% of the more than 250,000 people being English. The lowest proportion of English was in Maine, with 60%, but its population was only about 31,000. Scots accounted for about 4% and the Scots-Irish for about 3%. Interestingly, the 16,000 Africans in New England represented slightly more than 2% of the total, more than the combined numbers of Irish, Dutch, and Germans also living in New England at that time.

By 1775, this region contained a greater share of fifth- and sixth-generation Americans than the Middle or Southern Colonies. Most of these New England inhabitants had coalesced into reasonably unified communities, shaped in part by their consensus-driven town meetings that allowed widespread public participation in the discussion of local issues.

The Middle Colonies

The Middle Colonies were the most diverse of the three regions (see Figure 3.2). Here, the English, totaling almost 41%, did not constitute a numerical majority. About 15% were German, and more than 12% were African. The Dutch, Scots, and Scots-Irish were each slightly more than

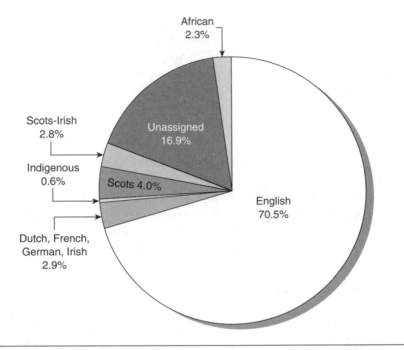

Figure 3.1   New England Colonies, Approximate Population in 1776

SOURCE: U.S. Bureau of the Census, *Historical Statistics of the United States, Part II,* Series Z 20-132 (Washington, DC: Government Printing Office, 1976).

6% of the total. Notably, ethnic clannishness prevented any cohesive cultural evolution as occurred in New England.

Throughout the New York–New Jersey region, the Dutch remained socially insulated and maintained ethnic solidarity up through the Revolutionary period. Buoyed by their numbers (one in six residents in New York and New Jersey was Dutch), their culture flourished. Amid the steep-roofed houses—with double doors, blue-tiled fireplaces, and built-in cupboards—stood the Dutch Reformed churches and parochial schools. Endogamy was the norm, and Dutch endured as an everyday language, with English not even introduced into Dutch schools until 1774.

President Martin Van Buren illustrated Dutch endogamy and social isolation during the colonial and federal periods when he wrote in his autobiography that his family was "without a single intermarriage with one of different extraction from the time of the arrival of the first emigrant to that of the marriage of my eldest son, embracing a period of over two centuries and including six generations."[10]

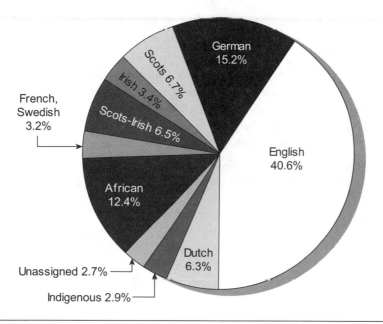

Figure 3.2   Middle Colonies, Approximate Population in 1776

SOURCE: U.S. Bureau of the Census, *Historical Statistics of the United States, Part II,* Series Z 20-132 (Washington, DC: Government Printing Office, 1976).

Van Buren's comment could have applied to most of the Dutch families and other ethnics of his time. Fluent in Dutch, Van Buren was chided, rather unfairly, by critics such as John Randolph for his inability to "speak, or write, the English language correctly," a complaint often made today about newcomers.[11]

It was in Pennsylvania, the most heavily populated of the Middle Colonies with almost 300,000 residents, where the most ethnic and religious diversity existed on the eve of the Revolution. Its Quaker-inspired religious tolerance and liberal land policies serving as important lures, Pennsylvania superseded all other colonies in attracting a mixed group of non-English immigrants. In 1766, Benjamin Franklin reported to the House of Commons that the Germans and Scots-Irish each comprised one third of Pennsylvania's population.

The Germans were splintered into numerous religious groupings. They were Lutherans, Reformed, or pietists: Quakers, Moravians, Mennonites, and Dunkers. Like the Dutch, the different German groups lived in community clusters, persevering as vibrant, distinct subcultures. Countering German pacifist sentiments were Scots-Irish Presbyterians, whose fierce anti-Anglican feelings and swift alignment with the rebel cause were key elements in tipping the Pennsylvania colony into a revolutionary posture.

Although some, like the French Huguenots and Welsh, were quickly absorbed into the dominant Anglo-American mainstream, others, such as the Germans and Scots-Irish, created separate and distinct communities for themselves where they maintained cultural cohesiveness, despite their close proximity to other ethnic groups nearby. United by their strong ethnic ties, they practiced a voluntary allegiance to their own distinct social groups. The Scots-Irish would eventually assimilate more quickly than the Germans, who remained clustered within a persistent subculture for several more generations.

In Delaware, the lowest populated colony with slightly more than 41,000, the Swedes were the second largest ethnic group, with about 9% of the total. Delaware was where the short-lived colony of New Sweden (1638–1655) had existed before Dutch takeover. The English were clearly dominant, however, with 60% of the total, and the Scots were a close third at 8%.

The Southern Colonies

In the Southern Colonies, the English, at 37% of the total, were also in the numerical minority, but, as in the Middle Colonies, they were the largest single group. From a sociological viewpoint, they were the dominant group in terms of power and control in both regions.

Slavery made the Africans the second largest group, at 39% (see Figure 3.3). Virginia, the most populated colony with more than a half-million inhabitants, had about two fifths of all slaves in the region, but in South Carolina, the Africans outnumbered the Europeans. If we include the approximately 40,000 Native Americans estimated to be living in the Southern Colonies at the time, this makes the Southern Colonies the most racially diverse of the three regions. Here, the non-White population was about 42%, or two of five inhabitants. The remaining 21% of the inhabitants were non-English Whites. Numbering more than 300,000, they were mostly Scots, Scots-Irish, Germans, Irish, and French Huguenots.

African Diversity on the Plantations

Cultural diversity also existed among the African slaves, who came from different tribal backgrounds in western Africa—particularly Angola, the Gold Coast, Nigeria, and Senegambia. Because of this cultural mixing,

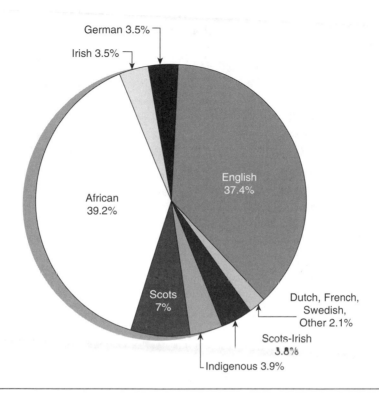

German 3.5%

Irish 3.5%

English
37.4%

African
39.2%

Scots
7%

Dutch, French,
Swedish,
Other 2.1%

Scots-Irish
3.8%

Indigenous 3.9%

Figure 3.3   Southern Colonies, Approximate Population in 1776

SOURCE: U.S. Bureau of the Census, *Historical Statistics of the United States, Part II,* Series Z 20-132 (Washington, DC: Government Printing Office, 1976).

no tribe or language group predominated, with the newly transported slaves speaking about 100 languages or dialects. The colonists, however, did not look on the Africans as a diverse group, instead viewing them as a single racial collectivity as well as less than human.

It was not simply the slave system that caused the colonists to ignore African diversity and generalize, for they did the same thing with Native Americans. Nor was it simply a racist response or a premodern lack of sophistication. Ingroup members typically generalize about outgroups, failing to note their diversity. Other examples of unnoticed diversity are when Americans a few generations ago viewed the many diverse peoples from central, southern, and eastern Europe as a single entity, or people today generalizing about all Asians or Hispanics.

In colonial times, the Africans adapted to their harsh new reality and, interacting with one another, soon overcame their tribal barriers through the process of ethnogenesis.[12] The Africans became bilingual, even trilingual, conversing in their native tongue to members of their tribe or language group, and in broken English to their owners. To converse with other slaves in the Carolinas, the Africans created *Gullah*, a dialect amalgamating some English and many African words into an African grammatical structure.[13]

By the 1730s, an African American culture began to evolve that became more cohesive after the end of the legal slave trade in 1808. In a harsh, arbitrary world separated along racial lines, enslaved Blacks developed a peasantlike culture. Like European peasants, they, too, formed close-knit communities based on family and kinship, with religion as an important center of their lives. Although Gullah gradually faded away, many elements of African origin remained in music, dance, marriage rituals, and housing floor plans (front-to-back rooms instead of two rooms side-by-side in front). Africans held on to their incest taboo as well. Rarely did marriage occur between cousins, unlike such common practice among the slaveowners, who usually did so to maintain inherited property and power.

Three Regional Cultures

By 1725, regional differences in the New England, Middle, and Southern Colonies led to distinct cultures evolving in each of those areas.[14] New England, with its unified farming societies, maintained a strong religious orientation. Its high educational standards, even in rural areas, resulted in a literacy rate of about 90% for men and 50% for women in 1790. Here, a more integrated society functioned and shared, for the most part, a common ancestry.

In the Southern Colonies, a different culture emerged. Most adult White women and more than one third of the White men could not read or write, not even their own names. Illiteracy occurred because a large number of White people, mostly tenant and small, independent farmers, lived in poverty and had little or no formal schooling. A small, aristocratic elite ruled this socially stratified and racially divided region, with its ethnically distinct backcountry inhabitants, over others for whom education was a low priority.

Within the Middle Colonies, the ethnic clannishness of the diverse groups prevented any cohesive regional culture from developing. Thus, 18th-century colonial America was literally a multicultural place, a fact frequently commented upon by European visitors and congressional representatives in the 1790s who noted the significant cultural differences among the three regions.

Throughout the three regions, regional residence and social class greatly affected the quality of women's lives. Most spun thread and made clothing, candles, and soap, but rural women had to be even more self-sufficient in a variety of productive tasks. These might include milking goats or cows, churning butter, working in the fields, or other farm tasks.[15]

Women in affluent families had servants to do menial tasks while they devoted their free time to such activities as playing a musical instrument, creating fine embroidery, or perhaps reading good books, particularly Scripture. Working-class women more likely produced goods for sale (cheese, cloth, shoes, yarn) or rendered services (working as cooks, domestics, or possibly servers at inns, restaurants, or taverns).

Ethnic background was another important variable in determining women's place in the social order. Those of English descent were most likely to be found indoors, either engaged in duties in and about the house or, if working class, in such public establishments as those mentioned previously. Those ethnic groups living even just a short distance away from these English-dominated settlements—the Germans, Scots-Irish, and French-Canadians especially—would normally have their women performing a variety of agricultural tasks, as they worked in the barns, fields, meadows, and stables, wherever they were needed.[16]

Religious Diversity

Religious diversity was another significant component of cultural pluralism throughout colonial America. Religion played a major role in colonial life, from its importance as a force for initial settlement by many different Christian groups, to its influence upon the everyday life of the settlers. Clergy were highly honored members of the community, and their advice extended beyond spiritual matters to include economic and political concerns, as well as gender relations.

Religious values—echoing such teachings as Paul's assertion that "wives should submit to their husbands in everything" (Ephesians 5:24)—greatly influenced social norms in most colonial communities. When Anne Hutchinson, a middle-aged midwife and wife of a merchant, challenged both her subordinate status and the traditional teachings of Puritan clergymen by holding weekly prayer meetings in her house, she was banished in 1637 for heresy. Afterwards, Governor John Winthrop declared that she could have lived "usefully and honorably in the place God had set her . . . if she had attended her household affairs, and such things as belong to women."[17]

Most women were the social products of their times and did not challenge the pervasive male authority promulgated by the clergy. Illustrative is *The Well-Ordered Family* (1712), in which its author, Reverend Benjamin Wadsworth, counsels his female readers, "Tho possibly thou has greater abilities of mind than he has, are of some high birth, and he of a more mean extract, or didst bring more Estate to Marriage than he did; yet since he is thy Husband, God has made him the head and set him above thee."[18] What a woman could only do, he admonished, was to fulfill her "duty to love and reverence him."

Religious Intolerance

Seventeenth-century religion was an all-encompassing force that helped people endure the hardships and sacrifices of daily life in settlements. Moreover, colonial religiosity instilled a narrow, intolerant view of other faiths. The expulsion of Roger Williams and Anne Hutchinson from the Massachusetts colony as religious dissidents is well known. Less known is the fact that many colonies at this time enacted discriminatory legislation against Catholics and Jews, usually by banning their immigration or right to vote.

Seventeenth-century English settlers were mostly Puritan in New England, Anglican in the South, and a variety of religious sects in the Middle Colonies, reflecting the population diversity and liberal stance of the governments, particularly in Pennsylvania. The American beginnings of the Baptist Church commenced in 1639 in Rhode Island with Roger Williams. After that, Baptists became the most persecuted sect in New England for the rest of the century. Fines, beatings, and whippings were not uncommon, and not until 1708 could Baptists legally have a house of worship in Connecticut. In contrast, Baptists thrived in the more tolerant Middle Colonies, establishing in Philadelphia by 1700 the strongest Baptist center in the colonies. And when the 1691 Massachusetts charter extended "liberty of conscience" to all Christians, including Baptists, it specifically excluded "Papists" (Catholics).

Dislike of Catholics was one common ground on which all the Protestants could agree. The Presbyterians, Baptists, Quakers, German Reformed, and Lutherans along the "frontier" were intolerant of one another, yet often shared a strong dislike of Anglicans. The Anglicans, strongest in Virginia but prevalent throughout the South, disdainfully looked down on the New England Puritans, while the New Englanders reciprocated and jealously guarded their communities against the Anglicans achieving any inroads.

By the 18th century, secular forces lessened the force of religion, although it remained an important social influence. A lessening of religious devotion and church attendance, together with the advance of humanitarianism and rationalism in this Age of Enlightenment, combined to make this so. As a consequence, religious tolerance increased, but only slightly. There were still conflicts to come.

The Great Awakening

A momentous, far-reaching religious revival movement in the 1740s, known as the Great Awakening, brought even more conflict and diversity onto the American religious scene.[19] It was initiated by Massachusetts preacher Jonathan Edwards (1703–1758), who proclaimed that an individual's "born again" spiritual awakening was strong evidence of a predestined life of heavenly bliss. Other clergy picked up this theme, but the most influential was George Whitefield (1714–1770), an eloquent English evangelist who tirelessly and effectively spread this message of revivalism from Maine to Georgia.

The new movement generated much bitterness between "Old Light" traditionalists and the "New Light" evangelists. The emotional preaching and theme of individual salvation through the Bible appealed to many and challenged the formal services and conservatism of the churches dominated by the elite. The movement spread rapidly, with memberships increasing dramatically among the evangelical sects. Baptists benefited the most from these gains, often at the expense of Anglicans and Congregationalists. The Great Awakening also caused schisms in the Congregationalist, Dutch Reformed, and Presbyterian churches, further increasing the bitterness of the established churches against the dissenting sects.

Significantly, the Great Awakening brought democratization to religion as the general public gained a larger voice in the church. In doing so, it strengthened the trend toward liberty of conscience as it raised fundamental questions about the nature of God and human behavior, about moral and political authority, and about economic comportment. Another interesting consequence was that revivalists boldly went into any hospitable church regardless of creed. Thus, they helped break down provincial barriers to create a more unified evangelical Protestantism that became part of the American character. Furthermore, the Great Awakening reinforced strong community values held by Americans outside the coastal towns and cities.

During this tumultuous religious period, every major Christian sect, concerned about preserving its faith and transmitting its values and beliefs to future generations, took steps to ensure its survival. Each established its own college to educate new clergy and, as noted historian Daniel J. Boorstin states, "to save more Americans from the untruths of its competitors."[20]

The Legacy of Religious Pluralism

No single religion dominated, and the proliferation of sects and the growth of religious enthusiasm in 18th-century America produced an unplanned, often undesired, religious tolerance. Religious pluralism slowly, sometimes painfully, led to tolerance because no one group was powerful enough to coerce the others. One example is the early creation of interdenominational boards of trustees at the previously mentioned denominational colleges, partially in response to the reality that no single sect could supply its entire student body from the limited population base in its area.

United by their nationalism after winning their war for independence, the colonists put aside their prejudices by institutionalizing that tolerance and establishing a bedrock principle of American culture: separation of church and state. Freedom of religion was more an act of practical necessity than of democratic ideals. It is one legacy from America's multicultural past.

A Kaleidoscope Society

Some historians have found colorful expressions to describe the diversity of colonial America on the eve of the Revolution. Michael Kammen calls it an "invertebrate" society composed of disconnected religious, ethnic, and racial groups lacking a "figurative spinal column."[21] James Stuart Olson describes the colonies in 1776 as "a cultural kaleidoscope of three races and dozens of ethnic and religious groups."[22]

English Americans may have held political power in the 13 colonies, but they constituted less than half the total population. In the Middle and Southern Colonies, they were decisively outnumbered by the combined racial and ethnic groups, and in South Carolina by African slaves alone. However, the Anglo Americans were the dominant group, holding political and economic power, and backed by the English military.

Their language and culture constituted the mainstream, but the English did not force other White ethnics to assimilate, allowing them instead to retain their own schools to teach their children in their native languages.

Minority Separatism

Ethnic colonials thus lived under this tolerant English rule, typically residing apart in culturally distinct ethnic communities. If geographically isolated, they also remained culturally insulated as well. If living within the English American cities, they adapted as urban ethnics always have, but also retained many vestiges of their ethnicity and maintained an ingroup solidarity among their own kind.

Native Americans also desired to live among their own kind and maintain their way of life, but unlike White ethnics, they were not left alone to do so. African Americans, mostly enslaved, had no voice in their own welfare but, within the slave communities, developed their own subculture. Although relegated to a subjugated existence, racial diversity remained a reality in colonial America.

The separate White groups gave at least grudging tolerance to one another, united as they were in their fear and defense against the native peoples and the French. Later, with the threat from England, they put aside their differences to fight for their freedom and to maintain their rights through local politics.

The Multicultural Revolutionary Army

The success of Washington's troops in defeating the English lies partly in the multicultural elite, who played key roles in military training, strategy, and leadership. Baron Friedrich Wilhelm von Steuben (Prussia), Gen. Casimer Pulaski and Gen. Thaddeus Kosciuszko (Poland), and Marquis de Lafayette and Baron de Kalb (France) were the most prominent volunteers from Europe who were of great value to the American cause, although de Kalb's death in 1780 at the Battle of Camden, South Carolina, was a major blow to American efforts to recapture the South at the time.

Just as the military leadership consisted of non-English individuals, so, too, did the ranks of fighting men. More than 5,000 Blacks served in the colonial forces, fighting in every major battle from Lexington in 1775 to Yorktown in 1781. Some distinguished themselves in combat, such as Peter Salem and Salem Poore at the Battle of Bunker Hill, and Lemuel Haynes at the Battle of Fort Ticonderoga. James Lafayette, a Virginia slave, was so effective in gaining strategic intelligence about the English for Lafayette's troops that the Virginia Assembly purchased his freedom as a reward.

Patriotic groups formed within ethnic communities, often cooperating or even merging with similar nonethnic groups out of necessity. Numerous ethnic communities recruited their own companies or regiments, staffed with their own officers. Soon, they mixed with other ethnic groups or those of English ancestry as they united against a common enemy. Then, the cultural barriers and suspicions between groups faded as they shared common dangers, common hardships, and, ultimately, common victories.

The Next Horizon

The American Revolution would have both obvious and subtle consequences. Most obvious would be the birth of a nation, but one of the subtle outcomes would be the gradual acculturation of the ethnic minorities of that time. Scots-Irish and French Huguenots, both Calvinists who adapted easily to the individualistic, success-oriented society developing in the English colonies, would assimilate quickly. They did not maintain the ethnic isolation of the Dutch and Germans, whose cultural pluralism endured, but even for these ethnics, the cultural barriers and social distance would be reduced.

A process of cultural homogenization among the Whites would begin, bolstered by the attempt to build a national identity, but it would be short-lived. The catalyst was the new nation's audacious declaration that leaders ruled only by the consent of the governed, that all men were created equal and entitled to life, liberty, and the pursuit of happiness.

Those rights and privileges were not yet to be fully extended to women and racial minorities, but the promise of freedom and opportunity would soon attract thousands of hopeful others. Ethnic communities would be revitalized and new ones would form, rejuvenating diversity in a land where it had always flourished.

Notes

1. Mildred Campbell, "Social Origins of Some Early Americans," in *Seventeenth-Century America,* ed. James M. Smith (Chapel Hill: University of North Carolina Press, 1959), 63.

2. Stephen Steinberg, *The Ethnic Myth* (New York: Atheneum, 1981), 10.

3. Bruce Catton and William B. Catton, *The Bold and Magnificent Dream: America's Founding Years, 1492–1815* (New York: Doubleday, 1978), 165, 166, 168.

4. Lawrence H. Fuchs, *The American Kaleidoscope: Race, Ethnicity, and the Civic Culture* (Hanover, NH: Wesleyan University Press of New England, 1990), 12.

5. Maxine Sellers, *To Seek America: A History of Ethnic Life in the United States* (New York: James S. Ozer, 1977), 37.

6. Steinberg, *The Ethnic Myth*, 8.

7. Gary B. Nash, ed., *Class and Society in Early America* (Englewood Cliffs, NJ: Prentice Hall, 1970), 19.

8. Gary B. Nash, *The Urban Crucible: Social Change, Political Consciousness, and the Origins of the American Revolution* (Cambridge, MA: Harvard University Press, 1979).

9. U.S. Bureau of the Census, *Historical Statistics of the United States, Part II* (Washington, DC: U.S. Government Printing Office, 1976), 1168–72.

10. Donald B. Cole, *Martin Van Buren and the American Political System* (Princeton, NJ: Princeton University Press, 1984), 14.

11. See John C. Fitzpatrick, ed., *The Autobiography of Martin Van Buren* (New York: DaCapo, 1973), 9.

12. See Richard D. Alba, "Models for Viewing American Catholicism," chap. 1 in *Italian Americans: Into the Twilight of Ethnicity* (Englewood Cliffs, NJ: Prentice Hall, 1985), 9–12.

13. See Carl Bridenbaugh, *Myths and Realities: Societies of the Colonial South* (Baton Rouge: Louisiana University Press, 1952).

14. Lawrence H. Fuchs, "True Americanism: The Foundations of the Civic Culture," chap. 1 in *The American Kaleidoscope*.

15. See Nancy Woloch, *Women and the American Experience* (New York: McGraw-Hill, 1984); Laurel Ulrich, *Good Wives: Image and Reality in the Lives of Women of Northern New England, 1650–1750* (New York: Random House, 1982).

16. Gary B. Nash, ed., *Class and Society in Early America*.

17. James A. Henretta et al. *America's History to 1877* (Homewood, IL: Dorsey Press, 1987), 54–5.

18. Ibid., p. 93.

19. Edwin S. Gaustad, *The Great Awakening in New England* (New York: Harper & Row, 1957).

20. Daniel J. Boorstin, *The Americans: The Colonial Experience* (New York, Vintage, 1958), 179.

21. Michael Kammen, *People of Paradox: An Inquiry Concerning the Origins of American Civilization* (New York: Knopf, 1972), 49.

22. James Stuart Olson, *The Ethnic Dimension in American History* (New York: St. Martin's Press, 1979), 51.

4

Diversity in the Early National Period

Cultural differences had been put aside in the fight for independence, bringing previously isolated groups together in the common cause, reducing the social distance between groups, and lessening cultural barriers. Another effect had been disruption in the traditional division of labor and status between the sexes. Military service caused the absence of husbands, older brothers, or fathers, thereby requiring thousands of women to assume major responsibility for managing the shops or farms. Thrust into such unexpected roles, the women grew in decision-making skills and self-confidence in their leadership ability.

Traditional gender role expectations returned after the war, but the brief emancipation of women did not fade completely. Although their social and political subjugation continued during the early national period, the struggle for independence had sown seeds in women's minds. Many women, for example, freely discussed political issues in letters and social conversations, much to the dismay of the men. Complaining that the men thought women had no business talking about politics, Eliza Wilkinson wrote in 1783, "I won't have it thought that because we are the weaker sex as to bodily strength we are capable of nothing more than domestic concerns. They won't even allow us liberty of thought, and that is all I want."[1]

Although gender relations did not advance much, another social process was evolving. Cultural homogenization, begun with the intermingling of ethnic soldiers and support groups during the American Revolution, continued at a rapid pace between 1783 and 1820. These were crucial years in the development of the American political tradition and of a common culture. Strong efforts were made on many fronts to establish a civic culture and socialize the population into following common tenets.

The place of the United States in the world system at this time went from that of a colonial periphery to that of a semiperipheral republic. Even as it attempted to forge what would become a distinct culture, and even though the dynamics of open land and upward mobility opportunities would shape an "anything-is-possible" mind-set among many, global events still affected the new society.

Turmoil in France created political turmoil in the United States, as Federalists and Jeffersonians engaged in fierce rhetoric about the excesses of the French Revolution. A few years later, as France and England declared embargoes on one another, the United States was drawn into the conflict. After the British navy captured more than 400 U.S. merchant ships and forcibly impressed more than 10,000 U.S. seamen into its own navy, a new political faction—the War Hawks, led by Henry Clay—demanded a declaration of war against England.

Aiding their cause was the brutal violence in the Ohio River Valley, where Indian tribes that had backed the British during the Revolutionary War now attacked and killed many American settlers. Tacitly supported by the British seeking dominance in the lucrative fur trade, the Indians—uniting under the leadership of Tecumseh—fought for an independent Indian nation. Anger at England's actions on the high seas and in supporting the Indians led to the War of 1812; France and the United States were again allies in fighting the British. Eventually, the war ended in a stalemate, with the only losers those killed and the Indians, whose dream of an independent nation was dashed in military defeat.

A minority group's armed conflict and the actions of two European powers were just a few of the forces affecting U.S. society. Others included advances in ship design and the further spread of the Industrial Revolution that affected migration, trade, and the economy.

Building a National Identity

Throughout the new nation, a surge of patriotic pride prompted the severing of Old World ties in ways other than political. For example, in such areas as arts and letters, language usage, and religious authority, a distinctly American form emerged. National myth building, glorification of revolutionary heroes, and shaping of the public mind into a shared value orientation became part of building the nation.

Arts and Letters

The first American play was a 1787 comedy dealing with American life. In *The Contrast,* playwright Royall Tyler's contrast was between American worth and the affectation of foreign manners. His character "Jonathan"—the shrewd, yet uncultivated New England farmer—evolved into the "Stage Yankee" and served as a model for many editorial cartoonists for depicting the "real" American for about 200 years.[2]

Songs, poems, and essays appeared in the early federal years, but Washington Irving wrote one of the first pieces of imaginative prose in 1809. Interestingly, it was about an ethnic group, the Dutch. Called *A History of New York,* by Diedrich Knickerbocker, it is a delightful parody, now a classic of American humor and an early example of creative writing distinctly American in form and content. Painters, sculptors, and writers lionized the new national heroes and practically deified George Washington. Books about U.S., not English, history, and other books containing American essays began to appear. The Fourth of July became a national holiday as a cause for celebration and part of the concerted effort to build a national identity.

In Jefferson's inaugural address on March 1, 1801, he asserted that common identity when he stated, "We are all republicans—we are all federalists." The first political opponent in world history to replace a rival power as national leader through a peaceful election process, Jefferson affirmed the new reality.[3]

Linguistic Independence

In 1783, a native-born Connecticut Yankee, Noah Webster, gave American English a dignity and vitality of its own when he published the *American Spelling Book,* which became commonly known as the "Blue-Backed Speller." The book legitimized American English and provided Webster with most of his income for the rest of his life. Never out of print, its total sales exceed 100 million copies.

Webster followed with a grammar book (1784) and a reader (1785) with mostly American writings about democratic ideals and dutiful moral and political conduct. In 1828, he published a two-volume *An American Dictionary of the English Language,* and all 2,500 American copies sold out within a year. Advocating the superiority of language usage by the American commoner over the so-called artificiality of London, Webster successfully worked to have American language declare its independence from England.[4]

Religious Independence

Another manifestation of evolution into a distinctly American culture was in religion. One by one, the ethnic Protestant churches created local governing bodies to replace previous overseas authorities. Anglican churches, for example, renouncing allegiance to the Church of England, reorganized as the Protestant Episcopalian Church of America. Even conservative churches took this path. Dutch Reformed churches insisted on approving ministers ordained in Europe before they could preach from American pulpits. The German Lutheran Ministerium of Pennsylvania—a region previously mentioned as home of the largest German population— required a 3-year probationary period for European-trained ministers before they could be accredited for permanent assignment.[5]

In colonial times, there had been only about 25,000 Catholics, most of them living in Maryland, ostracized and out of the mainstream. After independence, Catholics established a special American liaison to the Vatican, headed by Bishop John Carroll in Baltimore. He pioneered in exploring positive relations between Catholics and their Protestant fellow citizens, seeking to overcome the exclusion of Catholics so common in many colonies where Congregational or Episcopal churches were supported by law. The actions of various Protestant denominations to sever Old World ties and of Catholics to seek a dialogue with Protestants contributed toward a further lessening of religious separatism. It would be short-lived, however. Beginning in 1820, the first wave of immigration to the new nation would revive the ebbing ethnnoreligious differences. The influx of millions of Catholic immigrants would launch the Protestant Crusade, as nativist suspicion and hostility effectively countered these early ecumenical efforts.

Social Structure and Social Class

The wealth and social status of 18th-century Americans varied according to where they lived: the frontier, small farm communities, commercial farm communities, or urban societies. Only a few individuals of considerable means might be found in the frontier or small farm communities, but the commercial farm communities contained larger concentrations of wealthy people in possession of large properties. Cities, whether small or major centers, typically contained a wealthy class larger and richer, in control of a greater proportion of the property, than in the other three communities.

On average, about one third of the White population living in the North in the revolutionary era was poor. Large property owners comprised about 30%, and small property owners almost as much. The wealthy elite comprised about 10%, a large proportion of them merchants benefiting from the growth and commercialization of port towns and their investments in city real estate.[6]

Lines of economic division and marks of social status, already evident prior to the Revolution, crystallized further afterwards. As Gary B. Nash observes,

> This social transformation is statistically measurable, though we can never obtain mathematical precision in these matters, given the selective survival of documents. In the inventories of estate and tax lists lies the silent record of the redefinition of class categories. Most notable is the parallel emergence of the fabulously wealthy and the desperately poor.[7]

Within the cities, this growing void between the elite and the laboring class became more evident with the increase in urban mansions and four-wheeled carriages. Cities were less the repositories of ethnic Americans than they were of an economically stratified order of English Americans. Cultural pluralism was to be found in distinct subcommunities outside the cities, more often in rural and frontier communities.

Among the working-class, rural, and frontier families, the women continued working at many tasks that the genteel ladies of the mercantile and upper classes did not. There was, however, one commonality almost all women shared, regardless of social class or residence. They married at a young age, had many children, and were usually grandmothers by the time they were 40. By 1820, the number of children under age 5, per 1,000 women between the ages of 20 and 44, was 1,295, about triple what it is today. Child rearing, keeping of home and hearth—and working in the fields if you were a farmer's wife—were the areas of responsibility for most women. Only 6% of the women were in paid employment outside the home. For most women, the house, perhaps farm, was their world, their reality, their fate.[8]

Religion, Power, and Group Consciousness

In time, increased diversity and a political system allowing for freedom of choice prompted many changes involving religion. As more non-English Americans gained political power, they supported dominant group politicians promoting religious equality and sought to punish those who did not.

Religion and Politics

In the previous chapter, I mentioned that the doctrine of separation of church and state was a consequence of religious diversity. In all of New England except Rhode Island, however, the Congregational Church maintained its privileged position and public support from tax revenues. This close church-state relationship, made possible because of the predominance of English Americans, remained until the 1830s.

Complete separation of church and state was not exactly the case in most other states when it came to qualifications to run for office. Full political rights were bestowed only on Protestant Christians. Some states were even more specific. Delaware required belief in the Trinity; North Carolina and Pennsylvania stipulated belief in the divine inspiration of both Testaments; New Jersey allowed only Protestants conforming to certain religious beliefs; New York mandated only Christians who renounced all foreign rulers, whether civil or ecclesiastical, thereby eliminating Catholics and Jews.

The Virginia planter elite, as members of the Anglican/Episcopalian Church, had long dominated the political scene, despite frequent conflicts with Baptists and Presbyterians. So, when Virginians Thomas Jefferson and James Madison led the successful struggle to secure separation of church and state, their efforts brought these men the enduring support of ethnic Americans throughout their political careers.

In a second Virginia action with national consequences, the state legislature rejected a bill supported by George Washington and Patrick Henry for a "general assessment" tax to provide funds for all religious groups. Jefferson then successfully sponsored a state bill in 1786 that endorsed the principle of individual liberty of conscience in religious matters, made all churches equal before the law, and stipulated no direct financial support to any religion. Jefferson considered passage of this religious liberty statute (a precursor of the national principle) as one of his three major achievements, and had it so inscribed on his tombstone.

In Pennsylvania, that old critic of the Germans, Benjamin Franklin, joined with Robert Morris and Dr. Benjamin Rush to rally German support for the new constitution by endorsing the establishment of a German-sponsored college. Appreciative Germans named the institution Franklin College. Franklin further endeared himself to the various German denominations when he successfully led the opposition in overturning the "Test Act," which had required several religious oaths as a prerequisite to holding any office.

In contrast, Rufus King, the American minister to London, was one of the more vocal opponents of Irish Catholic immigration to the United States. His protests that the country wanted no more "hordes of wild Irishmen" because they would "disfigure our true national character" were printed in the Irish-American press.[9] Offended ethnics can have long memories. When King ran for the presidency against James Monroe in 1816, the Irish voted against him en masse and reveled in his defeat.

Parallel Religious Institutions

In the late 18th century, two groups of northern African Americans illustrated the conflict view of a rising group consciousness promoting social change from their previously accepted subordinate status. No doubt the new national doctrine of equality and the subsequent assertiveness of American churches from European dominance influenced two different

Black groups, fed up by subtle and overt forms of racism within the integrated churches they attended, to split from these churches.

In 1787, a group of African Americans withdrew from St. George's Methodist Episcopal Church in Philadelphia and formed their own congregation. They built their own church (Bethel) in Philadelphia, had their first ordained minister by 1799, and formally organized as the African Methodist Episcopalian Church in 1816. Today, their membership exceeds 2.2 million members.

The origins of the African Methodist Episcopal Zion Church, a different entity, trace back to 1796, when the African American members of the John Street Methodist Church in New York City terminated their membership. They, too, formed their own congregation, built their first church (Zion) in 1800, and formally organized in 1821. Today, their church membership exceeds 1.2 million members.

Creation of these separate churches was by no means the first nor the last instance of minority groups establishing parallel social institutions. Because racial discrimination is more likely than ethnic discrimination to be a multigenerational reality, these Black churches became part of a larger pattern of racial segregation and isolation that would continue for generations, unlike ethnic churches that often ceased to exist after a few generations. Both Black churches, as their memberships attest, remain viable today.

The Nation's First Census

The 1790 census, with the exceptions of the survey of England conducted in 1086 during the reign of William the Conqueror and the registering of people in Sweden in 1749, was the first national counting of a population.[10] That first U.S. census revealed a decidedly rural society. Only 3% lived in cities of 8,000 or more residents, and only 5% lived in towns of 2,500 or more. Most Americans lived in much smaller communities, sometimes in ethnic enclaves where language and Old World customs still prevailed.

If we rely only on the commonly reported census data of 1790 (see Figure 4.1), we can fall into the trap of the cultural homogeneity myth. These data emphasize that the English, Scots, and Scots-Irish comprised 75.2% of the White ethnic population. This grouping makes some sense, for by then, these previously distinct cultural groups had begun to coalesce into a White-Anglo-Saxon-Protestant (WASP) collectivity. Moreover, as the culturally dominant group, they became the essence of the new

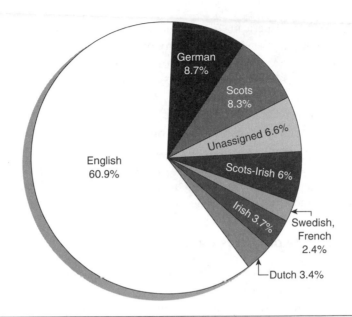

Figure 4.1   White Population Distribution in 1790

SOURCE: U.S. Bureau of the Census, *Historical Statistics of the United States, Part II,* Series Z 20-132 (Washington, DC: Government Printing Office, 1976).

national identity and remain to this day as the reference group for comparison with subsequent demographic changes.

This Eurocentric view is misleading, however, for it ignores the actual diversity that prevailed. Herein lie the origins for the Dillingham Flaw. It is one thing to speak of the culturally dominant group, but quite another to generalize about the entire population to argue cultural homogeneity.

The Other Side of the Coin

If 75% of the White population was White-Anglo-Saxon-Protestant, then 25% were not. This is one in four individuals, approximately 793,000 people of 3.1 million. Who were these non-Anglo-Saxon 25%? They were Dutch, French, German, Irish, and Swedish mostly, and they remained distinguishable in language and/or lifestyle from Anglo Americans. In smaller numbers, they were also Belgian, Danish, Flemish, Italian, Norwegian, Polish, and Swiss, plus scatterings from many other locales. Together, they were the ethnically diverse population segment that did not fit into the WASP category, and so contradict the false portrait of a new nation peopled almost entirely by Anglo Americans.

With so many Americans from ethnoreligious and linguistically diverse groups living outside the mainstream, any discussion of late 18th- and early 19th-century Americans as alike becomes an application of the Dillingham Flaw. Too much cultural heterogeneity within socially isolated subcultural groups prevailed at this time. Too many differences in economic and political power, in social status and stratification, and in lifestyle and outlook comprised this period to contradict erroneous generalizations about cultural consistency within a supposedly homogeneous population.

Yet it is not just that too many people forget about the many White ethnic Americans living in this era. These commonly reported data distort the past even more because they do not include racial minorities!

Eurocentric Use of Census Data

When we move past the Eurocentric presentation of 1790 census data to include non-Whites, we acquire a more complete understanding of the extensive diversity in America at that time.[11] By doing so, we not only find a smaller proportion of society of dominant Anglo-Saxon groups, but also further dispel mistaken assumptions about our past that enable the Dillingham Flaw to affect past-present comparisons.

Census tabulations in 1790 counted 757,208 African Americans, including about 60,000 nonslaves living primarily in the North. This increases the total population to 3.9 million, of whom 1.5 million are not White-Anglo-Saxon-Protestants. This means that instead of the 25% of American society previously identified as not fitting the mold of an Anglo-Saxon populace, the figure becomes 38%.

We can go higher if we include Native Americans. They may not have been included in the census, nor protected by the Constitution, nor even then considered part of "American" society, but they were nonetheless part of the total population. Most may have lived apart from the Whites, but they still lived within the states' boundaries and were a factor in trade, land disputes, and warfare.

Exact numbers on Native Americans in 1790 are not available. According to many anthropologists, a conservative estimate of those living east of the Mississippi River at this time is about 70,000. Adding that number to our previous numbers, we reach a total U.S. population of approximately 4 million people.

If we include all the people living in what was the United States in 1790—African, European, and Native Americans—we find that about 40% were not Anglo Americans (Figure 4.2). This is hardly the picture many Americans have today about that time. In 1790, two out of five

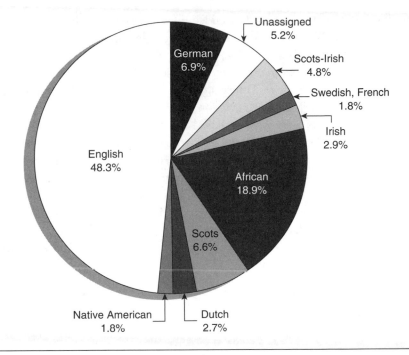

Figure 4.2   Total Population Distribution in 1790

SOURCE: U.S. Bureau of the Census, *Historical Statistics of the United States, Part II,* Series Z 20-132 (Washington, DC: Government Printing Office, 1976).

Americans were outgroup members whose race and/or culture set them apart from the dominant group of Anglo-American Protestants.

Expanding Territory and Diversity

Between 1783 and 1820, the United States doubled its size. Each expanse, the result of diplomatic treaties, brought even greater cultural diversity within the nation's changing borders. Tens of thousands of farmers moved into the Northwest Territory (later Ohio, Indiana, Illinois, Michigan, and Wisconsin), where 57% of the White population in 1790 was French, reflecting that nation's prior control of this region. Only 30% were English, the smallest proportion anywhere in land claimed by the United States. Germans and Scots each accounted for about 4%, the Scots-Irish for 3%, and the Irish for about 2%. Clearly, this region possessed significant White ethnic diversity.

This westward migration—into lands inhabited by the Shawnee, Chippewa, Ottawa, and Potawatomi—brought frequent conflict into the

Northwest Territory. The warfare ended with federal troops led by General "Mad Anthony" Wayne defeating the Western Indian Confederacy at the Battle of Fallen Timber in 1794. Another effort by a new confederacy leader, Tecumseh, to stop White encroachment of Native American lands was stopped at the Battle of Tippecanoe Creek in 1811, thereby sealing the fate of Native Americans with eviction from their ancestral lands.

In 1803, when Jefferson purchased the Louisiana Territory (865,000 square miles of dazzling country), he incorporated even French into the United States. French influence in architecture, language, and culture, including Catholicism, remained vibrant in the Mississippi Delta, its presence still felt today. Also absorbed were many new Native American tribes, many of them encountered by Meriwether Lewis and William Clark in their expedition to chart the new American region.

Another acquisition—the forced ceding of Florida to the United States in 1819—brought the Seminole and some Spanish inhabitants under U.S. authority. By 1820, the United States differed greatly from its 1783 beginnings. Twice as large as before, its newest territories contained mostly French, Spanish, and Native Americans. In fact, some of the new regions had no Anglo-American presence at all.

The Drop in Immigration

About 250,000 new immigrants came to the United States between 1790 and 1820. Because no detailed records were kept, we can assume that these newcomers were in reasonable proportion to the nationalities of those already living in the United States, thus suggesting that about three fourths of the new arrivals were British. Two other nationalities also came in significant numbers. About 25,000 were French-speaking immigrants, not refugees from the French Revolution, but mostly from the French islands in the Caribbean, where slave uprisings caused an exodus of almost the entire White population. Thousands of others were Irish revolutionaries fleeing the failure of a major rebellion begun in 1798 against English rule.

Despite the arrival of political refugees, U.S. immigration was low at this time, averaging only 8,300 annually. One factor in the drop in immigration was an English law passed in 1788 prohibiting the emigration of skilled artisans from Ireland and England. Then, in 1803, England drastically lowered the maximum number of passengers permitted in a ship, thereby reducing the profit margin for shipping companies. The resulting higher fares lessened the demand for indentured servants because increased costs were passed on to purchasers of the indentured contracts. Consequently, this form of migration decreased.

Other European countries also tried to restrict the emigration of skilled artisans, as well as men of military age. Furthermore, the French Revolution and Napoleonic Wars (1802–1815), eventually embroiling the United States in the War of 1812, disrupted European travel. Uncertainties and political turmoil in the United States between Federalists and Republicans also reduced the attraction of emigration.

The Significance of Natural Population Growth

Although immigration lessened in 1790–1820, the nation's population increased significantly from 3.9 million to 9.6 million in that same period. Only a small fraction was due to the territorial expansion, for it was in the older territories and states where population growth primarily occurred. Natural increase from high birth rates and the tendency to have large families were the main reasons for this rise in population.

This growth spurt of mostly "American stock," itself a composite of many ethnic groups, enabled cultural homogeneity to evolve to a degree never before attained and never again realized after 1820. Without a significant influx of new ethnics to reinvigorate the ethnic communities, a new generation emerged with a new identity. Reared by parents who lived through the Revolution, taught in schools where all things American were emphasized, and attending churches where clergy preached about God's blessings upon America, these children were the first to be socialized into the newly developing American culture.

Emergence of a Common Culture

Two other factors helped break down the walls of ethnic isolationism. First, fewer new arrivals meant no renewal of ethnic subcultures, thereby allowing acculturation of ethnic Americans to proceed unimpeded. Second, as western expansion continued, helped in part by lands given to Revolutionary soldiers in lieu of cash, many ethnic enclaves broke up as individuals and families left their old communities for the frontier.

The emerging American culture contained three major beliefs or value orientations. Political democracy had been at the core of the nation's founding, and it was indelibly reaffirmed with the peaceful transfer of power from Federalists to Republicans after the presidential election of 1800. Individual enterprise was the second hallmark and became an inspiration for both immigrant and native-born, as well as the basis for countless private economic initiatives. Third was the institutionalization of a Protestant culture, quite understandable in a society comprised almost entirely of Whites sharing that religious orientation, along with some converted African and Native Americans. Soon, the influx of millions of Catholic immigrants would challenge this cultural attribute.

Even as a common culture emerged, French influence was evident in cooking, fashions, and manners. French ads in American newspapers advertised "restauranteurs" who had previously been conventional American cooks and bakers. French chefs and recipes were popular. Inns and taverns renamed themselves "hotels." Americans became eager to learn from French dancing and fencing masters, or have their children become ladies and gentlemen by learning French manners and grace. French books, customs, dress, and music were all fashionable in the early 19th century.

As Americans sought to establish their own national identity, the prevalence of French influence on the public served to alarm some, particularly the Federalists. "Medusa's snakes are not more venomous," declared one Federalist writer, "than the wretches who are seeking to bend us to the views of France."[12]

Decline of Foreign Languages

Foreign language usage usually retains its vitality only under certain conditions. A continual inflow of compatriots will preserve the vitality of the alien language. Geographic isolation will prevent the typical pattern of children learning the host country's language. Social isolation may allow a persistent subculture to retain its language as part of its outgroup norms. In the United States in the early national period, none of these conditions prevailed to any large degree. On the frontier, pockets of ethnic isolation still existed, and in those regions, foreign language remained vigorous, everyday realities. Elsewhere, though, without an influx of new arrivals to sustain their resiliency, foreign languages went into decline.

A good example is the Germans, who comprised the largest non-British population segment. Prior to the Revolution, Baltimore, New York, and Philadelphia each had two or three German-language newspapers, but by 1815, none was left. Other languages declined in use as well, because by now, the Dutch schools, the Scandinavian schools, and others had introduced English into the classrooms.

This is not to say that the old languages died out completely, for that was not the case. Many of the older adults, unable to master the English language to any appreciable degree, held on to their native tongues. Some churches held duplicate services in both languages, enabling worshippers to have a choice.

Antiforeign Responses

Even though immigration was lighter than in earlier years and the populace was coalescing into a common culture, a visible foreign segment remained. It was comprised mostly of the French and Irish, whose numbers and buoyant ethnicity gave cause for alarm to some of the native-born.

The excesses of the French Revolution and growing support for the Jeffersonians among the Irish and French foreign-born alarmed the Federalists, who sensed a weakening of their power. In fiery speeches and newspaper editorials, they argued that these immigrants would "contaminate the purity and simplicity of the American character." One Federalist wrote, "Generally speaking, none but the most vile and worthless, none but the idle and discontented, the disorderly and the wicked, have inundated upon us from Europe." Noah Webster admitted that some immigrants were industrious, peaceable, and even voted the Federalist ticket but, he warned, "For one such 'good' European, we receive three or four discontented, factious men—the convicts, fugitives of justice, hirelings of France, and disaffected offscourings of other nations."[13]

Controlling the three branches of the federal government, the Federalists used their power to eliminate what they viewed as a threat to American society and to their own privileged position. Their actions were the first of several instances in the nation's history when the dominant group would successfully legislate against an "undesirable" foreign-born element. In 1798, President John Adams signed three bills passed by Congress. The Naturalization Act extended the residency requirement for citizenship from 5 to 14 years, in the hope of curtailing this new voter base of the Republicans. The Alien Act gave the president the power to arrest and deport undesirable aliens at his discretion. The Sedition Act prescribed fines and imprisonment for anyone criticizing the government.

Although Adams never used the Alien Act, his administration did implement the Sedition Act—a serious invasion of individual rights and liberties—arresting several foreign-born newspaper editors for seditious writings. Despite this law's blatant violation of the First Amendment provision for freedom of the press, a principle originating with the celebrated court victory of Peter Zenger in 1734, Federalists enforced it. The Alien and Sedition Acts expired after 2 years and faded away forever. As president, Jefferson succeeded in revising the Naturalization Act back to its 5-year residency requirement, where it remains.

The False Horizon

No one living it really knows when an era is drawing to a close. Only when it is past can we look back and mark the moment when the change occurred. So it was in 1820. That year saw James Monroe reelected, surely one sign of continuity. However, it was the first presidential election in which the Federalists did not field a candidate, for they had virtually disappeared as a political force by then. New, still unfelt, political winds were blowing. Even though the Democratic-Republican Party seemed invincible, before the decade ended, it too would be gone.

A whole generation had grown up, knowing nothing but independence. Older adults could look back on the far-reaching changes since their youth. Three states had been added to the first 13 by the turn of the century, and by 1820, that number had grown to 23.

Commerce was flourishing in the Northeast, agriculture under an entrenched slave system was prospering in the South, and westward expansion at the expense of Native Americans was continuing unabated. Canals, railroads, highways, and steamboats—plus such inventions as the reaper, the cotton gin, and the telegraph—were helping create an enormous economic empire rich in natural resources.

Probably many White Americans envisioned a tomorrow that would be better and essentially a continuation of what they knew. It would not be so, however. In 1820, a new era was dawning, some of it to be influenced by babies born that year, such as Florence Nightingale, William Tecumseh Sherman, and the daughter of Massachusetts Quakers Daniel and Lucy Anthony, whom they named Susan.

Thanks to low immigration and high natural population growth, together with the pervasive acculturation process, society had become more culturally homogeneous. Assimilation and societal cohesiveness were far more prevalent than White ethnic pluralism. And, because religious intolerance and conflict between the different Protestant denominations had virtually ended, many Americans may have deceived themselves into thinking that their society had evolved into its final synthesis.

This, too, was an illusion, for beyond the horizon that Americans could see was the first great wave of immigrants to come since the nation began. The sheer numbers of these culturally distinct newcomers would pose enormous challenges to U.S. institutions, embroil many in violent conflict, and change forever the America that these Americans of 1820 knew.

Notes

1. James A. Henretta et al., *America's History to 1877* (Homewood, IL: Dorsey Press, 1987), 196.

2. Arthur H. Quinn, *Representative American Plays* (New York: Appleton-Century-Crofts, 1957), 45.

3. Stanley Elkins and Eric McKitrick, *The Age of Federalism* (New York: Oxford University Press, 1993), 190.

4. "Noah Webster," *The New Encyclopaedia Britannica,* ed. Peter B. Norton (Chicago: Encyclopaedia Britannica, 1990), 12:550.

5. Henretta et al., *American History to 1877,* pp. 258–60; Sidney A. Ahlstrom, *A Religious History of the American People* (New Haven, CT: Yale University Press, 1972).

6. Jackson T. Main, "The Economic Class Structure of the North," chap. 1 in *The Social Structure of Revolutionary America* (Princeton, NJ: Princeton University Press, 1965).

7. Gary B. Nash, *The Urban Crucible: Social Change, Political Consciousness, and the Origins of the American Revolution* (Cambridge, MA: Harvard University Press, 1979), 257.

8. U.S. Bureau of the Census, *Historical Statistics of the United States, Part II,* Series Z20-132 (Washington, DC: U.S. Government Printing Office, 1976).

9. Vincent N. Parrillo, *Strangers to These Shores,* 7th ed. (Boston: Allyn & Bacon, 2003), 162.

10. U.S. Bureau of the Census, *Historical Statistics of the United States, Part II,* 1168.

11. Gary B. Nash, *Red, White, and Black: The Peoples of Early America* (Englewood Cliffs, NJ: Prentice Hall, 1974).

12. John C. Miller, *Crisis in Freedom* (Boston: Little, Brown, 1951), 41–2.

13. Ibid., 51–2.

5

Diversity in the Age of Expansion

At first glance, the 8,385 immigrants entering the United States in 1820 may have seemed just a continuation of similar numbers for the preceding 30 years. Few paid much attention then, judging by the lack of printed commentary. Perhaps some commented to friends that they detected a few more Irish, but if they did, they probably attributed it to the 3,000-strong Irish labor crew building the Erie Canal.

We now know it was more than just a case of a few more Irish arriving. In 1820, 47% of the emigrants from Europe were Irish Catholics. That proportion, almost one out of two, was significantly larger than the fairly small Irish presence of about 4% among the population at that time. In hindsight, we recognize that this ratio in 1820 was a clear signal of something new happening. That Irish group of newcomers became the vanguard of almost 2 million Irish who followed in the next 40 years.

A then-record influx of more than 5 million immigrants entered the country between 1820 and 1860. From 9.6 million inhabitants in 1820, the nation grew to 31.4 million by 1860. In the 1820s, immigration totals represented less than 2% of the total population, but by the 1850s, that decade's immigration total constituted more than 11% of the total population.

A young core power on the world stage, its vast resources and opportunities attracting both farmers and mill workers, the United States continued to experience the effects of social forces exerting pressure elsewhere in the world. Newcomers mostly arrived from Ireland—driven out by famine, poverty, and oppression—and from Germany, where economic conditions and civil unrest prompted many to leave. It was not yet a dominant force in the international community, but the United States clearly was a magnet for the disaffected of the world. Then, as now, migration patterns resulted as much from the "push" factors in the world as they did from the "pull" factors of freedom and opportunity in the United States.

As usual, dual patterns of assimilation and pluralism flourished. For the new arrivals in cities and in self-contained communities elsewhere, ethnicity was an everyday reality. As Joshua Fishman observed, the persistence over generations of Dutch, French, German, Navajo, and other languages became a normal fact in American life.[1] It is also true, as Calvin Veltman showed, that with some exceptions, a language shift to English was usually a two- to three-generation phenomenon.[2]

Travelers Discover the Ethnic Mosaic

Intrigued by the dynamics of a new nation and the diversity of its people and landscape, Europeans came to visit and record their impressions, many of which included comments on the many displays of ethnicity that they found.

Tocqueville's Dismay at Racial Suffering

After a 9-month visit in 1831–1832, Alexis de Tocqueville produced *Democracy in America* (1835), a masterpiece in political sociology for its analysis of the vitality, excesses, and potential future of American democracy. His observations about American associational life, collective pressures, individualism, competition, and materialism remain the bedrock for modern analyses of the American character.

Witnessing a band of Choctaw crossing the Mississippi at Memphis as part of the government's Indian removal policy, and also seeing the effects of slavery, Tocqueville observed, "I saw with my own eyes many . . . miseries . . . and was the witness of sufferings that I have not the power to portray." He envisioned a bleak American future with Native Americans perishing in isolation and African Americans, if freed from the slavery he condemned, continuing to experience racial prejudice. As Tocqueville explained, *1835 – 2006*

Still true today

> The prejudice of race appears to be stronger in the states that have abolished slavery than in those states where servitude has never been known. . . . Thus it is in the United States that the prejudice which repels the Negroes seems to increase in proportion as they are emancipated, and inequality is sanctioned by the manners while it is effaced from the laws of the country.[3]

Martineau's Defense of Immigrants

Harriet Martineau was a remarkable Englishwoman who wrote fine analyses on social, economic, historical, philosophical, and religious topics. After her visit to the United States (1834–1836) in her early 30s, she wrote *Society in America* (1837), in which she offered many of her observations about the American people, including the immigrants. To those critics of the immigrants, she countered,

> It would certainly be better if the immigrants should be well-clothed, educated, respectable people (except that, in that case, they would probably never arrive). But the blame of their bad condition rests elsewhere, while their arrival is, generally speaking, a pure benefit.

She went on to illustrate the value of immigrants to America:

> Every American can acknowledge that few or no canals or railroads would be in existence now in the United States, but for the Irish labor by which they have been completed; and the best cultivation that is to be seen in the land is owing to the Dutch and Germans it contains.[4]

how about Chinese labor?

how about Chinese & Japanese?

Another European visitor, Frederika Bremer, offered a warm and astute commentary about the ethnicity in midwestern cities in *The Homes*

OK – Published in 1857?

of the New World (1853). One city that appealed to her was St. Louis, Missouri, with its "interesting mixture" of French, German, Irish, and Spanish characteristics, as illustrated in the diversity of books and magazines sold, the variety of retail stores, and languages spoken on the street.[5]

Olmsted's Reaction to Isolated Ethnic Communities

Frederick Law Olmsted, later to become the famed landscape architect of many city parks, surprised himself by unexpectedly stumbling upon isolated ethnic communities in his travels. He described in *A Journey Through Texas* (1860) his seeing a farming community of Silesian Poles, as well as numerous German farming settlements throughout west Texas, where their homes, work, and leisure activities reflected their native origins.[6] He was especially impressed with New Braunfels, a German town named after Braunfels, Germany, located to the southeast of Bonn. He also chanced upon the village of Castroville, Texas, founded in 1844 by Alsatian French. Its population of 600 still spoke French and read French newspapers, and maintained two churches with worship services conducted in—what else?—French.

The French

French cultural influence, so popular among the public in the early national period, diminished by the 1820s but retained its vitality in the many areas where the French were concentrated. In the Mississippi Valley region, for example, elements of French influence from colonial times continued throughout the 19th century. Many rivers and towns bore names indicating their French origin, as did the names of the largest cities: Detroit, Michigan; New Orleans, Louisiana; and St. Louis.

America's "Flanders"

Flanders extends along the North Sea in northern France and western Belgium and still retains its medieval appearance. When Charles Dickens visited St. Louis in 1842, he went into the older section of the city long ago built by French settlers. He would write in *American Notes* that it reminded him of Flanders.

> The thorough-fares are narrow and crooked, and some of the houses are very quaint and picturesque; being built of wood, with tumble-down galleries before the windows, approachable by stairs, or rather ladders,

from the street. There are queer little barbers' shops, and drinking-houses too, in this quarter; and abundance of crazy old tenements with blinking casements, such as may be seen in Flanders. Some of these ancient habitations, with high garret gable windows perking into the roofs, have a kind of French shrug about them; and, being lop-sided with age, appear to hold their heads askew besides, as if they were grimacing in astonishment at the American improvements.[7]

The large presence of French Catholics in St. Louis prompted the Vatican to create a new diocese there in 1823. Here, as in many other American cities, French priests dominated the American Catholic hierarchy until midcentury, when massive Irish immigration ended their power.

America's "Little Paris"

New Orleans remains foremost in its preservation of French architecture, language, and culture. A picturesque reminder of Old World cities, it did not yield to Sunday "blue laws," as Boston, New York, and Philadelphia did in the early 19th century. On Sundays, New Orleans stores remained open, street musicians continued to play and sing, the markets were busy, and the theatrical performances drew large audiences.[8] The richness of French culture is partly revealed through the abundance of productivity, as seen in the New Orleans Theatre St. Pierre, which offered 70 operas in 1806–1811. Also, French historians, novelists, and poets created a vast outpouring of distinguished French literature between 1820 and 1860.

French Immigration

The French subculture remained resilient in part because of the steady arrival of new immigrants. More than 316,000 immigrants from France came in the period from 1820 to 1880, almost half of them arriving from 1840 to 1860. Much of this latter immigration resulted from the political disturbances preceding the Second Republic in 1848 and the dictatorship of Louis Napoleon, who became emperor in 1852. The previous year, 1851, was the single greatest year of French immigration to the United States, when more than 20,000 arrived.

Typically, the French preferred city life, and so most settled in many American cities. Sizable French populations in pre-Civil War cities could also be found in Charleston, South Carolina; Chicago; Cincinnati, Ohio; New York; and Philadelphia. French newspapers and social organizations were commonplace. With the outbreak of the Civil War, French military battalions formed in many cities to join in the cause on both sides.

The Irish

The Irish dominated U.S. immigration statistics from 1820 to 1860, when almost 2 million came, with 1.2 million of them concentrated in the years between 1847 and 1854.

America's First Ghetto People

Although mostly tenant farmers in their homeland, the Irish were ill equipped for U.S. agriculture. Potato farming in Ireland required only rudimentary skills and equipment, for it was all manual labor on fairly small plots of land. American farms required capital investment in larger tracts of land, and in axes, saws, seed, horses, mules or oxen to pull the plow, and a means to survive until the harvest. Impoverished, the Irish had neither money nor credit. Moreover, the low population density of rural America was quite different from home, where they lived in tight clusters in their villages, about 300 per square mile.

With no capital to become farmers and industrial America offering lots of jobs in the cities, others settled in what became known as "Dublin Districts," living in overcrowded tenements, dirt-floor cellars, converted warehouses, or shanties made of wooden crates and tar paper. Conditions were deplorable. Poor ventilation, heating, and lighting were common, and so were the open sewers in the streets and poor sanitation systems that contaminated drinking wells. Epidemics of cholera, typhoid, diphtheria, smallpox, and tuberculosis caused thousands of deaths among the immigrants. In 1849, for example, 5,000 people, mostly Irish immigrants, died from cholera in New York City. In 1860, the mortality rate in Boston, New York, and Philadelphia was 34 deaths per thousand, more than twice that in rural regions.

Labor, Religion, and Politics

Some Irish males worked as farmers, miners, or businessmen, but most worked at manual jobs in or near cities. They were in all types of construction: paving roads; laying down railroad track; digging out canals; building dikes, houses, or ships. They loaded or unloaded freight on trains and ships; cleaned streets and other people's houses, laundry, and chimneys; and they labored in the factories and mills.

Many Irish were single women taking jobs as domestics or nannies for the native-born urban elite. In 1800, there was one domestic servant for every 20 families, but by 1840, the ratio had dropped to one servant for every 10 families. Unmarried Irish (and Scandinavian) young women often came first to work in families' homes. Their typical workload was a 16-hour, 6-day week of cooking, cleaning, child care, and nursing the sick. The loss of husbands through accident, desertion, or sickness left many women without means to support large families except, perhaps, by taking in boarders or hiring out to do others' laundry or sewing at home. Among the Irish, female-headed households reached 18% by 1855. Although dropping to 16% by 1875, this proportion remained significantly higher than the national average.

It was the Irish, more than the French and Spanish, who brought Catholicism to Protestant America on a large scale. Bringing along their priests and nuns, building churches, convents, and parochial schools, they established a church hierarchy that would dominate American Catholicism for generations, which would later create some occasional interethnic resentment by Catholic immigrants of other nationalities.

Andrew Jackson's election in 1828 opened the political door to the common man, and the Irish hastened through. Using their political organizational skills, they forged a powerful voting bloc, city political machines, and a spoils system second to none. Graft and corruption may have been an integral part of machine politics, but so, too, was the proactive aid to the poor with food, fuel, and jobs.

The Germans

By 1820, German Americans were assimilating so rapidly that the Lutheran and Reformed churches were not only offering regular worship services in English, but had also opened their memberships to those of English, Scottish, Welsh, and Scots-Irish descent as well. As the wave of German immigration rose to tidal proportions in the 19th century, however, German culture quickly revived and flourished. Driven by hunger, political discontent, and a series of wars, 1.5 million Germans entered the United States between 1820 and 1860, followed by another 1.5 million in the next 20 years. Some came for political reasons, but economic reasons motivated most. By the 1850s, newly arriving German immigrants outnumbered Irish arrivals, a lead they would sustain for the next 60 years.

Massive German immigration and widespread settlement patterns made the German presence felt almost everywhere.[9] They entered through almost every eastern or southern port city, some to put down roots in those areas and others to move inland by train or boat along the Erie Canal or Ohio and Mississippi rivers. The Midwest attracted many, particularly Ohio, Indiana, Illinois, and Wisconsin. Large concentrations lived throughout the South before the Civil War, including Wheeling, West Virginia; Mobile, Alabama; Richmond, Virginia; Charleston; Louisville, Kentucky; Nashville, Tennessee; New Orleans; and Stuttgart, Arkansas. Some Germans went west, as did John Sutter, on whose land the discovery of gold touched off the California gold rush.

The "German Athens"

If New Orleans was the definitive French city of the United States in the 1850s, then Milwaukee, Wisconsin, was the definitive German city. Two thirds of the city's 13,000 inhabitants in 1850 were foreign-born, and Germans accounted for two thirds of this number. The city became the distributing center of German settlers throughout the north central states. In contrast to the coarseness and dullness of most frontier towns, Milwaukee was an oasis of culture in the 1850s. Its musical and literary cultural level shone so brightly that travelers called it the "German Athens." The city possessed numerous German organizations, including a highly respected German American Academy, a freethinkers club, a *Sangerbund* (singing society), a theatre, and a *Turnvereine,* which blended physical fitness and German patriotism. A brewery, beer gardens, pork stores, mutual aid societies, and fire and militia companies were other aspects of the German presence.

German Diversity

Nineteenth-century German immigrants defied categorizing because of many differences within their own group, which impeded any sense of pan-German ethnicity. An extreme cultural gap existed between the Catholics, mostly from the southern and southwestern provinces, and the Protestants, who were mostly from the northern provinces.[10] Yet the Protestants themselves were distinct subcultures. The Calvinists—Baptists, Presbyterians, and Reformed—did not share the cultural nationalism espoused by the German Lutherans, and all of these religious groups were less culturally isolated than the Pietists—Amana, Amish, Hutterites, and Mennonites—who lived in separate but closely knit (*Gemeinschaft*) communities.

Other distinctions among the Germans were occupational and residential patterns. In rural areas throughout the land, Germans turned uncleared, partly cleared, or waste lands in productive farms with their agricultural aptitude. These industrious and conservative Germans were knowledgeable in livestock, dairying, and crop raising, but they were far less cosmopolitan than their city-dwelling compatriots.

These were the artisans and merchants who settled in Germantown sections in virtually every American city. As their numbers increased, their many social and cultural activities sometimes replaced the preeminence of an earlier group, as in St. Louis, where French music and customs yielded to those of the Germans. Not all Germans in the cities were economically secure people enjoying social and cultural activities, however. Some lived in abject poverty and struggled each day just to survive.

For most German immigrants, the reunification of Germany in 1871 intensified their sense of German ethnicity. The common German language reinforced that awareness and militated against going to a non-German church regardless of faith. A German Reformed Church not Dutch, a German Lutheran Church not Norwegian, or a German Catholic Church not Irish, made one feel more comfortable by practicing the faith in one's native language. A common expression in those times for German Catholics was "language saves the faith," and so German-language masses continued despite the protest of the Irish American-dominated church hierarchy to Rome.

Native Americans

White attitudes toward Native Americans were mixed in the 19th century. Whereas some simply wanted them out of the way, idealists sought to integrate the indigenous peoples through assimilation. Various missionary groups attempted to make them into individualist Christian farmers who spoke English instead of communal, foreign-speaking "heathens" who depended on hunting and subsistence agriculture.

Assimilation Efforts

Some Native Americans in the old Northwest Territory did convert to Christianity and attempt to assimilate. In doing so, they found themselves to be a dually marginal people, for they were now social outcasts from their own tribes, victims of ridicule and even physical abuse, and also not accepted by the Whites. Confronted by a double dose of discrimination, many chose to return to their old ways rather than suffer a lifetime of social isolation.

By 1820, hundreds of thousands of Whites lived in Georgia, Tennessee, and the brand-new states of Alabama and Mississippi. Their food source and lifestyle endangered by White encroachment, five tribes—the Cherokee, Chickasaw, Choctaw, Creek, and Seminole—tried to keep their lands by adopting the White man's way of life. Greater power comes to those who assimilate into a society rather than live on its fringes, and these tribes thus sought power through integration to control their destinies rather than face loss of power through resistance and thus have no voice in their future. Because of the tribes' conversion to their culture and Christianity, White Americans gave them the ethnocentric appellation of the "Five Civilized Tribes."

"As Long as Grass Grows and Water Runs"

Living on rich, fertile land at a time of agricultural growth, particularly in cotton, the tribes stood in the path of further White settlement. President Jackson sent agents to negotiate, offering them lands west of the Mississippi River where "their white brothers will not trouble them" and where they "can live upon it, they and all their children, as long as grass grows and water runs."[11]

As a witness to one small part of this expulsion, Tocqueville offered this poignant commentary:

> It is impossible to conceive the frightful sufferings that attend these forced migrations. They are undertaken by a people already exhausted and reduced; and the countries to which the newcomers betake themselves are inhabited by other tribes, which receive them with jealous hostility. Hunger is in the rear, war awaits them, and misery besets them on all sides. To escape from so many enemies, they separate, and each individual endeavors to procure secretly the means of supporting his existence by isolating himself, living in the immensity of the desert like an outcast in civilized society. The social tie, which distress had long since weakened, is then dissolved; they have no longer a country, and soon they will not be a people; their very families are obliterated; their common name is forgotten; their language perishes; and all traces of their origin disappear. Their nation has ceased to exist except in the recollection of the antiquaries of America and a few of the learned of Europe.[12]

For those tribes not pressured into agreeing, Jackson ordered the military to expel them from their lands and to force-march them into Oklahoma Territory to live.[13] Despite a U.S. Supreme Court ruling in favor of the tribes, Presidents Jackson and Van Buren, the Congress, and the public sided with economic expansion instead of cultural accommodation. By 1838, Indian removal was complete except for the Seminole, who, aided by runaway slaves who had married into the tribe, waged guerilla warfare until 1842, when they, too, were defeated and removed to Oklahoma. In the old Northwest Territory, only the Sauk and Fox, led by Chief Black Hawk, fought against removal until their defeat in 1832. Like the Delaware, Kickapoo, Miami, Ottawa, Peoria, Potawatomi, Shawnee, Winnebago, and Wyandot tribes before them, the Sauk and Fox were also moved across the Mississippi.

All that now remained east of the Mississippi were the Iroquois of upstate New York, whose land was not coveted, and remnant bands from the expelled tribes who had escaped detection. Most Native Americans now lived in the western half of the nation on lands that were supposed to be theirs forever.

The End of Forever

"Forever" was less than 20 years. Acquisition of Oregon in 1846 and the Southwest in 1848 extended the U.S. border to the Pacific Ocean. Native Americans found new pressures for their land from a relentless White migration, encouraged by discovery of gold in California in 1848, the Homestead Act of 1862 giving 160 acres of free land in the Great Plains to migratory Whites, and completion of the transcontinental railroad in 1869.

Skirmishes, massacres, and major battles erupted throughout the West. Deliberate, large-scale slaughter of the buffalo made them nearly extinct, devastating the culture and economy of the Plains tribes. In time, the independence of all the tribes ended, and they began a new life as dependent wards of the government, segregated on open-air slums called reservations.

Because ethnic Americans, mostly German and Irish, served in the U.S. army in numbers greater than their proportion in the population, they played a major role in the bloody Indian wars of the 19th century. Military service offered them a well-paid job without discrimination and enabled them to assert that they were "real" Americans. Adapting to the cultural biases of their new country, they saw it as their duty to kill the "bloodthirsty savages."

The Africans

Of the 1.8 million African Americans in 1820, all but about 230,000 were slaves. By 1860, the slave population increased to almost 4 million, and free Blacks grew to about 488,000. Virtually all of this growth was due to natural population increase, because Congress outlawed international slave trade in 1808.

Southern Blacks

Three separate cultures evolved in the South among (a) the nonslave-owning Whites primarily living in the back country, (b) the plantation owners, and (c) the slaves. Even among the slaves, diversity existed. Most were field hands working from sunup to sundown, but a small number were domestic servants or skilled workers. Of the tens of thousands of skilled workers, some lived and worked on plantations, but many were artisans hired out in the cities. In some cities, notably New Orleans, these artisans had a remarkable degree of free physical movement and personal behavior, but they were slaves nonetheless.[14]

In 1860, when about 4 million African Americans lived in the South, Whites totaled only 7 million. In South Carolina and Mississippi, Blacks far outnumbered Whites, whereas in Georgia, Florida, Alabama, and Louisiana, the two races were about evenly divided in numbers. Only in Virginia, Arkansas, and Texas did Whites outnumber Blacks, by about a three-to-one ratio.

Life as a slave was a blend of labor exploitation, sexual exploitation, illiteracy, limited diet, and primitive living conditions. Only in their private times of leisure in the evening or on Sundays and holidays could slaves find respite from the relentless demands of bondage. It was then that they could hunt, fish, gamble, visit, gossip, sing, dance, picnic, or attend church. Essentially, slave culture revolved around three elements: family, music, and religion.

The family was the primary institution of slave society despite the breakup of families through sale or transfer of ownership, or White sexual exploitation of Black women. The typical slave household had two parents, fulfilling their traditional gender roles with the male as disciplinarian and head of the family, and the female in charge of their home and children. We have several clues to the strength of Black family norms in the antebellum South. Their sexual mores allowed premarital sex but condemned adultery. This commitment of a man and woman to one another, first legitimized in the "jumping over the broomstick" ceremony, was reinforced by tens of thousands of former slaves legalizing their marriages through an official ceremony after the Civil War. Moreover, many actively searched for children, spouses, and parents after the war to reunite separated families.

African music has a rich history and variety. Beginning with the recorded observations of Hanno the Carthaginian in the 5th century B.C., many have written about the varied African musical instruments, including flutes, lutes, fiddles, lyres, reed pipes, drums, xylophones, and musical bows. African music is also different from Western music in that one cannot separate music from dance or bodily movement; even the playing of an instrument involves a complex combination of body movements.

Music is a reflection of the life and times of a people. In their slave society, African music was an important component of work, leisure, and worship. Using the forms, tones, and rhythms of their heritage, African Americans expressed their emotions and feelings through songs and spirituals. Frederick Douglass—whose rise from an illiterate slave to an articulate abolitionist writer and speaker is an inspiration to anyone born into poverty—noted the importance of music to his brothers still in bondage: "Slaves sing most when they are most unhappy. The songs of the slave represent the sorrows of the heart, and he is relieved by them, only as an aching heart by its tears."[15]

Religion was another outlet where slaves could express their deep feelings, bond together, and find hope. Traditional African cultures are rooted in a worldview of continuous interaction between spiritual forces and the community. Thus, it was a logical step for slave religion to blend the spiritual and secular worlds, connecting themselves to both a glorious past and a more rewarding future. Converting mostly to the Baptist and Methodist faiths because they permitted Black clergy, African Americans used their Christian faith to sing the joys of God's love for all and of the promise of glory and salvation in heaven.[16]

Northern Blacks

Theoretically, Northern Blacks were free, but in reality, they were not equal. Most states passed laws denying them the right to vote, serve on juries, or migrate from another state into theirs. Segregation was the norm in public facilities and residential areas. Job discrimination was widespread. Confined primarily to menial occupations, the Northern Blacks also fought a losing battle in the northeastern cities against the inroads of Irish competition.

Socially ostracized, disenfranchised, and economically discriminated against, Northern Blacks created their own subsociety. Parallel social institutions, comparable to those of White ethnics, sprung up. Besides Black churches, there were the fraternal and mutual aid societies. These organizations offered educational programs and medical and burial services, and provided forums to air grievances and enhance self-esteem.

The Chinese

Just as many Americans, both native-born and foreign-born, went west across land to seek their fortune, so, too, did the Chinese go east across the Pacific Ocean to seek theirs. Only 88 Chinese immigrants entered the United States between 1820 and 1853, but in 1854, 13,100 arrived, attracted by the discovery of gold. When the 1850s ended, more than 41,000 Chinese had come, followed by another 64,000 in the 1860s.

Most Chinese came to the United States in the 19th century as sojourners, intending to work for a limited time and then return home. Few women came; about 1 in 20 arrivals from China was a female. The men worked as miners, farm laborers, and fishermen. Soon, many were employed as railroad workers and builders of dams, levees, and irrigation systems.

Obviously, the Chinese brought a new element to an already diverse U.S. society. They were a non-Western, non-Christian people whose appearance (race, clothing, hair); belief system; food; language; music; and other cultural attributes clearly set them apart from the rest of society.

Another distinction was their social structure.[17] Traditional clans were a primary source of identity and emotional ties to family. Settlement patterns depended upon clan location, as each tended to take up residence in selected areas. The *hui kuan* associations were mutual aid societies that represented six sending regions of China. With wider influence than the clans and often mediating disputes between clans, the *hui kuan* played a key role in helping Chinese newcomers find work and lodging; they also lent money, provided health care and burial arrangements, and met other social needs as necessary.

The tongs, or secret societies, brought a disruptive element to the Chinatowns. Involved in such organized crime activities as gambling, heroin, opium, and prostitution, the tongs challenged clan and *hui kuan* leadership, resulting in frequent bloody clashes. Because the tongs were better organized, they were more effective at offering welfare assistance to the sick, disabled, and unemployed, as well as life insurance, thus mixing fear and support to gain influence.

These three groupings—clans, *hui kuan,* and tongs—provided the Chinatowns with an infrastructure that resulted in self-sufficient ethnic communities. Ignored by politicians because they could not become citizens and vote, the Chinese in 19th-century America preserved their way of life much as Germans in isolated rural communities, for example, sought to preserve theirs by different means.

The Mexicans

Beginning in the 1820s, thousands of American settlers crossed the Louisiana border into the Mexican land of Texas, starting hundreds of cotton plantations in that fertile region. A decade later, more than 25,000 Americans lived in eastern Texas. Their presence set a chain of events in motion that would result in the U.S. annexation of Texas from Mexico, war with Mexico, and the subsequent acquisition of New Mexico and California territories. With the signing of the Treaty of Guadalupe Hidalgo in 1848, 80,000 new ethnics became part of the American population.[18]

The new Americans were mostly a blend of a small group of wealthy landowners, a much larger group of artisans, ranch hands, or farmers, who lived in an area also occupied by tens of thousands of Native Americans. Soon, widespread land fraud, expensive litigation, or forced land sales under violent duress caused almost all the Mexican American elite to lose their land titles by 1880 to squatters or emerging White land barons for little or no money. Federal troops would eventually subdue the tribes as they had others.

Northern California and Texas were the locales of the most violent episodes of interethnic conflict with the Spanish-speaking Catholic residents. Banditry, riots, terrorism, vigilantism, even open warfare were common throughout the 1850s. In southern California and New Mexico, ethnic relations were more peaceful because arid conditions there attracted far fewer White settlers. Completion of the southern transcontinental railroad in the 1870s, however, brought in many new settlers and a repetition of the cycle of ethnic hostility and loss of land titles to the Whites.

Although some *mexicano* landowners managed to keep their property, most did not. Gradually, the Mexican Americans took on the status of a colonized people. School segregation, political disfranchisement, and economic dependence as laborers upon the now powerful Whites changed the Mexican Americans into essentially a suppressed minority. One telling statistic about the impact of colonization and poverty on family organization was the increase in Mexican American female-headed households, which numbered one third of the total by 1880.

Intergroup Conflicts

Numerous interethnic clashes occurred throughout the 19th century, such as those previously mentioned as occurring in the West and Southwest between the dominant group and Mexicans or Native Americans. Greatly upset about the large influx of Chinese, Irish, and German Catholics, and other foreigners, a right-wing reactionary group formed, calling itself the Supreme Order of the Star Spangled Banner. Dubbed "Know-Nothings" for their refusal to talk about their secret activities, they lobbied extensively for strict immigration laws and discrimination against Catholics.

Their vicious hate campaign was often accompanied by brutal violence, with mobs raiding Irish and German homes, churches, schools, and businesses. Arson, vandalism, beatings, and murders occurred throughout the 1850s, with virtually every large northeastern city experiencing major disturbances.[19]

Organizing as the American Party, they elected 75 congressmen in 1854. By the next year, they had elected six governors and many local officials. In 1856, their presidential candidate, ex-President Millard Fillmore, ran a distant third to James Buchanan and John C. Fremont, although he did receive about 22% of the vote. This movement afterwards faded into oblivion as North-South antagonisms mushroomed into civil war. It was not the last time American minorities would face right-wing extremists.

The Next Horizon

In this era, the large numbers of Asians, Hispanics, and Europeans, particularly Germans and Irish, brought significant cultural diversity into the land. Some assimilated, but the numerous pockets of ethnic pluralism returned an expanded America to a new version of its earlier colonial patchwork ethnic quilt. On the negative side, the violence perpetrated by antiforeign or anti-Indian forces and the exploitation of racial minorities scarred the American minority saga. Yet it was also a time when the national conscience was stirred into various social reforms, including the end of slavery, and when feminists organized and launched a campaign for women's rights, though with only limited success. Of course, much more was to come.

The Civil War curtailed immigration, but did not stop it completely. When the awful carnage had ended and the nation was reunited, immigration resumed even stronger than before. Where it had taken 40 years before the war to absorb more than 5 million immigrants, that figure was surpassed in just 20 years, with the arrival of 5.1 million between 1861 and 1880.

Irish immigration, however, had peaked and was now about half what it had been in the 1850s. German immigration dropped too, but not as much, and exceeded the Irish by more than 630,000 from 1861 to 1880. Other groups were beginning to make their presence felt more, most notably the Chinese, French Canadians, Russians, Scandinavians, and Swiss. By 1880, the U.S. population exceeded 50 million, more than five times what it had been in 1820. It was filled now with millions of Irish and German Americans, tens of thousands of Chinese, Mexican, and Native Americans, plus many other White ethnics, none of them Anglo Americans, and most of them still unassimilated.

Yet even though the process was incomplete, this era was drawing to a close and a new one beginning. In 1890, the Census Bureau would declare that the frontier no longer existed; in urban areas, steel girders and elevators would dramatically alter the cityscapes and population density; and inventions such as the telephone (1876) and incandescent light (1880) were beginning to revolutionize life at home.

An industrializing America would now roar into an industrial age, with new factories opening almost daily. The world would become a smaller place, thanks to advances in transportation and communications. Steamships would soon fill their holds with human freight, as millions of "new immigrants" from Asia, Europe, and the Middle East would seek the American Dream.

The America to which they would come would be vastly different from what earlier immigrants had found. And these new immigrants would be vastly different from what Americans had known of immigrants. Physically and culturally distinct, the newcomers would bring even greater diversity, challenges, and progress to the American scene than ever before.

Notes

1. Joshua Fishman, *Language Loyalty in the United States* (London: Moulton, 1966).

2. Calvin Veltman, *Language Shift in the United States* (New York: Moulton, 1983).

3. Alexis de Tocqueville, *Democracy in the United States,* 1835, ed. Phillip Bradley (New York, Knopf, 1960), 359–60.

4. Harriet Martineau, *Society in America,* 1837, ed. Seymour M. Lipset (Garden City, NY: Anchor Books. 1962), 183.

5. In Carl Wittke, *We Who Built America,* rev. ed. (Cleveland: Case Western Reserve University Press, 1967), 207–8.

6. Frederick Law Olmsted, *A Journey Through Texas, or a Saddle Trip on the Southwestern Frontier,* 1860 (New York: Burt Franklin, 1969), 169–83, 276–8.

7. Charles Dickens, *American Notes,* 1842 (Greenwich, CT: Fawcett, 1961), 201.

8. Wittke, *We Who Built America,* 318.

9. Robert H. Billigmeier, *Americans from Germany: A Study in Cultural Diversity* (Belmont, CA: Wadsworth, 1974).

10. Jay P. Dolan, *The Immigrant Church: New York and German Catholics, 1815–1865* (Baltimore: Johns Hopkins Press, 1975).

11. James A. Henretta et al., *America's History to 1877* (Homewood, IL: Dorsey Press, 1987), 359.

12. Tocqueville, *Democracy in America,* Vol. 1.

13. See Dale Van Every, *Disinherited: The Lost Birthright of the American Indian* (New York: Avon Books, 1966).

14. Eugene D. Genovese, *Roll Jordan Roll: The World the Slaves Made* (New York: Pantheon, 1974).

15. Henretta et al., *America's History to 1877,* 417.

16. C. Eric Lincoln and Lawrence H. Mamiya, *The Black Church in the African American Experience* (Durham, NC: Duke University Press, 1990).

17. Stanford M. Lyman, *Chinatown and Little Tokyo* (Millwood, NY: Associated Faculty Press, 1986).

18. Ellyn R. J. Stoddard, *Mexican Americans* (New York: St. Martin's Press, 1994), 66–9, 206–12.

19. See Carleton Beals, *Brass Knuckle Crusade,* rev. ed. (New York: Hastings House, 1960).

6

Diversity in the Industrial Age

Astounding changes occurred between 1871 and 1920. Railroad track miles tripled from 53,000 in 1870 to 167,000 in 1890, creating an efficient transportation system that welded the nation into a unified, enormous market.[1] The spectacular growth of cities dramatically altered the American way of life. Industrialization brought the majority of the labor force into manufacturing, creating thousands of jobs and a labor shortage.

In this era, the United States became an industrial giant and a world influence. Sometimes, it was the initiator, as when it altered sea travel by building the Panama Canal or when it defeated Spain in the War of 1898 and acquired Spain's island possessions in the Caribbean and Pacific. At other times, global forces beyond the control of the United States—such as the social upheavals in southern, central, and eastern Europe, or World War I—dramatically affected the country by changing migration patterns, which in turn affected the country's population composition and inter-group relations.

The influx of 26.3 million immigrants in this period filled America's desperate need for labor. Whether they worked in the mines, on railroad construction, or in the factories and mills, the immigrants helped the nation come of age industrially. In a pattern comparable to today, they were obliged to take jobs of low status, low pay, long hours, and difficult work that were shunned by the native-born. By their presence, the immigrants represented the paradoxical duality of opportunity and exploitation.

Exploitation often matched the economic opportunities that the immigrants found. Large-scale immigration enabled industrialists to keep wages low and circumvent labor union organization efforts. This split labor market was a constant reality, as employers hired newcomers as strikebreakers or as lower-paid workers to replace higher-paid ones.[2] The result was ethnic antagonism of native-born or older immigrant workers against the new arrivals for either taking their jobs away or else depressing their wage scale.

Minority Family Economies

Gender played an important role in family economic activities. Whereas the men sought employment in a variety of occupations, cultural norms dictated that married women should not work outside the home. Indeed, less than 5% did so in 1890, often only because their husbands were disabled, missing, or unemployed. Typically, the wife's role was to maintain the house. If family needs required her income because the children were too young to work, then she would take on work at home (such as laundry or sewing) or else care for boarders (a common practice given the high number of male immigrants).

The world of work for women thus fell mostly to the young and single. More than half of all gainfully employed women at the turn of the century were between 16 and 24 years of age. These young women were often employed in factories or mills in "suitable" positions as machine tenders or seamstresses perhaps, or else as assemblers, inspectors, packers, and so on in various types of plants.[3]

About one third of all employed female workers were blue-collar workers. Another third were domestic workers: maids, cooks, nannies, and so on. In the North, many were single Irish or Scandinavian women who had journeyed without family to begin life anew. In the South, African American women held similar positions. The final third of female workers were usually not first-generation Americans. This category of employed women was in such white-collar positions as nurse, teacher, or sales clerk.

Children, usually at about the age of 8 or 9, often went to work in the mills and the mines. With no child labor laws yet to protect them, they worked the same long hours under harsh working conditions as did the adults, but usually for one tenth an adult's wages. Economic necessity dictated their working, however, for without the children's small wages, families could not survive.

In nonurban settings—whether the family be African, Asian, Hispanic, White ethnic, or native-born American—the entire family unit worked every day, each family member—man, woman, and child—performing necessary farm tasks for the welfare of all. Here, too, the work was hard, although one's labors were at least within a family environment.

An expanding economy and population, and the institution of child labor laws (not applicable to agriculture), brought about an increase in jobs for women. Included in this significant rise in female participation in the nonfarm labor force were married women as well. By 1920, 1 in 5 paid workers was a woman, and 1 in 10 married women, twice that of 1890, had become a wage earner.

Population Diversity

In addition to the great influx of southern, central, and eastern Europeans in this period, it was also a period of high immigration from northern and western Europe, and other parts of the world. Evidence is found in the 1.7 million Canadians, 840,000 Asians, 277,000 Mexicans, 307,000 West Indians, and 90,000 Central and South Americans. In cities, towns, and reservations, America's racial minorities lived segregated and socially isolated from White America. Some were former slaves or their descendants. Others were a conquered people. Still others were voluntary immigrants seeking their fortune. All shared, however, a common fate. As Robert Blauner observed, most were relegated to primary occupations that did not provide the same upward mobility opportunities as industrial jobs did for Europeans.

In an historical sense, people of color provided much of the hard labor (and the technical skills) that built up the agricultural base and the mineral-transport-communication infrastructure necessary for industrialization and modernization, whereas the European worked primarily within the industrialized, modern sectors. The initial position of European ethnics, while low, was therefore strategic for movement up the economic and social pyramid. The placement of nonwhite groups, however, imposed barrier upon barrier on such mobility, freezing them for long periods of time in the least favorable segments of the economy.[4]

The "new" immigration encouraged by a rapidly expanding economy brought considerable cultural diversity into the country. Previously little-known nationality groups now flocked to the nation's shores, establishing their ethnoreligious cultural marks. By the turn of the century, most northeastern cities would contain two thirds or more of a foreign-born population.

Yet even as pluralism manifested itself in new or revitalized ethnic communities, ethnicity was beginning to fade among other groups. Second- and third-generation Americans of northern and western European ancestry were less inclined to retain an ethnic identity. Even though they had not yet become fully assimilated, the Irish and Germans were gaining political power and moving toward economic equality with older groups. The native-born of Dutch, French, and Scandinavian ancestry were more likely to have attained structural assimilation, even as new arrivals from those areas replenished the ethnic mosaic.

In short, the dual realities of assimilation and pluralism were once again evident. The following pages offer a brief look at various groups who comprised that diversity.

African Americans

For a while after the Civil War, interracial cooperation offered promise of a new era in race relations in the South. Blacks and Whites worked side by side in coal mines and lumber camps, and on waterfront docks, their efforts encouraged in the mid-1880s by the interracial unionism of the Knights of Labor. White and Black dirt farmers formed separate Farmers' Alliance organizations, but the two worked together for agrarian reform. They united behind the Populist Party in 1891, but vicious opposition and voter fraud resulted in defeat almost everywhere. The embittered poor

Whites turned against their Black allies as the cause of their losses, strongly encouraged in this direction by the White conservative elite.

Out of this struggle was born a malicious form of White supremacy, determined to establish a rigid color line. As George M. Fredrickson succinctly said,

> In the late nineteenth century, when blatant racism was reaching the extreme point of its development, the resurgent white supremacists of the South put new and more stringent laws on the books. Not only were anti-miscegenation statutes re-enacted or reaffirmed, but more rigorous definitions of whiteness were put into effect. By the beginning of the twentieth century most southern states were operating in accordance with what amounted to a "one-drop rule," meaning in effect that a person with any known degree of black ancestry was legally considered a Negro and subject to the full disabilities associated with segregation and disfranchisement.[5]

Poll taxes, initiated in some districts in 1877 to disenfranchise Black voters, now spread. Literacy tests were another effective means enacted, because about 75% of Black Americans were illiterate. (Illiterate poor Whites were exempted by "grandfather clauses," if their grandfathers had been eligible to vote in 1860.[6]) Beginning in Florida in 1887, mandatory segregation laws regarding train passengers were passed in several states. When the U.S. Supreme Court upheld such laws in *Plessy v. Ferguson* in 1896, the "separate but equal" doctrine became institutionalized. Between 1901 and 1910, most Southern states passed a wide array of Jim Crow laws, bringing racial segregation into all places of public accommodation.

Racism manifested itself in its ugliest form in violence. From 1892 to 1921, almost 2,400 Blacks were lynched, most in the South. The growing presence of Blacks in the cities and perceptions of them as an economic threat led to deadly race riots erupting in Georgia, Illinois, Indiana, and Ohio from 1904 to 1908. Fear of economic competition triggered another deadly race riot in East St. Louis in 1917. When union organizers placed a newspaper ad claiming that local industries were recruiting Blacks to reduce White wages, the workers attacked the Black ghetto. In the aftermath, 39 Blacks and 9 Whites had been killed. Two years later, riots exploded in 26 cities, leaving 38 killed in Chicago and 6 dead in Washington, DC.

The promise of better education and jobs kept luring Black migrants to the North. Their numbers were not that noticeable next to the large

European inflow, but the 80,000 migrants from 1870 to 1890 increased to 200,000 from 1890 to 1910, bringing the northern Black population to about one tenth of the total at the turn of the century.[7] Economic hard times and boll weevil destruction of cotton crops prompted more to head north in the next decade, raising the northern Black population from 850,000 in 1910 to 1.4 million in 1920.

Labor union hostility in the North and de facto segregation created a dual society there just as de jure segregation had done in the South. Black churches and other parallel social institutions formed the bedrock of the segregated racial community. A Black middle class, many of them graduates of Black colleges, emerged and achieved success in business and the professions. Black artists and writers creatively depicted Black life in America, while musicians contributed blues and jazz to the popular culture.

Southern Blacks remained a rural people, struggling within a system designed to keep them subjugated. Northern Blacks were an urban people, some of them poor, others working or middle class. A 1918 Census Bureau analysis showed that 79% of all Black males older than age 10 were gainfully employed, 49% of them in agricultural pursuits.

Economist Robert Higgs reports that, in more than a third of a century between 1867 and 1900, Black incomes more than doubled, thus increasing more rapidly than White incomes. He adds, however, that in absolute numbers, the Black income level in 1900 lay far below the White level:

> Even if the Blacks could have steadily raised their income per capita twice as fast as the Whites, about 70 years would have been required to close the gap. Black income per capita probably did not exceed four-tenths of the white level in 1914.[8]

Black exclusion from political influence and public discrimination in education and in law impeded their economic development. But even if there had not been racial discrimination, argues Higgs, the years of the industrial age were not sufficient to enable Blacks to acquire the literacy, skills, experience, and capital needed to close the economic gap with Whites. These "swift competitors" had too large of a head start.

Asian Americans and Pacific Islanders

Between 1871 and 1920, the Asian American population changed from a fairly small, mostly Chinese group to a significantly large, multi-Asian and Pacific Islander presence. Japanese, Filipinos, Asian Indians, and Koreans came to the U.S. mainland, as tens of thousands of others went to Hawaii, most to work there on the sugar and pineapple plantations.

Each of these nonwestern groups brought, and kept fairly intact, a racial and cultural diversity throughout the western states. Despite Asian American differences in nationality, language, and culture, to most Americans they all looked alike, they all were alike, and they all were unassimilable and undesired. Not surprisingly, fear, resentment, antagonism, and violence soon marked Asian-White relations.

National leaders fanned the flames of racial bigotry. U.S. Senator James G. Blaine, who narrowly lost the presidency to Grover Cleveland in 1884, declared in an 1879 Senate speech, "The Asiatic cannot go on with our population and make a homogeneous element."[9] Pressured by labor unions and newspapers, Congress enacted in 1882 the first national human embargo on a particular race. In 1924, spurred by the efforts of Senator Henry Cabot Lodge and Secretary of State Charles Evans Hughes, Congress specifically denied Japan an immigration quota in the Immigration Act of 1924.

What can we make of these actions? It is too simplistic to attribute them solely to racial bigotry, although it certainly was a factor. From an interactionist perspective, nonwestern differences in physical appearance, language, belief systems, customs, stoicism, and observable behavior affected social distance perceptions and resultant interaction patterns. Once removed from any affinity to the dominant group, the Asians were more likely to generate tensions, violent outbreaks, and governmental restrictions.

It would be a mistake, however, to confine interracial problems only to racist motivations and/or perceived cultural dissonance. Economic competition played a major role, as indicated by the rising intensity in demands for Chinese exclusion during the depression of the 1870s, when a lull in railroad construction brought the Chinese back into California. In another example, Roger Daniels describes a "crusade against Japanese contract labor" in the 1890s by the *San Francisco Morning Call,* which claimed that Japanese immigrants were taking work away from Americans.[10] Organized labor continually viewed the Asians as a threat to the American worker and lobbied extensively against their immigration.

Hispanic Americans

In the last two decades of the 19th century, approximately 300,000 Mexican Americans living in the Southwest continued to experience serious challenges brought on by thousands of Anglo-Americans and

European immigrants coming to settle in the region. Victims of drought, discriminatory taxes, foreclosures, questionable local judicial rulings, and violent intimidation, many lost their lands. Mexican Americans also fell victim to economic change, as the large commercial farms of agribusiness, with their extensive investments in machinery and irrigation systems, priced the small farmers out of business.

Decline of their rancho system played havoc with their traditional values, which had long sustained the cohesiveness of a paternalistic extended family system. A nuclear family pattern slowly emerged, accompanied by an increase in common law marriages and consensual unions. In urban areas such as Los Angeles, a startling increase in female-headed families occurred; by 1880, one third of the Mexican American families were matriarchal, most living in substandard conditions. Reduced to the status of low-paid laborers, Mexican Americans became stereotyped as lazy and backward. Living in the barrio of a city or town, or in rural isolation, they were virtually a colonial people lacking in economic or political power.

Elsewhere, the Hispanic presence was small. About 1,500 Puerto Ricans lived in the continental United States in 1910. Florida was home to most other Hispanics at this time, although a small Cuban community across the Hudson River from New York City continued to thrive since its 1850 beginnings.

Native Americans

This era was a bleak one for the indigenous peoples of the United States. Made dependent wards of the government in 1871, confined to reservations out of the White man's way, they would soon lose even two thirds of these reservation lands through deceitful and fraudulent real estate transactions. This followed passage of the ill-conceived Dawes Act of 1887, which attempted to divide tribal lands into individual tracts in an effort to "civilize" the inhabitants.

Whites' fears of a resurgence of Native American beliefs and practices, prompted by a Native American spiritual revival known as the Ghost Dance Religion, led to the tragic massacre at Wounded Knee in 1890 that killed 150 defenseless Sioux. It was the last violent episode, as the government continued its efforts at Anglo conformity through education and Christian missionary work. The northern Plains Indians were given the southern section of the Dakota Territory and the southern Plains Indians were placed in Oklahoma Territory along with the Cherokee, Chickasaw, Choctaw, Creek, and Seminole. The Navajo and Apache were on reservations in the Southwest, whereas other tribes were scattered in the Rockies and beyond.

Reservation life changed the tribes from self-reliant harvesters of nature's bounty to dependent wards of the government, obliged to rely on food shipments for sustenance. With their food-producing, often nomadic, lifestyle nullified, Native Americans also found their cultural, familial, and communal well-being subverted as well. Their social structure, with active roles for all within the tribe, collapsed under an imposed passive role. Loss of their independent male role as leaders, hunters, providers, protectors, and warriors denied the men any means of maintaining self-esteem. As an escape from their harsh reality, hopelessness, and despair, many thousands of Native American men turned to drink and drugs.

Despite laws against Native American possession of alcohol, it was readily available, even supplied by government agents to keep the reservations tranquil. Alcoholism became a problem, as did the chronic use of the hallucinogen peyote, a derivative of the cactus plant. Its use spreading through several decades from the Mescalero Apache to virtually all tribes, peyotism was institutionalized in the Native American Church. With no control of their lives, Native Americans struggled to maintain their sense of identity and oneness with the universe by any means possible.

As the Native Americans lived their lives in a reduced state of dependency, their population shrank to about 237,000 by 1900. (It had been 600,000 in 1776.) During the late 19th and early 20th centuries, they remained pockets of diversity, ignored by most of society, pacified through alcohol by government agents, and encouraged by assimilationist idealists and missionaries to divest themselves of their diversity and embrace "white civilization."[11]

Middle Eastern Americans

About 3,000 Arab immigrants came in the 1880s, followed by more than 30,000 in the 1890s. Another 70,000 followed until the outbreak of World War I in 1914. Most came from Syria and Lebanon, but because they lived in a region under the control of the Ottoman Empire, their passports designated them as "Turks." Not until 1899 did a separate category for "Syrian" appear on immigration rosters. Although about 85% came from Lebanon, identification of "Lebanese" did not gain acceptance until the 1930s.

About 10% were Muslims, a very small number were Jewish, and almost all the rest were Christians fleeing religious persecution from the Turks. The Christians divided into Maronites, Melkites, Orthodox, and Presbyterians. Their theological differences translated into social and structural separation in their ethnic communities in the United States, as it had in the Middle East. What bonded them together was a conviction that those sharing similar beliefs belonged to a social order qualitatively different from the rest. They looked upon themselves not as Syrians, but as coreligionists from a particular village. Americans lumped them together as the single entity of *Syrian,* much as they had combined other provincial groups into single nationality groups. And, as with other ethnic groups, these first-generation immigrants soon saw themselves as Americans perceived them.[12]

Most immigrants settled in a "Syrian belt" stretching westward from the textile mills of southern New England and New York–New Jersey through the steel towns in Pennsylvania and Ohio, to the automobile factories in Detroit. In each of these regions near the factories where they worked, the Syrians established their ethnic communities. Some Syrians became itinerant peddlers or salesmen. Once financially secure, they became shopkeepers, wholesalers, and fabric or department store owners. By 1911, Syrians were in almost every branch of commerce, including banking and import-export houses, and the government reported that Syrian American median income was only slightly lower than the $665 annual income of adult native-born White males.

Northern and Western European Americans

For many countries situated in the northwestern part of the European continent, the late 19th and early 20th centuries marked the time of their largest numbers of emigrants leaving for the United States. Belgium, Denmark, England, Holland, Norway, Scotland, and Sweden sent more emigrants at this time than in any other period.

Because more than 8.1 million immigrants arrived from this part of the world between 1880 and 1920, northern and western European cultural diversity was as marked a presence as that of other nationality groups. English immigrants, for example, numbered 1.5 million from 1881 to 1920, and other parts of Great Britain accounted for almost an additional half million. Almost a million Swedes, more than a half million Norwegians, and almost a quarter million Danes came. Germany sent more than 2.4 million immigrants, and Ireland supplied more than 1.5 million. More than 100,000 Belgians, 170,000 Dutch, and 216,000 French also came.

With large numbers coming in each of these four decades, the tight clusters of these ethnic communities made the vigor of their everyday ethnicity even more pronounced. In the 1880s, for example, the 5.2 million immigrants included approximately 1.5 million Germans, 655,000 Irish, 645,000 English, 177,000 Norwegians, 392,000 Swedes, 150,000 Scots, 88,000 Danes, 53,000 Dutch, and 50,000 French. From 1901 to 1910, the 8.8 million immigrants included about 388,000 English, 341,000 Germans, 339,000 Irish, 250,000 Swedes, 190,000 Norwegians, 120,000 Scots, 65,000 Danes, 48,000 Dutch, and 41,000 Belgians.

New Irish arrivals, in typical chain migration pattern, often settled near family or friends. Consequently, by the turn of the century, almost 7 million Irish Catholics were concentrated in the urban Northeast, living in "Paddy's Villages" or shantytowns usually located in older, less desirable residential sections of most cities. Experiencing job and social discrimination because of their religion, their full absorption into the mainstream was at least one generation away.

More than 9 million Germans, diverse in religions and backgrounds, lived in both rural and urban clusters. Most major cities throughout the Northeast had Germantown sections, but the greatest number remained in the German triangle of the Midwest (the area between Milwaukee, Cincinnati, and St. Louis). Wherever they lived, German Americans, particularly first generation, functioned in a culturally isolated ethnic world where a wide array of parallel social institutions helped maintain their language and customs.

The Midwest—particularly Illinois, Iowa, Michigan, and Wisconsin— also attracted the recent Dutch immigrants because of favorable soil and climate conditions. More than 1.5 million Danes, Finns, Norwegians, and Swedes lived on farms or in towns of the northern Midwest, retaining a vibrant Scandinavian imprint upon that region.

The residence in New England of more than a half million French Canadians and in Louisiana of about a quarter million Cajuns generated circumstances that would allow for the establishment of persistent ethnic subcultures lasting into present times. In addition, more than 150,000 French immigrants arriving between 1871 and 1900 were too recent to yet be fully assimilated.

Southern, Central, and Eastern European Americans

Whether for economic, political, or religious reasons, these "new" immigrants came to "Golden America" to seek a better life. They were Armenians,

Greeks, Italians, Portuguese, and Turks from the southern part of the European continent; Czechs, Hungarians, Poles, and Slovaks from the plains of central Europe; Austrians and Swiss from the high mountain country; Latvians and Lithuanians from the Baltic area; Byelorussians, Ruthenians, Ukrainians, and others from the western regions of czarist Russia; and Jews from all parts of eastern and central Europe, especially Russia. Even within these groups, much diversity could be found. Within the Slavic group, for example, were Bohemians (Czechs), Bulgarians, Croatians, Dalmatians, Montenegrins, Serbs, Slovaks, Slovenians, and still others. Each had their identity and culture, which they attempted to preserve in their adopted country.

Arriving in record numbers, these nationality groups were strikingly different in appearance, culture, customs, language, political experiences, and ideology. Physical appearance—whether the darker features of those from the Mediterranean region, or the eastern European women with kerchiefs on their heads, or Jewish men with yarmulkes and full beards—set them apart from native-born Americans. Because most were Catholics, Jews, or Orthodox Christians, Protestant America also reacted with disdain at this large display of diverse groups whose religious buildings and clergy were daily reminders of a change in U.S. society.

The largest nationality group was the Italians, who numbered more than 4.1 million arrivals between 1881 and 1920. Settling mostly in "Little Italys" in cities large and small, immigrants from the same region, even village, clustered in the same city sections. This chain migration pattern resulted in the creation of cohesive neighborhoods with village, family, and communal orientations built around their parallel social institutions of church, newspapers, social organizations, and stores. Although assimilation would gradually occur—particularly among their children pursuing *la via nuova*—in those communities, Italian was the daily language and ethnicity an everyday reality, leading many native-born Americans to view negatively the presence of so many "unassimilable" newcomers.

Native-born Americans, mostly of northwestern European descent, were aghast at the heavy immigration of dissimilar cultural types and blamed the new arrivals for all existing social discontents. They condemned them for the increase in crime, even though every objective investigation proved the crime rate among first-generation Americans was lower than for the rest of the country. (The increase occurred more typically among the second generation.) Labor disputes and calls for political and economic reform furthered criticism of the "un-American agitators."

Hundreds of thousands came as sojourners, or "birds of passage," as some called them. They came not to stay, but to make enough money to return home and to buy land, redeem the family mortgage, or provide dowries for sisters or daughters. They had less interest in learning English, getting involved in the labor movement, or acculturating. Greeks, Poles, and Italians particularly were sojourners. Half of all Italians to arrive in the 1880s and 1890s returned home, creating a "shuttle migration." Often, between 1908 and 1920, the number of Italians returning home reached between 60% and 70% of the new arrivals. More than 500,000 Poles returned between 1900 and 1915, as did tens of thousands of Greeks.

Gradually, many sojourners decided to stay. Others returned to the United States with their wives and children. As these joined other family groups putting down roots, their birth rates—considerably higher than for that of multiple-generation Americans—became a cause for nativist alarm. Some cited population statistics to project the "old" Americans becoming a minority to the "inferior" newcomers. Eugenicists like Madison Grant, president of the New York Zoological Society, argued in *The Passing of the Great Race* (1916) for those of Anglo-Saxon, Nordic, and Teutonic origins to marry only among themselves to prevent racial hybridism and reversion to the "lower type" through contamination of their "racial purity."[13]

Intergroup Conflicts

Nativist hostility and violent clashes marked the industrial age as they had the earlier part of the 19th century. In addition to the race riots previously mentioned, interethnic conflicts also arose. Organizations such as the American Protective Association (APA) and the Ku Klux Klan drew widespread popular support in their campaigns for a "pure" America.[14]

The APA began in Iowa in 1887, and by 1893, it claimed about 1 million members in 20 states, primarily in the midwestern "Bible Belt." An anti-Catholic organization, it particularly attracted the Scots-Irish, as well as Germans, Scandinavians, and English. Committed to an English-only school curriculum, removal of Catholic teachers and school board members, longer naturalization periods, restrictive immigration, and election of Protestant officeholders only, the APA claimed 100 members serving in the 54th Congress (1895–1896).

The Ku Klux Klan, reconstituted in 1915 after being sympathetically portrayed in D. W. Griffith's silent film classic *Birth of a Nation*, reached a membership of almost 5 million by 1926. Membership was strongest in Indiana and Ohio, with loyal support from thousands of Pennsylvania Dutch Klansmen, who held intense feelings against Roman Catholics. Dedicating itself to White supremacy, Protestant Christianity, and

Americanism, the new Klan used intimidation, violence, and politics to influence voters, employers, schools, and textbook content, seeking moral regulation and a stabilization of the old order.

American entry into the war in 1917 touched off an anti-German, patriotic hysteria. This ranged from renaming sauerkraut "liberty cabbage," to German Americans losing their jobs, to mob attacks on German establishments and communities. Anything German was eradicated: German-language publications, school courses, church services, concert music, street names, and organizations.

In each instance, these reactionary movements flourished and faded with a few years. Internal struggles, corruption charges, and the free-silver issue undermined the APA. Corruption among the leadership of the Ku Klux Klan and restrictive immigration laws lessening public concern hastened its decline. The end of World War I in 1918 soon enabled the German American community to reassert its ethnic marks of organizational activities, although its cultural resilience never sprang back fully to its former vitality.

The Next Horizon

A new flurry of immigration after the war brought calls anew for restrictions. Passage of the National Origins Quota Act of 1921 reduced immigration to 3% of any nationality living in the United States in 1910. Amended in 1924 to a temporary limit of 2% of those here in 1890, the limit was raised again to 3% in 1929 with a ceiling of 150,000 total immigrants. Designed to favor northern and western Europeans, this legislation was hailed by its supporters as a way to prevent further dilution of the U.S. population and its cultural composition. In their desire to "keep America American," nativists succeeded in ending the Great Migration.

Yet as William James once observed, "Change begets change." The labor market still needed workers in good economic times. With few Europeans to fill expanding needs, Mexicans and Puerto Ricans would meet the demand for new labor, setting in motion a greater Hispanic migration than ever before.

Ahead lay the Roaring Twenties, the Great Depression, and another world war, which would bring in about 400,000 Displaced Persons afterwards. It was a paltry number compared to past immigrant totals or to the nation's 150.7 million people in 1950.

Even though in 1930 almost one out of three Americans was foreign-born or the child of immigrant parents, ethnicity became less visible. With few new immigrants to renew them, ethnic communities would fade, causing a new generation of Americans to forget the great cultural diversity that had been such a dynamic part of U.S. society. Once again, as in the early 19th century, low immigration in the late 1920s and throughout the 1930s, together with the pervasive acculturation process, were creating a culturally homogeneous population. Even though assimilation remained the ongoing process it always had been, the ebb in immigration gave it preeminence over the ever-present reality of pluralism.

This time, though, there would be differences. Some groups—the Armenians, Greeks, and Jews—would quickly enter the middle class. Others—like the Italians, Poles, and Slavic peoples—would mostly remain in working-class occupations for another generation, as would Asian Americans. African Americans, Mexicans, and Native Americans—victims of racial discrimination and an internal colonization, would mostly struggle to survive in poverty or near-poverty circumstances.

Further ahead lay suburbanization, Vietnam, the civil rights movement, space exploration, the fall of communism, the end of the cold war, and the information age. Significantly, also ahead would be a new immigration law and a third wave of immigration that would once again bring widespread diversity to the land and test once more its people's acceptance of that diversity.

Notes

1. James A. Henretta et al., *America's History to 1877* (Homewood, IL: Dorsey Press, 1987), 515.

2. See Edna Bonacich, "A Theory of Ethnic Antagonism: The Split Labor Market," *American Sociological Review*, 37 (1972): 547–59.

3. See Alice Kestler-Harris, *Out to Work* (New York: Oxford University Press, 1982).

4. Robert Blauner, *Racial Oppression in America* (New York: Harper & Row, 1972), 62.

5. *African History* (New York: Oxford University Press, 1981), 130.

6. James S. Olson, *The Ethnic Dimension in American History* (New York: St. Martin's Press, 1979), 300.

7. See W. E. B. DuBois, *The Philadelphia Negro: A Social Study* (New York: Schocken, 1967).

8. Robert Higgs, *Competition and Conflict: Blacks in the American Economy, 1865–1914* (Chicago: University of Chicago Press, 1980), 125.

9. *Congressional Record* (February 14, 1879), quoted in Vincent N. Parrillo, *Strangers to These Shores*, 7th ed. (Boston: Allyn & Bacon, 2003), 296.

10. Roger Daniels, *The Politics of Prejudice* (New York: Atheneum, 1969), 20.

11. Frederick E. Hoxie, *A Final Promise: The Campaign to Assimilate the Indians, 1880–1920* (Lincoln: University of Nebraska Press, 1984).

12. See Philip M. Kayal and Joseph M. Kayal, *The Syrian-Lebanese in America* (New York: Twayne, 1975).

13. Madison Grant, *The Passing of the Great Race* (1916, reprint ed. New York: Arno Press, 1970).

14. See Donald J. Kinzner, *An Episode in Anti-Catholicism: The American Protective Association* (Seattle: University of Washington Press, 1964); Kenneth Jackson, *The Ku Klux Klan in the City, 1915–1930* (New York: Oxford University Press, 1967).

7

Diversity in the Information Age

As early as 1948, the invention of the transistor signaled the dawn of an electronic revolution. In the 1950s, numerous advances—the discovery of the structure of the genetic material DNA, the first successful transplant of an organ (the kidney), development of an effective polio vaccine and of an oral contraceptive, the building of atomic energy plants, and the successful orbiting of *Sputnik,* the first artificial earth satellite—all expanded the horizons for human achievement.

The 1960s, an incredible decade of turbulence and reform, also heralded new accomplishments once the sole province of science fiction. We developed the laser beam, transplanted hearts, and launched communication satellites instantly linking the world with images and sound from anywhere. Sending men in space and landing on the moon fired our imaginations even more. In the 1970s came microprocessors, test tube babies, space shuttles, and the eradication of smallpox. On the heels of those advances arrived VCRs, CDs, personal computers in the home and workplace, the Internet, and the information highway.

In this era, the United States became a global, hegemonic power, particularly after the collapse of the Soviet Union. Changes in immigration laws, declining birth rates in Europe, and numerous push factors in the developing world—high birth rates, weak economies, and political unrest, to name a few—resulted in a new migration flow to the United States. Asia and Latin America surpassed Europe as the primary sending areas of new immigrants, a process intensified by the chain migration pattern of family members reuniting with those who arrived before them. Living conditions in Mexico prompted an unauthorized migration flow northward across a convenient, porous border. Other factors—such as globalization disrupting local economies, and wars (Korea, Bosnia, Kosovo) or civil wars (Angola, El Salvador, Peru, Sierra Leone) forcing refugees to flee—played an additional role in changing the population composition of the United States. As before, social forces in many parts of the world affected the nation's multicultural evolution.

The Human Element

This exciting world of scientific advancement is, of course, only one part of the human dimension, and in many ways, other aspects of life are unchanged from past generations. People in the world still suffer from hunger, deprivation, persecution, and repression. They still dream of a better life for themselves and their children. And for many, that dream has a name: America.

In July 1963, when President John F. Kennedy urged an end to national quota restrictions in a special message to Congress, he initiated a change in our immigration policy that culminated with President Lyndon B. Johnson symbolically signing the new bill in 1965 on Liberty Island at the base of the

Statue of Liberty. With his signature, he ended a discriminatory immigration policy that emphasized place of birth and not individual worth or family reunification.

Unexpected Consequences

Most government officials expected the new legislation to open the doors to increased European migration. After all, there was an extensive waiting list for visas in many European countries severely restricted under the old quota system. Yet in a typical year, the British Isles, for example, was sending less than 40% of its allotted quota.

Immigrants from some countries—namely Greece, Italy, Poland, Portugal, Spain, the Soviet Union, and Yugoslavia—did increase notably. However, the "push" factors to leave were now greater in other parts of the world, and soon, European migration was quickly eclipsed. By the 1980s, European immigration represented only 10% of the total, with countries such as Greece, Italy, and Yugoslavia declining significantly in the number of emigrants leaving for the United States.

In the 1960s, emigrants from the Caribbean and Latin America outnumbered Europe for the first time and have done so in increasing proportion ever since. European immigration was more than two-and-a-half times Asian immigration in the 1960s, but only slightly more than half the Asian total in the 1970s. In 2003, Europe accounted for 15% of all immigration, Asia for 33%, and the Caribbean and Latin America for 41%. Canada, Africa, and Oceania accounted for the remaining 11%.

A Different America

The high-tech age dramatically altered American society just as the industrial age had. Previous emigrants from agrarian Europe had to make a triple adjustment to a new culture, an urban environment, and an industrialized society. Many of today's emigrants also make a triple adjustment, but for some, the third part is often a bigger leap, from a preindustrial background into a postindustrial society.

Gone are many unskilled and semiskilled jobs enabling the newcomers to gain even a toehold in their new society. Many factory and mill jobs, once plentiful in the cities a short distance from where immigrants clustered in ethnic urban neighborhoods, are now often in industrial parks away from where many of today's immigrants can afford to live. New types of jobs now exist in the service sector, but many are low-paying, dead-end ones.

Some immigrants arrive possessing entrepreneurial skills or the education and training needed for higher-status, higher-paying positions. Their income enables them to settle in residential areas unaccustomed to the presence of first-generation Americans, particularly racially and culturally distinct Asians. Many of our suburbs now have a racial and cultural diversity once mostly confined to our cities.

Today's diversity is visible everywhere, not just in a few geographic locales. Some states receive more immigrants than others, and some have greater numbers of one or more groups than others, but no state is immune to the influx of developing world immigrants. Each of the 50 states now contains an unprecedented mixture of racial and ethnic groups that reflects current immigration patterns.

For Americans lulled by 40 years of lower immigration totals, and new arrivals primarily from the sending countries of the past, the presence of so many different groups and languages is strange, but it is *deja vu* for this nation. Some of the groups may be new to the American scene, but the patterns of acculturation and ethnogenesis among them and of negative dominant responses are replays of yesteryear.

However, as this latest version of pluralism manifests itself, some new ingredients have been added. Government policy now supports pluralism instead of forced assimilation. Bilingualism in ballots, driver education manuals, education, and other public aspects are controversial realities. Social legislation from the 1960s ensures minority rights and opportunities as never before. Because diversity is more visible and protected than ever, some Americans fear the loss of an integrative, assimilationist force in the land.

Institutionalizing Minority Rights

Significant legislation passed in the 1960s brought American ideals about equality closer to reality for minorities long denied their rights. The Civil Rights Act of 1964 was the most far-reaching law against racial discrimination ever passed. It dealt with voting rights, employment practices, and any place of public accommodation, whether eating, lodging, entertainment, recreation, or service. It gave broad powers to the U.S. Attorney General to intervene in private suits regarding violation of civil rights and directed federal agencies to monitor state and local recipients of federal funds and withhold monies wherever noncompliance was found.

In 1965, Congress simplified judicial enforcement of the voting laws and extended them to state and local elections. In 1968, new legislation barred discrimination in housing and gave Native Americans greater rights in their dealings with courts and government agencies. Affirmative action, initiated by an executive order in 1963 by President Kennedy, became a powerful tool toward reducing institutional discrimination in hiring, promotion, and educational opportunities for minority group members or women.

In the decades since, important gains have been made, some of which will be delineated in the following sections on specific groups. For women, whether of the majority or of minority groups, we will note some progress now.

Females have achieved near parity with the males of their race in the level of educational attainment. A greater proportion than ever before are in the labor force, with growing numbers of women entering male-dominated occupations, including such advanced degree professions as medicine, dentistry, law, and engineering. Whereas only 9% of bachelor's degrees in business and management were awarded to women in 1971, almost half now are. Even in the male domains of mathematics and the physical sciences, where women earned 13% of the degrees in 1971, they now earn more than 42% and are steadily increasing in numbers.[1] The 109th Congress has the most female senators and representatives in its history (65 of 535), and the number of women serving in state legislatures is four times greater than the number 20 years ago. Two women now serve on the U.S. Supreme Court, and thousands of others hold judgeships at the federal, state, county, and local levels.[2]

All of these and many other gains too numerous to mention are very encouraging, yet there are many disquieting signs as well. Gender bias continues in the public schools, even among female teachers, according to a 1992 study by the American Association of University Women Educational Foundation.[3] Many occupational fields remain mostly sex-segregated, usually with lower pay levels than comparable male sex-segregated fields. Women face a "glass ceiling" in upward mobility, as illustrated in a Department of Labor report showing that only 3% of the top executive positions of the largest U.S. corporations are held by women, a figure unchanged in 10 years.[4] A few women may be U.S. Supreme Court justices, or governors, or in Congress, but their ratio is far lower than their population proportion.

Women of racial minority groups face the double problem of both racism and sexism. As in generations past, women from affluent, main-stream groups enjoy greater advantages and are often social activists in quest of gender equality. That destination has not yet been reached for many women, but their journey is nearer its destination than ever before.

The Europeans

Even though Europe is no longer the principal sending region for immigrants to the United States, it still continues to send a sizable number. Between 1993 and 2003, almost 1.5 million European immigrants arrived. Included were 174,000 Russians, 168,000 British, 166,000 Poles, 94,000 from Bosnia-Herzegovina, 88,000 Ukrainians, 75,000 Germans, 58,000 Romanians, and 25,000 Italians.

California, Texas, and New York, in that order, are typically the primary places of intended residence for the Germans. For the Irish, it is New York, Massachusetts, and California. Polish immigrants prefer Illinois, New York, and New Jersey, whereas former Soviet Union immigrants like better the states of California, New York, and Illinois. British immigrants mostly choose California, New York, and Florida.

According to the 2000 census, the states with the highest density of people with English ancestry were Utah (30%), Maine (25%), and Idaho (22%). Highest German densities were North and South Dakota (46% each), Wisconsin (43%), and Minnesota (38%). Highest Irish densities were Massachusetts (23%), New Hampshire (21%), and Rhode Island (20%).

Other significant ancestry densities were Italian in Rhode Island and Connecticut (20%), New Jersey (18%), and New York (15%); French in Vermont and New Hampshire (27%), Maine (25%), and Rhode Island (20%); and Polish in Wisconsin and Michigan (9%), Connecticut (8%), and Illinois and New Jersey (7%).

Asians and Pacific Islanders

As they naively once did with the Native Americans and the southern, central, and eastern European immigrants, many Americans view Asian Americans as a single cultural entity because they are of the same race. In fact, they are quite different from each other in their histories, languages, religious beliefs, and cultural attributes.

The earliest of the Asian immigrant groups to put down roots in the United States, the Chinese have become a very strong presence, numbering now more than 2.4 million. Although Chinese Americans live in all 50 states, their greatest concentrations are in California and New York, with high aggregates also found in Massachusetts, Illinois, New Jersey, and Texas. A bipolar occupational distribution exists for Chinese Americans. Their ratio of professional and technical workers is twice that of the White labor force, but they also have twice as many low-skilled service workers. About one in four works in a low-skilled service job, often for long hours and meager compensation. Many of these workers are (to use a Chinese American expression) "FOB" (fresh off the boat) immigrants living in overcrowded, dilapidated buildings in Chinatown districts. However, with about 30% of all Chinese Americans in professional or technical fields, the median family income for Chinese Americans is higher than the national figure.

Other than Mexican Americans, no other foreign-born group is as heavily concentrated in one state as are the 980,000 Filipinos in California. Other states where the remainder of the 1.9 million total live are Hawaii, New York, Illinois, New Jersey, Washington, Texas, and Virginia. Mostly Roman Catholics, American-born Filipinos tend to have less education and fewer occupational skills than do newcomers from the Philippines, and so they work in low-paying, private-sector jobs. Many of the new arrivals find work in professional and technical fields, especially in health care. Because of licensing and hiring problems, many are underemployed, unable to secure jobs comparable to their education, skills, and experience. Filipino Americans are fragmented linguistically, politically, and socially. Although they have strong loyalty to their family and the church, they generally avoid group separatism or an ethnic advocacy group. Although fraternal and social organizations do offer ethnic interaction opportunities, most Filipinos seem more desirous of broader participation in nonethnic associations.

Asian Indians are another sizable presence, now numbering about 1.7 million. California is home to the largest cluster of Asian Indians, with other high population totals found in New York, New Jersey, Illinois, and Texas. Most Asian Indian immigrants are Hindi-speaking, but many others arrive who speak Gujarati, Punjabi, or Bengali. About half of all working Asian Indians are in managerial or professional occupations, more than any other group in the United States, including Whites. About 20% of the nation's convenience stores, gas stations, or family-managed hotels and motels are operated by Asian Indians, giving them a family-labor economic niche. This ethnic group has the smallest proportion of its members in low-paying, low-status jobs.

In 1970, Japanese Americans constituted the largest Asian American group, totaling 591,000. Although they increased to 701,000 in 1980, they dropped to third behind the Chinese and Filipinos. In 2000, Japanese Americans numbered 798,000, with between 7,000 and 9,000 new immigrants arriving in recent years. As with other Asian groups, the largest concentration of Japanese Americans resides in California. Other high population areas are New York, Hawaii, Texas, and Washington. The Japanese presence is augmented by nonimmigrant, intracompany transferees, about 15,000 arriving annually with their families on 2- or 3-year assignments.

Although a significant presence in some states, Japanese Americans are the most widely dispersed of all Asian groups throughout the 50 states. They are the most highly educated of all U.S. groups, including Whites, and their economic success has enabled assimilation to continue at a rapid pace. Younger Japanese Americans seem more interested in their structural assimilation, as indicated by their high rates of outgroup dating and marriage. Despite occasional outbreaks of "Japan-bashing" because of trade competition and Japanese corporate takeovers of some U.S. companies, this group shows less desire than most racial and ethnic groups to retain or revive its cultural ties to its past.[5]

Korean Americans were once one of the fastest growing Asian immigrant groups in the United States, but in recent years, their annual immigration totals have lessened and now fluctuate between 12,000 and 21,000 a year. Only 12,500 new immigrants arrived in 2003, the lowest total in more than a decade. However, they are now the fifth largest Asian American group (behind the Chinese, Filipinos, Asian Indians, and Vietnamese), numbering more than 1 million.

Among first- and second-generation Korean Americans, 33% live in California, 11% live in New York, and about 4% live in each of the following states: New Jersey, Texas, Virginia, Washington, and Maryland. About 70% of the 1.1 million Korean Americans are Christian, mostly Methodist and Presbyterian. Church affiliation is about four times greater than in Korea, for the church serves also as a communal bond for ethnic identity and culture.[6] Koreans can be found in a variety of occupations, but one striking aspect is their self-employment rate of about 12%, far greater than any other group. One out of eight Korean Americans is a business owner. These family-owned businesses are found in both cities and suburbs, more likely serving other minority customers or mainstream Americans than fellow Koreans.

Vietnamese Americans, now exceeding 1.1 million, live in all 50 states. Half of them live in California, with 10% in Texas and other sizable numbers in Virginia, Washington, New York, and Pennsylvania. Their acculturation is similar to other Asian groups.[7] The older adults—particularly the women, who are less likely to be in work situations interacting with outgroup members—display little grasp of English or American ways, but the children and younger adults, more exposed to

American life, learn quickly. Scholastic achievement by Vietnamese youth is strong, well above the national average.

More than 168,000 Laotians, 172,000 Cambodians, and 113,000 Thai also call the United States home. Many are refugees and more likely to live on welfare or in near-poverty conditions, these adults thus rebuking the "model minority" stereotype of Asian American success. Also comprising part of the cultural diversity of Asian Americans are Afghanis, Burmese, Indonesians, Malaysians, and Pakistanis (the largest of these five groups); they number in the aggregate more than 300,000, about half of them living in California.

Black Americans

Use of the term *African American* is somewhat problematic, because we need to distinguish between those who are American-born of long-ago African ancestry, those who are recent African immigrants, and those who are from a Caribbean background or elsewhere. Even within these three main groupings, enormous diversity exists in the lives of the different social classes of American-born Blacks, and in the languages, cultures, and adjustment patterns of Black immigrants from the different countries. Moreover, as for other racial groups, social stratification creates separate worlds for the American-born, and ingroup loyalty and social isolation among many first-generation Americans often keeps them apart from others.

American society is far from eliminating racism as a serious social problem, and Black Americans are still disproportionately represented among the nation's poor, with all the attendant problems of that sad reality. Billions of dollars have been spent on social welfare programs and economic incentives, and yet one fourth of Black Americans remain mired in poverty. Yet this is not the complete picture. Black America is really two societies, one poor and the other nonpoor. Thanks to civil rights legislation and other social reforms, remarkable gains have been made, especially in education and occupational representation. Nevertheless, a disturbing gap remains between Black Americans and White Americans.

One of the more encouraging social indicators for Black Americans is educational attainment, but even here the message is mixed. From a high school dropout rate of 22% in 1970, double that of Whites in 1970, both are now closer—10.1% for Blacks and 8.7% for Whites in 2002. In 1970, 4% of Blacks and 11% of Whites completed college; by 2003, this level was achieved by 17.3% of Blacks and 27.6% of Whites, or a quadrupling of the Black rate to a doubling of the White rate. Black enrollment in college increased from 25% in 1975 to 35% in 2001. However, this increase has not kept pace with that of White students, whose college enrollment grew from 35% to 44% in the same period.[8]

Black representation in managerial and professional specialties is steadily growing, now at about 18% for males and 26% for females. About 19% of the males and 36% of the females are in technical, sales, or administrative support positions. For Black females, this is a dramatic change in occupation patterning from just a little more than one generation ago, when two in five worked in domestic service. As of now, Black and White females are less different from one another than are the males. About two out of five Black males work in service or blue-collar jobs as compared to two out of three White males working in white-collar jobs.[9]

Continued increase in the number of Black elected officials is another positive indicator. With 40 of 435 representatives in the 109th Congress, Blacks are nearing a total proportionate to their population ratio, although only 1 presently serves in the U.S. Senate. More than 9,000 elected Black officials now serve in the U.S. or state legislatures, in city or county offices, and in law enforcement or education. This number has grown consistently for more than 30 years.[10]

On the negative side are the data for Blacks living in the central cities: higher rates of poverty, unemployment, infant mortality, miscarriages, and mortality than Whites. Of particular concern is the high proportion of female-headed families. Of the 8.9 million Black families in 2003, women headed 45% of them, compared to a total of 14% female-headed White families. Adding strength to Black American families is the extended family household. About 60% of children with only the mother present live in the home headed by a grandparent; among teenage mothers, this figure increases to 85%, allowing for greater child care.[11]

Many Black immigrants add to the diversity found among the U.S. Black population. About 372,000 Haitian immigrants have arrived since 1981. About 91% of all Haitian Americans, most of whom are Roman Catholics, are concentrated in just four states: New York, Florida, Massachusetts, and New Jersey. Most live in social isolation in tightly clustered neighborhoods. Speaking Haitian Creole, most have a very limited command of English when they first arrive. They usually work in low-paying jobs in service industries or as farm laborers.

Jamaican Americans are the largest non-Hispanic group from the Caribbean now living in the United States. Of the approximately 681,000 here, about 80% are foreign-born. Now averaging less than 20,000 immigrants annually, they continue to grow as a sizable minority group. About 40% of all Jamaican Americans live in New York. Florida is home to another 26%, with other large Jamaican populations found in New Jersey, Connecticut, California, Maryland, Massachusetts, and Pennsylvania.

Immigration from Africa remained low until the 1980s, but since 1981, more than 700,000 immigrants have arrived. Nigerians constitute the largest group, with about 149,000 claiming Nigerian ancestry in the 2000 census, compared to 78,000 Ethiopians and 42,000 Ghanaians. African immigrants face two handicaps while trying to make a cultural adjustment to life in the United States. In their homelands, they were a racial majority, but here, they are not. In various social and work settings, many encounter racism for the first time. Second, because of their cultural distinctions, many Africans do not identify with either American Blacks or Africans. Successful American Blacks interested in helping the less fortunate of their race usually concentrate on the American-born poor, not on newcomers from Africa. As a matter of preference and necessity, the African immigrants seek out one another for mutual support and refuge.

An important lesson emerges from the last point. Culture is an important determinant in how groups relate to one another. *Black* may be a convenient racial category, but it is a simplistic generalization that ignores cultural differences. Blacks born in Ethiopia, Ghana, Haiti, Jamaica, Nigeria, the United States, or any other country each belong to distinctive groups whose cultural differences make them unlike one another and, to some extent, more likely to have social distance barriers between them. Multiculturalism thus takes many forms, both between and within all races.

Hispanic Americans

Hispanic is a broad term that encompasses the Hispanos of the Southwest whose family roots predate the nation's expanding borders, U.S. nationals such as the Puerto Ricans, Latino immigrants and refugees, and their descendants. This generic term suggests a common Spanish language and cultural influence, but it is deceptive because it ignores the Portuguese Brazilians and the many cultural and class distinctions among the various Spanish-speaking nationalities.

Although some non-Hispanic Americans view the Hispanic American population as a collectivity of similar groups, their differences are consequential enough to prevent the evolution at this time of a cohesive entity.

Cultural orientations, social class divisions, and first-generation American ingroup loyalties create considerable diversity within this rapidly growing ethnic group, presently comprising about one tenth of the total U.S. population.

Excluding the Mexican Americans, more than 3 million people are first- or second-generation Americans from Central or South America.[12] Salvadorans are the largest group, with about 655,000, followed by Colombians with about 471,000, and Guatemalans with about 372,000. Other larger groups include those from Ecuador (261,000), Peru (234,000), Honduras (218,000), and Nicaragua (178,000). Central and South Americans are very diverse and defy generalization, except to say that they tend to be better educated and less susceptible to poverty than all other Latinos except Cubans, and also fall behind Anglos in both categories. Otherwise, differences in the economic development in their homelands, their rural or urban backgrounds, social class, or racial composition make for numerous dissimilarities.

Since 1971, more than 641,000 Cubans have come to the United States, and those of Cuban ancestry now exceed 1.2 million. Two out of every three Cuban Americans live in Florida, with other large concentrations in New Jersey, New York, and California. In Miami, the Cubans have stamped a positive imprint. Its "Little Havana" section is now a 600-block area, and more than 25,000 Cuban-owned businesses operate in the Miami metropolitan area. The Cuban influence has transformed Miami from a winter resort town to a year-round commercial center with linkages throughout Latin America, and made it into a leading bilingual cultural center. Cubans have a lower fertility rate and a much higher proportion of people 65 years old and older than other Hispanic groups. They also have a lower unemployment rate, higher median family income, and greater middle-class composition.

A major sending country of recent immigrants is the Dominican Republic, which has sent more than 805,000 immigrants since 1971. Two out of every three live in New York. Their large numbers and settlement patterns have enabled the Dominicans to establish viable ethnic neighborhoods, often adjacent to Puerto Rican ones. Although the two groups coexist and essentially keep to themselves, intergroup marriages and consensual unions are becoming common. Low educational attainment and limited job skills result in high unemployment rates and poverty-level living standards among many Dominicans.

Most of the 23 million Mexican Americans are concentrated in the southwestern states, with the largest concentrations in California, Texas, and Arizona. All 50 states contain appreciable numbers of Mexican

Americans, with the largest concentration living outside the Southwest in Illinois (1.1 million). Nine out of 10 reside in metropolitan areas, and some of them are realizing the American Dream in rising educational levels, occupational opportunities, and incomes. However, Mexican American gains as a group have not kept pace with Anglo gains because of the large influx of unskilled, poorly educated newcomers. Almost half of urban Mexican Americans live in central cities, where life in the barrio is one of substandard housing, high unemployment rates, poverty, school dropouts, crime, and gang violence. One source of strength, however, is the family. Mexican Americans' divorce rate is well below the national level, and the percentage of their family units headed by both a husband and a wife is comparable to the national average.

Of the total Puerto Rican population of 3.4 million living on the mainland, one third of them live in New York. Other states with large concentrations are Florida, New Jersey, and Pennsylvania. In comparison to other Hispanic groups, Puerto Ricans have the lowest median family income, the highest poverty rate, and the highest proportion of female-headed families. Puerto Ricans have a higher educational attainment level on average than Mexicans, but lag far behind non-Hispanic Americans. As with the Mexican American urban poor, the Puerto Rican urban poor live in areas of limited job opportunities, making them more vulnerable to welfare dependency. Some segments of the Puerto Rican community are doing well. Almost 40% of all Puerto Rican families earn as much or more than the national median family income level, and about 10% have incomes that classify them as affluent.

The rapid increase in the Hispanic population (a 58% increase from 22.4 million in 1990 to 35.3 million in 2000) led to their becoming the largest minority group in the United States. Because of a higher birth rate than African Americans, a high immigration rate, and a low average age of these immigrants (more than 40% are under 21), the Hispanic American population will continue to grow significantly in the foreseeable future.[13] Their growing numbers have enabled them to gain political power in many cities and increased their labor market competition. Both of these developments have occasionally generated some tensions with the African American community, and it remains to be seen whether such problems are fleeting adjustment issues or a portent of greater problems to come in minority relations between African Americans and Hispanic Americans.

Perhaps the analogy of the *nopales* is apt here.[14] Nopales are cactus with a rather prickly exterior, but they are also edible treats if one proceeds with patience, caution, and determination. In previous eras, a new group's arrival often created tensions with an older minority group, particularly in economic competition, but in time, the situation improved as both groups moved past the sharply contested points and "digested" their share of the American Dream. That was not always simply accomplished, but neither was it usually a prolonged encounter. Hopefully, African and Hispanic Americans will similarly move past the prickly experience in short fashion and into that place where both can enjoy the fruits of their labors.

North Africans and Middle Easterners

Immigration from Islamic countries of North Africa and the Middle East has been of such sustained strength that these ethnic groups have become a visible presence in many states. More than 182,000 immigrants arrived in the 1970s, followed by the next wave in the 1980s that increased to almost 343,000, with a slightly higher number coming in the 1990s. Not all are Muslims, particularly the many Christians from Lebanon and Coptic Christians from Egypt.

Although the single largest concentration of Arab Americans is the more than 250,000 living in southern Michigan, the largest proportion of the approximately 1.2 million Americans claiming Arabic ancestry in the 2000 census are the 27% living in the Northeast. About 24% live in the Midwest, 26% in the South, and 22% in the West. More than one third of all Arab Americans, about 440,000, are of Lebanese descent. Syrians are the next largest group, approximately 143,000. Other sizable groups are Egyptians, Palestinians, Jordanians, Moroccans, and Iraqis.

Largest of all groups, but neither Arab nor Arabic-speaking are the Iranians. With their distinct culture and Farsi language, about 60% of the more than 338,000 Iranian Americans live in California. Other large enclaves are in the New York and Washington, DC, metropolitan areas. Many are middle-class professionals, and their children are becoming extensively Americanized, despite their parents' efforts to preserve their culture.

Turks also are neither Arabs nor Arabic-speaking, but tend to settle near other Arabic and Islamic immigrants in working-class urban neighborhoods. Along with their Arabic neighbors, they work as tradespeople and laborers.

Native Americans

In 2000, the Native American population increased 19%, rising from 2.1 million in 1990 to 2.5 million, thanks to a birth rate higher than the national average. Their quality of life varies from tribe to tribe. Some reap large profits from gambling casinos, whereas others languish in poverty. Nationwide, the Native American poverty rate hovers at nearly three times the national average. Equally depressing are statistics showing Native American life expectancy about 10 years less than the national average. Their death rates from diabetes, liver disease, and alcohol-related accidents are two to three times the national average.[15]

Twenty percent of Native Americans are aged 10 to 19, compared to 14% of other U.S. racial/ethnic groups. Yet compared to those same minority groups, fewer Native American teens will graduate from high school (72% vs. 84%), and fewer still will complete college (22% vs. 26%), given current patterns.[16]

Disputes about water rights, fishing rights, natural resources, landfills, and upwind or upstream pollution of tribal lands continue in many states. However, legal efforts to honor treaty rights have been more numerous and successful in recent years.[17] Those successes have led state officials to respect the growing power of Native Americans and to negotiate directly with tribes in their borders to avoid costly and possible court defeats on environmental issues, health policy, child welfare agreements, and water rights.

Religious Diversity

The United States is now probably the most religiously diverse country in the world, with more than 1,500 religious groups. About 200 of these are conventional Christian and Jewish denominations, with 26 of them having memberships exceeding 1 million.[18] Although the country remains mostly Christian (83% claim this faith), the forces of immigration, intermarriage, and disenchantment with some of the oldest religious institutions are redefining the country's religious composition. For example, the United States now contains 7 times more Muslim Americans (6 million), 10 times more Buddhists (2 million), 9 times more Hindus (1 million), and 220 times more Sikhs (220,000) than it did in 1970. Religions once on the periphery of mainstream Christianity are growing vigorously: Mormons by 90%, Jehovah's Witnesses by 162%, and the Pentecostal Assemblies of God by 267%. In contrast, the once dominant Episcopal, Presbyterian, and Congregational churches have declined in membership by 20% to 40%.[19]

A curious paradox now exists. Perhaps the fastest growing group of all are those opting not to belong to any church, these "unaffiliated" now totaling 32 million Americans, including 11% of all Christians.[20] At the same time, the proportion of Americans attending a weekly service has increased by three percentage points in the past decade, from 44% to 47%, the highest of all developed countries. (England reports only 10%, for example). Moreover, 64% of all Americans say religion is "very important" in their lives, up from 60% a generation ago, and two to three times higher than in other Western nations.[21]

The growing diversity in religion and its increased importance for many often have a pronounced effect on numerous societal issues and on race and ethnicity. Such "hot-button" topics as abortion, gay marriage, Nativity displays on public property, and school prayer, for instance, fuel intense and bitter debate, political pandering, and extensive lobbying. Erection of non-Western houses of worship in mostly Christian suburban communities can trigger a backlash of resentment and hostility. Seemingly minor issues, such as Sikh males insisting on maintaining their religious beliefs in wearing a turban and having the right to be, say, a police officer, can spark controversy and criticism.

In many ways, U.S. society is more religiously tolerant than in past centuries. However, the efforts of some religious groups to impose their values on the rest of society create both division and conflict. A multicultural society continually faces the moral challenge of encouraging norms and laws for the common good while simultaneously respecting the different religious values of others.

The Next Horizon

A new wave of immigrants arrives on U.S. shores in pursuit of the same dreams of a better life that motivated millions of other immigrants before them. A new generation of native-born Americans, the descendants of those older immigrants, observes the present immigration with apprehension, concerned and alarmed about what they fear is an undermining of the American culture and character. That was the past nativist reaction to previous immigrations also.

Some demographers, historians, and politicians point with alarm to tomorrow's reality, given today's trends. Misgivings about the multiple losses of White numerical superiority, preeminence of Western culture and the Judeo-Christian heritage, and preservation of the existing social order are heard from many sections of the country. There is distress about group separatism and use of languages other than English. On another front, feminist advocacy also draws negative responses in some quarters.

Some of the resistance is from well-intentioned individuals who view the changes as altering the nation's identity too dramatically. Some of that concern is rooted in racial fears, as the White majority sees its numerical superiority and its economic and political dominance threatened by the continued arrival of so many non-White immigrants.

At the heart of most of these feminist, ethnic, and racial issues is the struggle for power. Challenges to the status quo—as vocal and visible minority groups seek economic, political, and social power—prompts resistance by those unwilling to yield their advantages. Their real fears of loss of hegemony are masked in dire predictions about loss of societal cohesion.

Multiculturalism is evident in the land once again, and we can find many examples of both accommodation and conflict. Which trend will prevail? Will our future be one of greater discord or greater unity? What does lie beyond the next horizon? Fortunately, we have some clues from our past and present that may offer us a glimpse of that future. In the next three chapters, we shall seek that understanding.

Notes

1. National Center for Education Statistics, *Digest of Education Statistics, 2003* (Washington, DC: U.S. Government Printing Office, 2005).

2. Center for the American Woman and Politics, Eagleton Institute of Politics (information releases, Rutgers University, 2005).

3. Barbara Kantrowitz, "Sexism in the Schoolhouse," *Newsweek* (February 24, 1992): 62.

4. Amy Saltzman, "Trouble at the Top," *U.S. News & World Report* (June 17, 1991): 40–48.

5. See Harry H. L. Kitano and Roger Daniels, *Asian Americans: Emerging Minorities* (Englewood Cliffs, NJ: Prentice Hall, 1988).

6. Ill Soo Kim, *New Urban Immigrants: The Korean Community in New York* (Princeton, NJ: Princeton University Press, 1981).

7. Paul J. Strand and Woodrow Jones, Jr., *Indochinese Refugees in America* (Durham, NC: Duke University Press, 1985).

8. U.S. Bureau of the Census, *Statistical Abstract of the United States 2004* (Washington, DC: U.S. Government Printing Office, 2004), Tables 212, 255, 264.

9. Ibid., Table 597.

10. Ibid., Table 405.

11. Ibid., Table 33.

12. See Nora Hamilton and Norma Stoltz Chinchilla, "Central American Migration: A Framework for Analysis," *Latin American Research Review*, 26 (1991): 75–110.

13. U.S. Bureau of the Census, *Census 2000 Brief: The Hispanic Population,* C2KBR/01–3, May 2001.

14. My thanks to Gonzalos Santos at California State University Bakersfield for suggesting this concept.

15. National Center for Health Statistics, *Health, United States 2004* (Hyattsville, MD: NCHS, 2004), Table 30.

16. U.S. Bureau of the Census, *Census 2000 Supplemental Survey Summary,* Table PCT035C.

17. See "Dances with Lawyers," *The Economist* (August 10, 1991): A18.

18. Eileen W. Lindner, ed., *Yearbook of American and Canadian Churches, 2004* (Nashville, TN: Abingdon Press, 2004).

19. Mary Rourke, "Redefining Religion in America," *Los Angeles Times* (June 21, 1998): 1.

20. Ibid.

21. The Gallup Organization, *Religion in America.* Available at http://www.gallup.poll/indicators/indreligion.asp [Accessed August 1, 2004].

8

Intergenerational Comparisons

Each generation of Americans experiences anew the influx of immigrants arriving in pursuit of the American Dream. Each new generation also contains native-born Americans who have not only been denied fulfillment of that dream, but also witnessed newcomers who succeed where they do not. This has been the case since colonial beginnings and appears likely to continue far into the future. It is an old story and yet incredibly fresh each time to those who live or observe it.

When we examine what has prompted people, past and present, to forsake their homelands and begin new lives elsewhere, we find a remarkable consistency in their motives.[1] Many entered on their own initiative, lured by the promise of a better life. Others were recruited by labor agents, enticed by the media, or encouraged to leave by their own governments that were seeking a lessening of social unrest or economic distress. Still others, forced to flee their native lands as refugees, had little choice.

Whatever the reason, whenever the time, the United States has always served as a destination for these adventurous, desperate, or determined people. Yet despite the immigrant ancestry of most Americans, many times in the past and present they have wanted to pull in the welcome mat for new immigrants.

Why Are Voices Raised Against Immigration?

Too often, the native-born react with fear and anxiety, perceiving some groups as "unassimilable" and their presence in large numbers as a threat to societal cohesion.[2] Other Americans are apprehensive about these groups' possible integration, believing such an eventuality would somehow destroy or undermine the "purity" of the American character. So it was with American ambassador to England Rufus King, who wrote in 1797 to Secretary of State Timothy Pickering that the Irish immigrants would "disfigure our true national character."[3] Ever since, others have expressed concerns about this or that group of immigrants as wrong for the nation's well-being.

Religious, Racial, and Cultural Biases

Sometimes, these reactions reveal a religious bias: against Quakers, Shakers, or Catholics in the 18th century; against Catholics, Jews, or Mormons in the 19th century; or against Catholics, Jews, or Sikhs in the early 20th century. Other negative responses reflect a racial bias: against African and Native Americans throughout the nation's history, and against Asians and dark-complexioned southern Europeans in the late 19th and early 20th centuries. There have been other varieties of bias: religion and race (Rastafarian), and culture and religion (Irish, Italian). Today, other nativist voices express the old fears about other religiously, racially, or culturally different newcomers: Muslims, Asians, or Latinos.

Economic Competition

Past or present targets have also induced alarm because others see them as a danger to their own livelihood. This perceived economic threat may result from the scarcity of jobs, affirmative action hiring or promotion policies, or the recruitment of cheaper labor or strike breakers. Since the mid-19th century, employers have often used newly arrived groups, including migrating Black Americans, to keep wages low or to break a strike.

The resulting ethnic antagonism can be of three types. Native-born Americans may resent the immigrant influx, as when West Coast labor unions in the late 19th and early 20th centuries fought against Asian workers. An interethnic rivalry may develop, such as the importation of Syrian-Lebanese immigrants in an effort to break the 300-mill shutdown in the Paterson, New Jersey, region in 1913, caused by striking European immigrant textile workers. Same-group members can pose a third variation of an immigrant economic threat. Economist Vernon Briggs, for example, has shown the negative influence on employment conditions for legal Mexican Americans by undocumented Mexicans working in the food and fiber industry.

The "Tipping Point"

Sometimes, biases are so deeply ingrained that people will respond negatively to the presence of even one member of a despised outgroup. More often, however, if the number of outgroup members is few, people tend to be more receptive to less-alike strangers, or at least indifferent or begrudgingly tolerant. When the numerical increase reaches the tipping point, hostile responses become more likely. As Luigi Laurenti's classic study on property values and race revealed, that tipping point has no exact number; it is a perceptual stage when the ingroup believes "too many" of "those people" are in its midst and "something needs to be done."[4]

Today Isn't Yesterday, or Is It?

If 10 generations of Americans have followed similar patterns of response to immigrants who have subsequently blended into the mainstream, why can't we recognize that fact and be less fearful about today's newcomers?

Today's nativists dismiss any effort to compare past immigrant concerns with their own. Past objectors, they argue, were narrow-minded bigots opposed to people who have since proven their ability to assimilate. They contend that today we are "inundated" with racially different Asians who lack a Judeo-Christian heritage, whose culture is radically different from ours. Hispanics, they add, are holding on to their language and customs, thereby presenting a real threat to the cohesiveness of U.S. society.

With the 1990s now the decade of the greatest number of immigrants ever to arrive (9.1 million), and with about four in five from developing world countries, nativists consider current immigration as a serious threat to the population composition of U.S. society as we have long known it. Furthermore, with a lower national birth rate among the native-born, the higher birth rate among the foreign-born enables them to have a stronger impact on natural population growth. Moreover, the nation has not satisfactorily dealt with the unemployment and poverty of its native-born Americans, they contend, to continue to admit large numbers of immigrants to intensify further an already difficult problem.

Questions about America's racial mix, natural population increase, unemployment, and poverty do offer some new wrinkles to old arguments, and need to be addressed. However, despite nativist disclaimers of new and different elements, these arguments share many commonalities with those of similar-minded alarmists of previous generations. All have seen newcomers as a threat to the "purity" of the American character, and to the stability and economic welfare of the society. All have seen the newcomers as inferior additions and complained about their retention of language and customs. All have assumed acculturation and assimilation would not occur. As Rita J. Simon states,

> These have been the arguments used against all of the "current cohorts" from the time the new immigrants began arriving, first from Ireland, then a decade or two later from Southern and Eastern Europe. . . . Contemporary immigrants are no less popular than the immigrants who began coming to this country after the Civil War and for all the years in between. The only popular or valued immigrants are those who came long ago, whenever "long ago" happened to be.[5]

I would suggest that, when nativists argue that today's situation is far different from past years, their perception reflects the Dillingham Flaw. They tend to view past fears as ignorant or irrational nativism against White ethnics who actually shared far more similarities with their hosts than any differences. However, what we perceive today as their mutual similarities were not viewed as such in those times. It is past perception, not present-day perception, that matters when examining past behaviors.

So are things different today or not? We need some comparative data to determine where the truth lies. To relate the present with the past, I'll focus on several aspects of nativist fears: the significance of immigration totals, the foreign-born presence, racial population changes, and assimilation.

Immigration Rate

Legislation in 1990 set a limit of 700,000 immigrants for 1992 to 1994, and of 675,000 thereafter. Because immediate family members are not included in these caps, annual figures have actually been higher, as they were in 2001 and 2002, when more than 1 million immigrants were admitted both years. Those numbers, about 214,000 higher than in 2000, reflected efforts to address the application backlog as well as adjustments of status from temporary visa status to legal immigrant. In 2003, legal immigration dropped to 705,827. Even so, such numbers provoke that nativist alarm, but it is a misleading statistic by itself. Much more informative about the impact of immigrants on society is the immigration rate. This measurement tool allows for comparisons of different eras while enabling us to specifically address vague nativist fears that the United States is being overwhelmed by a large influx of foreigners. It thus serves as a concrete aide in objectively describing a reality that may or may not differ from perceptions.

The immigration rate per 1,000 persons in the general population is computed by dividing the sum of the annual immigration totals by the sum of annual U.S. population totals for the same number of years. Collection of such data began in 1820, when new regulations required shipmasters to submit passenger lists to customs officials. What is particularly useful about this measurement tool is that it allows us to relate immigration totals to population totals and to do so in a way that provides a comparative means for analysis. Immigrant totals for any particular year or decade become more relevant if we know the size of the population the newcomers are joining. To be more specific, if 1 million people enter a society that totals 50 million people, the immigrants' presence will be more keenly felt than if 1 million people enter a society that has a population of 250 million.

As can be seen in Figure 8.1, the 1990s were the highest decade in total number of immigrants arriving. However, in terms of its immigration rate of 3.4, the 1990s actually tie for ninth out of the 17 decades. Immigrants in the 1990s were less than one third the proportion found in 1901–1910.

What are we saying? First, we are saying that the earlier waves of immigrants in each of the decades between 1841 and 1920 had a more

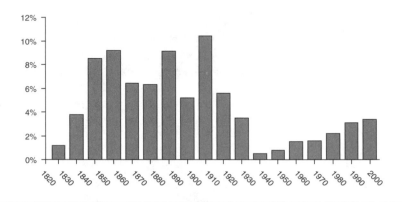

Figure 8.1   Immigration Rate, 1820–2000

SOURCE: U.S. Immigration and Naturalization Service, *2004-2005 Statistical Yearbook* (Washington, DC: Government Printing Office, 2004), Table 5, p. 8.

immediate effect on the nation's population composition. That is, the ratio of immigrants to the population receiving them was greater in the past. Such a higher ratio means that those immigrants from 1840 to 1920 proportionately and visibly changed America's population mix to a greater degree than the recent immigrants have.

We are also saying that a major factor in examining the immigration rate is immigration law. With the current ceiling of 675,000 immigrants annually, the general population will experience natural increases annually while the immigration cap remains constant. The result therefore must be a decline of the immigration rate in the years to come, as the population (denominator) increases while the number of immigrants (numerator) remains fairly constant. (In 2003, for example, the immigration rate dropped to 2.4 after a 3.7 rate for the previous 2 years.) Until new legislation raises that immigration cap, we can expect a steady reduction in the immigration rate, one measurement of alien impact on the host society.

Immigration Rate Caveats

Although the immigration rate is a helpful comparative measurement, it cannot stand alone. Too many other factors need to be considered as well. Perhaps most important is how much immigration contributes to population growth in an era of declining birth rates. Because immigrants have a higher birth rate than the native-born, their group numbers will grow at a faster rate. Using a formula of births plus immigration minus deaths and emigration, the Population Reference Bureau reports that immigrants currently account for about 23% of U.S. population growth.[6] Demographer Leon F. Bouvier says immigration will thus affect the nation's future ethnic population mix, a topic coming up in the last chapter.

Another consideration is that the United States is now a postindustrial society. Many manufacturing jobs no longer exist that immigrants with few skills and limited command of English could once attain. The ability of a nation to absorb its newcomers is thus dependent upon how well they can find their niche in the workplace, as well as on the proportion of immigrants to the total population.

Some states—such as California, Texas, Florida, and New York—receive so many immigrants that they are severely overburdened in education and social welfare costs. Nationwide, the data are much more positive. One study found that, between 1970 and 1992, immigrants generated a surplus of $25 billion to $30 billion in taxes paid over social services costs.[7] In 1997, the National Research Council reported similar findings, stating that immigrants may add as much as $10 billion to the economy each year.[8]

Foreign-Born Population

A companion set of data to immigration rates is the foreign-born population in various time periods, because they represent the cumulative totals of immigrants residing in the United States. Therefore, by determining what percentage of the general population is foreign-born at any given time, we can discern the extent of their presence as a basis for comparing the past with the present.

Data on the foreign-born were not gathered until the 1850 census. This year marked the close of the first decade with more than 1 million immigrants—1.7 million, to be exact. (In the 1830s, there were about 600,000 and about 143,000 in the 1820s.) So, 1850 serves as a good starting point for examining times of higher immigration.

Because immigration rates were higher in the past than in the present, as we have just seen, it is therefore not surprising to see in Figure 8.2 that the foreign-born segment of the population has been higher in 10 of the past 15 decennial censuses, consecutively from 1850 to 1940.

In Figure 8.2, we can see that the percentage of foreign-born living in the United States between 1860 and 1930 was greater than in 2000. In the

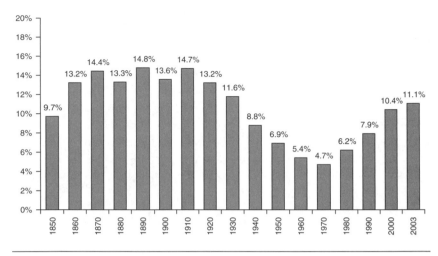

Figure 8.2   U.S. Foreign-Born Population as a Percentage of the Total Population, 1850–2000

SOURCE: "The Foreign-Born Population in the United States: 2003," August 2004, U.S. Census Bureau, Series P20-551.

1890 and 1910 censuses, one in seven was foreign-born; in 1860, 1870, 1880, 1900, and 1920, it was one in eight. The Census Bureau reported that the foreign-born population in 2003 totaled 33.5 million, or 11.7% of the population, a lower percentage than existed between 1860 and 1920.[9]

At the beginning of the 20th century, most cities in the Northeast contained a foreign-born population that comprised two thirds to three fourths of the cities' total populations. In contrast, the cities in 2000 with the most foreign-born populations were Miami (60%), Los Angeles (41%), San Francisco (37%), and New York (36%).[10] Although these are significant proportions, they pale alongside the data of 100 years ago.

From another viewpoint, the approximately 31.1 million foreign-born identified in the 2000 census are the largest numerical total ever, but in proportion to the entire population, that figure ranks eighth among the 16 decades for which this information is available.

Because these statistics do not include American-born children being raised in immigrant family households, the proportion of those living in various ethnic subcultures has been greater, especially among past generations, when family size was typically larger than today. Regardless of acculturation patterns, different languages, customs, and traditions from the old country have always prevailed to some extent among a sizable part of U.S. society, more so in the past than the present.

At its lowest point in 1960, the foreign-born component has since been moving upward again, reflecting the recent increases in the immigration rate. Similarly, the foreign-born percentages will continue to rise for a while but will eventually level off and decline, for the same reasons enumerated for the immigration rate.

Race in America

U.S. race relations have a violent, exploitative past and an often-troubled present. Racism finds many forms of expression ranging from verbal put-downs to killing, producing disturbing consequences not only for its victims but also for the society itself in economic, health, and social welfare costs.

At first, only Whites among the native-born enjoyed the privileges of citizenship and voting rights, and only White aliens could become naturalized citizens. In time, following the pain of the Civil War, the Fourteenth Amendment (1868) granted citizenship to anyone born or naturalized in the United States, and the Fifteenth Amendment (1870) extended voting rights to every male regardless of race or color. After an arduous struggle, non-White exclusion yielded under force of law to inclusion.

Advances against other areas of exclusion—notably in education, employment, housing, and public accommodation—occurred only a generation ago, growing out of the civil rights movement of the 1960s. Gaining legal rights and political participation did not necessarily mean social acceptance, however. Just as Crèvecoeur overlooked the disenfranchised racial U.S. minorities of his time, so too have many White Americans avoided any inclusion of non-Whites in their daily lives. Lack of interaction helps perpetuate stereotypes and allows racial prejudice and discrimination to thrive.

Although succeeding generations of America's people of color have made significant gains in education, employment, income, and political participation, problems remain. Many forms of institutionalized racism have been eliminated, but structural discrimination—the differential treatment of racial groups that is entrenched in our social institutions—remains. One out of four African and Hispanic Americans still lives in poverty, three times that of Whites, a ratio that has been consistent during the lifetime of most readers of this book.

Racism manifests itself in negative reactions to the number of immigrants in general who are non-White, or of one race such as Asians, of one group such as Haitians. It finds expression also in fears that American society's racial mixture is changing too dramatically.

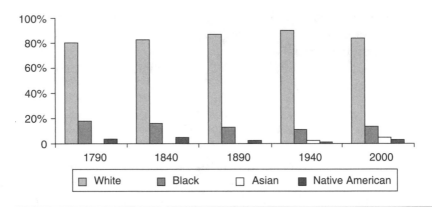

Figure 8.3   U.S. Population by Race as a Percentage of the Total Population

SOURCE: U.S. Bureau of the Census, *Historical Statistics of the United States, Part I,* Series A91-104 (Washington, DC: Government Printing Office, 1976); *Statistical Abstract of the United States 2003* (Washington, DC: Government Printing Office, 2004).

If we look at some of the data about past and present racial groups in the United States, we can dispel some of the generalizations and unfair comparisons (the Dillingham Flaw) that engender some of the unfavorable responses to the presence of people of color. Our focus once again will be on proportional representation within the total population through the years. Is the non-White to White ratio greater than ever? Exactly how is our society changing in its racial mixture?

After increasing proportionately since 1790 and peaking in 1940 at 89.8%, the nation's White population has since been decreasing steadily, as Figure 8.3 reveals. At this point, however, the 2000 percentage of 75.1 is only a slightly smaller portion of the total population than the 79.3% of Whites living in the United States in 1790.

The reason there was a smaller percentage of Whites in 1790 is that there was a greater percentage of Blacks. Then, African Americans constituted almost one in five residents, at 18.9%. That was the peak year for African Americans. Thereafter, elimination of the slave trade in 1808 and mostly White immigration slowly but steadily reduced African American apportionment within the society.

Even though the percentage of African Americans continually declined until reaching its lowest point in 1940 at 9.8%, their percentages did not drop below current figures until 1890. Before then, African Americans comprised a greater share of the total population.

Since 1950, their ratio has been slowly climbing from 9.9% to 12.3% in 2000, with the Census Bureau projecting an increase to 15% by 2050. Part of that increase is due to the presence of more than 1 million residents of West Indian ancestry and more than 881,000 immigrants from Africa.

Virtually nonexistent in the United States in 1790, Asians have been steadily increasing in numbers and proportion since their first tallies in the 1860 census. Since the liberalization of immigration regulations in 1965, their growth has been dramatic, and their visible concentration in certain regions of the country—particularly on the east and west coasts and in the Chicago metropolitan region—makes their 4% of the total population seem much greater to residents of those areas.

After experiencing a calamitous decline in population from first contact with Europeans until the 20th century, Native Americans have a high birth rate and are now steadily increasing their numbers. Their recent population growth has stabilized their proportional place in U.S. society at 1%.

What can we conclude from this information? Perhaps one surprise is that the United States is less Black today than it was from 1790 to 1890. However, it is also true that the White population percentage of the total is shrinking and the Black population percentage is increasing. Also, the increase in Asians, Hispanics (who can be of any race), and Native Americans—when combined with the increase in African Americans—means that the United States today is more of a multiracial society than ever before. What will the changing racial composition mean for the future of race relations? As the ratio of Whites declines, Whites will no doubt become more aware of their race instead of just paying attention to the visibility of other racial groups. Will this lead to greater understanding or to a racial backlash? This is part of the challenge before us.

In the last chapter, we shall explore more fully the implications of current birth and migration rates upon the future of U.S. society, including racial composition.

Mainstream Americans

Rarely are cultures or societies static entities. In the United States, the continual influx of immigrants has helped shape its metamorphosis. Part of this tempering has been the evolving definition of the mainstream ingroup, or identifying who was "really an American."[11]

In the initial conception of mainstream Americans, the English comprised virtually all of this ingroup. Gradually, this ingroup expanded from

English American exclusivity to British American or White-Anglo-Saxon-Protestant, thus including the Scots-Irish and Welsh previously excluded. This reconceptualization was triggered by the rapid Americanization of these groups after the Revolutionary War and by nativist reaction to the first large-scale wave of immigrants whose culture, religion, and, in the case of the Irish, peasant class set them apart from the mainstream.

By 1890, the "mainstream American" ingroup did not yet include many northwest European Americans. Although some multigenerational Americans of other than British ancestry had blended into the mainstream, millions had not. These Americans remained culturally pluralistic, their separateness resulting from race, religion, or geographic isolation. In addition, more than 9 million foreign-born—one in seven, perhaps one in five if we include their children—also lived outside this mainstream society then.

In 1890, the "melting pot" had not yet absorbed the 80,000 Dutch, 200,000 Swiss, or 1.2 million Scandinavians in the Midwest, most of whom had arrived after 1870. Likewise, the 150,000 French immigrants, 200,000 Cajuns in Louisiana, and 500,000 French Canadians in New England and the Great Plains remained culturally, linguistically, and religiously separated from the larger society. So, too, did many of the 8 million Germans in the rural Midwest or who were concentrated in many large cities. Their poverty and Catholic faith kept 6 million Irish in the Northeast and 300,000 Mexican Americans in the Southwest in social isolation. About 7.5 million African Americans, 248,000 Native Americans, and 110,000 Asians also lived as mostly impoverished racial minorities separate from the mainstream.[12]

Race, culture, and/or social class origins shaped group relations in the United States in 1890, keeping the nation a patchwork quilt of cultural diversity. All three variables influenced perceptions, receptivity, and interaction patterns.

In the 1890s, the tide of immigration began to change. The turning point came in 1896, when immigrants from the rest of Europe surpassed those from northern and western Europe. These "new" immigrants soon caused a redefinition of a mainstream American, bringing those of north and west European origins (including Australian and Canadian) into this classification in contrast to the newer, "less desirable" newcomers. Because this redefinition did not necessarily reflect cultural or structural assimilation, Figure 8.4 shows two groupings for 1890. The first indicates the more probable actuality of mainstream Americans, and the second suggests the perceptual reality.

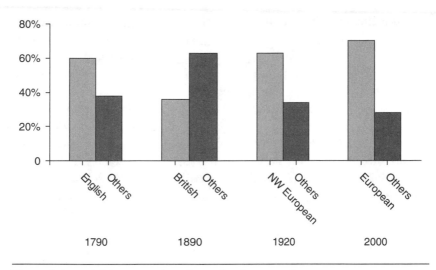

Figure 8.4   Mainstream Americans, by Ancestry Group

SOURCE: Based on data from U.S. Bureau of the Census, *Historical Statistics of the United States, Part I,* Series A91-104 (Washington, DC: Government Printing Office, 1976); *Statistical Abstract of the United States 2004–2005* (Washington, DC: Government Printing Office, 2004).

By 1970, a new turning point in immigration had been reached, with third world immigrants outnumbering European immigrants. Once again, partly through a reaction to this change and partly due to acculturation, education, and upward mobility, the concept of "mainstream American" expanded. This time, it included anyone of European origin, thus setting them apart from the people of color now arriving in great numbers, as well as the still nonintegrated African Americans and Native Americans.

Mainstream American Caveats

Figure 8.4 illustrates these mainstream American and outgroup classifications. Admittedly, these groupings are somewhat arbitrary. For example, some non-English were clearly mainstream Americans in 1790, such as Welsh Americans William Floyd, Button Gwinnett, Thomas Jefferson, Francis Lewis, and Lewis Morris—all signers of the Declaration of Independence. However, there still were many 18th- and 19th-century segregated Welsh settlements of Quakers, Baptists, or Congregationalists scattered in numerous regions where Welsh-language newspapers, even books, helped maintain a distinct ethnic minority group. Similarly, 19th-century German industrialists such as H. J. Heinz, Frederick Weyerhauser, John J. Bausch, and Henry Lomb typify non-British individuals who wielded considerable power and influence; yet most Germans remained socially isolated in rural or urban subcommunities.

The 2000 mainstream category is also an arbitrary oversimplification because it overlooks the religious and cultural differences among White ethnics that set them apart from fully assimilated European Americans. For example, mainstream Americans view the Amish, Mennonites, and Hasidic Jews as culturally distinct groups living within their own subcultures outside the mainstream. Therefore, the categories cannot be taken literally.

Even so, these categories still serve a useful purpose. They address the perception, acceptance, social distance, and therefore the basis upon which people react positively or negatively to physically or culturally distinct others. Some people here included in the mainstream group may not actually be a part of it and vice versa, yet these groupings offer an approximation of who are seen as "Americans" and who still remain as outsiders. The social distance scores reported by Emory Bogardus and other researchers since 1926 are a helpful indicator of these groupings.[13] Comparatively, the studies reveal a lessening of social distance among all groups through the decades, but nevertheless a consistent clustering of non-White groups farther away in social acceptance than White ethnic groups.

One can, of course, create other configurations and numbers. For example, one could introduce social stratification as a variable and make an effective argument for social class designation affecting mainstream acceptance and thereby altering the ingroup-outgroup memberships. Such a position has some merit, although it opens the door for counterarguments involving racism and structural assimilation, which would affect acceptance regardless of social class. Even so, with a smaller proportion of people living in poverty today than in 1890, and less in 1890 than in 1790, the pattern shown in Figure 8.4 of an increased proportion of mainstream Americans through the centuries would likely remain, and perhaps be even greater.

These statistics serve as a guide to our understanding and not as an absolute identification. Avoiding the Dillingham Flaw and identifying mainstream Americans through the eyes of each period's contemporaries, we find that the expanding American identity has resulted in a greater ingroup totality today than ever before. Despite recently expressed fears about the United States becoming a polyglot society of dissimilar peoples (a historically recurring anxiety), the nation's mainstream group has expanded, not contracted.

The "Wall"

What do we learn from this focus on mainstream Americans? As the nation's population mix has changed through the generations, so, too, has its definition of national cultural identity. Groups once excluded, once considered unassimilable, and even sometimes reviled, became included. In time, this socially constructed new reality seemed natural, especially with the appearance of a new group perceived as "different" and/or as economic competitors. A long, sometimes conflict-ridden process unfolded. Eventually, the newer group also became part of the ingroup and was replaced by another outgroup.

The concept of an expanding mainstream American identity is similar to the history of the walled medieval cities. Only so many inhabitants could fit within the protective wall that surrounded the city. The lack of available space forced newcomers to settle outside in *fauborgs* (the first suburbs!), where they could participate in the city's daily activities although they were not really a part of the city itself.

Hawking their wares like merchants inside the city's gates, they no doubt were resented by some as economic competitors. When trouble came in the form of marauders, all united in a common cause, but the newcomers were more likely to suffer the most in loss and destruction of their property outside the walls. In time, as the outsiders became a more integral part of the city, a new encircling wall was built farther out, as the old wall was torn down. With the previously excluded inhabitants now safely ensconced within the city's new walled perimeter, others would soon settle outside and begin the process anew.

The wall is an apt metaphor. In intergroup or gender relations, too often we still build protective walls of isolation, avoidance, or exclusion. Whether physical or social, walls do more than separate people: They limit one's field of vision, restrict movement, create a "they" and "we" mentality, and inspire conflict. Walls of prejudice keep people apart from one another, making those on one side more susceptible to victimization, as those *fauborg* dwellers once were. Just as economic growth brought the medieval walls down, so, too, does it help bring down our walls of prejudice. Conversely, economic decline helps erect walls between groups as people compete for jobs.

The social barriers we erect can sometimes be just as insurmountable and long lasting as many of those medieval walls still standing these many centuries later. Sometimes, though, those walls can be scaled, their gates opened, the ramparts destroyed. It is a paradoxical tribute to the dynamics of U.S. society that its cultural identity walls of exclusivity have been weak enough to overcome several times, thereby producing a stronger nation and a more vibrant American character than could have existed without such expansiveness.

Perception and Reality

Americans' perception of the foreign-born population is affected by how they become aware of the diversity that is the United States. The growing presence of first-generation Americans in previously homogeneous suburban locales brings a changed reality into the residents' taken-for-granted world. How that translates into interaction patterns determines the positive or negative reactions. On the other hand, news about illegal aliens almost always triggers a negative response, as Americans typically resent people violating their laws who also cost them money as well.

Concern about illegal aliens is nothing new. After passage of the Chinese Exclusion Act in 1882, Americans faced the problem of Chinese illegally entering the United States through British Columbia. Today, with a porous border with Mexico, illegal crossings are constant. Federal agents now apprehend more than 1 million aliens each year, but an estimated 200,000 successfully elude detection.[14]

Controversy about these undocumented aliens—particularly with the education, health, and social welfare costs they create—distorts the public image of legal immigrants. A 2002 Gallup poll, for example, found Americans divided on whether immigration is a good thing for the country.[15] Those expressing negative views frequently cite reasons such as immigrants being unskilled and using too many tax-supported services, factors that are more likely to be associated with illegal aliens than immigrants whose skills or family sponsorship clears them for admission legally. Unfortunately, many Americans do not make a distinction between these two very different groups of newcomers.

Today's Patterns in Perspective

Many Americans believe we are living in the midst of the greatest immigration ever. In actual numbers, that appears to be true, but in relation to the total population, the current immigration rate is lower than that of an 80-year period stretching from 1840 to 1920. Those higher rates meant a much greater ratio of immigrants to the population than at present.

Similarly, today's foreign-born population, so easily visible, is, in fact, less in relation to the native-born population than in 8 of the last 16 censuses. Put plainly, we have a lower foreign-born ratio today than we have had throughout most of the past 150 years.

We are indeed becoming a more multiracial society, and we have more Africans, Asians, and Hispanics than ever before. The trend toward more people of color will continue. As Whites decline as a percentage of the total, they may feel threatened economically and politically, and could act to reverse or slow down this demographic change. Perhaps California, where Whites first became a minority, will become the bellwether state for a national response. Florida and Texas are other states to watch for nativist reactions.

Acculturation and assimilation have resulted in a greater inclusiveness of previously excluded groups into the mainstream American category. Up until now, however, that process has not included people of color. If the process is to continue, a sea of change in racial attitudes will be required to allow today's outgroup members to become part of the American mainstream.

Our discussions about the statistics relating to immigration, foreign-born census counts, and racial proportions all addressed aspects of the pluralism that has been, and continues to be, the reality of the United States. Commentary on the expanding definition of mainstream Americans points to the ongoing assimilation process that continues through the generations. So, while dispelling some of the myths that immigration will get out of hand or that the proportion of foreign-born is higher than ever, the data also offer quantitative insights for avoiding the Dillingham Flaw. Peter Berger was right. Things are not necessarily as they seem. The pluralism of today in many ways does not surpass that in our nation's past, and assimilation is not endangered by numbers because it has successfully continued as a dynamic force under more overwhelming proportionate numbers of years ago.

Left unsaid in this discussion is whether the agendas of separatist multiculturalists create a real danger to societal cohesiveness, regardless of comparative statistics. We turn next to that topic.

Notes

1. See Vincent N. Parrillo, *Strangers to These Shores*, 7th ed. (Boston: Allyn & Bacon, 2003), 184–5, 340–1, 447–8.

2. See John Higham, *Strangers in the Land: Patterns of Nativism, 1860–1925* (New York: Atheneum, 1971).

3. James M. Smith, *Freedom's Fetters* (Ithaca, NY: Cornell University Press, 1956), 25.

4. Luigi Laurenti, *Property Values and Race: Studies in Cities* (Berkeley: University of California Press, 1960).

5. Rita J. Simon, "Old Minorities, New Immigrants: Aspirations, Hopes, and Fears," *The Annals of the American Academy of Political and Social Science,* 530 (1993): 65, 73.

6. Philip Martin and Elizabeth Midgley, "Immigration: Shaping and Reshaping America," *Population Bulletin,* 58 (June 2003): 21.

7. Jeffrey S. Passel, *Immigrants and Taxes: A Reappraisal of Huddle's "The Cost of Immigrants,"* PRIP-UI-29 (Washington, DC: Urban Institute, 1994).

8. "Immigration's Costs and Benefits Weighed," *Population Today* (July-August 1997): 3.

9. U.S. Bureau of the Census, "The Foreign-Born Population in the United States: 2003," *Current Population Reports,* Series P20-551, August 2004.

10. U.S. Bureau of the Census, *Profile of Selected Social Characteristics: 2000,* Summary File 3.

11. See Martin E. Spencer, "Multiculturalism, 'Political Correctness,' and the Politics of Identity," in Vincent N. Parrillo (guest ed.), "Multiculturalism and Diversity" [special issue], *Sociological Forum,* 9 (1994): 547–67.

12. James S. Olson, *The Ethnic Dimension in American Society,* 2nd ed. (New York: St. Martin's Press, 1994), 102–4.

13. Emory Bogardus, "Comparing Racial Distance in Ethiopia, South Africa, and the United States," *Sociology and Social Research,* 52 (1968): 149–56; Carolyn A. Owen, Howard C. Eisner, and Thomas R. McFaul, "A Half-Century of Social Distance Research: National Replication of the Bogardus Studies," *Sociology and Social Research,* 66 (1981): 80–97; Parrillo, *Strangers to These Shores,* 5–8.

14. U.S. Immigration and Naturalization Service, *2003 Statistical Yearbook* (Washington, DC: U.S. Government Printing Office, 2004), Table 40.

15. June 2002 Gallup Organization Poll reported by Public Agenda, "People's Chief Concerns: Immigration." Available at http://www.publicagenda.org [Accessed December 27, 2004].

9

Is Multiculturalism a Threat?

Multiculturalism is taught in academia, debated in government, promoted by ethnic leaders, reported by the media, and discussed among the citizenry. Few are indifferent to a subject with so many proponents and opponents. Some see multiculturalism as the bedrock upon which to build a society of true equality, whereas others see multiculturalism as a sinkhole that will swallow up the very foundation of U.S. society.

At its very core, the multiculturalism debate is a polarization of the centuries-old dual American realities of pluralism and assimilation into competing forces for dominance. As this book has shown, pluralism has been a constant reality in the United States since colonial times, and assimilation has been a steady, powerful force as well. There have always been both assimilationist and pluralist advocates, as well as both nativist alarmists and minority separatists.

Resentment and hostility about multiculturalism result from several factors. Rapid communication and televised images have heightened public consciousness of the diversity within U.S. society, but without placing it in the continuity of the larger historical context. Government policies and programs, particularly those dealing with bilingualism, become controversial when viewed as more than transitional aids by both pluralists and assimilationists. Vocal advocates for each position arouse strong feelings in their listeners in suggesting an "either-or" stance of supposedly diametrically opposing forces.

What raise reactions toward multiculturalism to a firestorm level are still other factors. First are the radical positions either anti-immigrant or racist, or else anti-White male or nonintegrationist.[1] Another is revisionist history or literary anthologies that downplay "DWMs" (dead White males) or else Western civilization, and heavily emphasize women, people of color, and non-Western civilization. Add furor about political correctness—whether in the guise of speech or behavior codes, curricula offerings, or selective emphases. The result is controversy of a (dare I say it?) white-heat intensity.

Multiculturalism is a stance taken by pluralists. Does that mean it imperils the process of assimilation? The answer is, basically, no, but the explanation is a complicated one. Multiculturalism, as mentioned in the first chapter, is a newer term for cultural pluralism, not a new phenomenon. Large foreign-speaking communities, foreign-language schools, organizations, and houses of worship, even pluralist extremists, are not new to U.S. society. Is, then, the new version not to be feared any more than its precursor, or is this more than a "new suit"? Is this thing we call multiculturalism a clear and present danger? Before we can address this concern, we need to understand exactly what multiculturalism is.

The Umbrellas of Multiculturalism

Multiculturalism does not mean the same thing to everyone. Even the multiculturalists do not agree with one another as to what they are advocating. Before we can address the advantages or disadvantages of a multicultural society, therefore, we need to understand these differing viewpoints.[2]

The Inclusionists

During the 1970s, multiculturalism meant the inclusion of material in the school curriculum that related the contributions of non-European peoples to the nation's history. In the next phase, multiculturalists aimed to change all areas of the curriculum in schools and colleges to reflect the diversity of U.S. society and to develop in individuals an awareness and appreciation for the impact of non-European civilizations on American culture.[3]

Inclusionists would appear to be assimilationists, but they are more than this. Assimilationists seek elimination of cultural differences through loss of one's distinctive traits that are replaced by the language, values, and other attributes of mainstream Americans. Although inclusionists share assimilationists' desire for national unity through a common identity, they also promote a pluralist or multiculturalist perspective. This finds expression by recognition of diversity throughout U.S. history and of minority contributions to American art, literature, music, cuisine, scientific achievements, sports, and holiday celebrations.

In the 1990s, this viewpoint perhaps found its most eloquent voice in Diane Ravitch.[4] She, too, emphasized a common culture but one that incorporated the contributions of all racial and ethnic groups so that they can believe in their full membership in America's past, present, and future. She envisioned elimination of allegiance to any specific racial and/or ethnic group, with emphasis instead on our common humanity, our shared national identity, and our individual accomplishments.

Inclusionist multiculturalists thus approach pluralism not as if it were groups each standing under their own different-colored umbrellas, but of all sharing one multicolored umbrella whose strength and character reflect the diverse backgrounds but singular cause of those standing under it together.

The Separatists

The group of multiculturalists that generates the most controversy is people who advocate "minority nationalism" and "separate pluralism." They reject an integrative approach and the notion of forming a common bond of identity among both the distinct minority groups and mainstream Americans. Instead of a collective American national identity, they seek specific, separate group identities that will withstand the assimilation process. This form of multiculturalism is the most extreme version of pluralism.

To achieve their objective and create a positive group identity, these multiculturalists seek to teach and maintain their own cultural customs, history, values, and festivals, while refusing to acknowledge those of the dominant culture. For example, some Native Americans raise strong objections to Columbus Day parades, while Afrocentrists downgrade Western civilization by arguing that it is merely a derivative of Afro-Egyptian culture—a claim, by the way, that is not historically accurate.[5]

Separatist multiculturalists do not want to stand with others under one multicolored umbrella. Not only do they wish to be under their own special umbrella, but they also want to share it only with their own kind and let them know why it is such a special umbrella. One may walk the same ground in the same storm, but shelter is to be found under a group's personal umbrella.

What particularly infuriates the assimilationists about the separatists' position is their concern that such emphasis on group identity promotes what Arthur Schlesinger calls "the cult of ethnicity." In *The Disuniting of America* (1991), a book widely discussed in both Europe and North America, Schlesinger warned that the Balkan present may be America's prologue.[6]

It is precisely that devastating warfare in the Balkans between Bosnians, Croatians, and Serbs in the former Yugoslavia that prompted so many voices in Canada, Europe, and the United States against multiculturalists who espouse separate pluralism. The "balkanization of society" is the most common expression that critics of multiculturalism use to suggest the threat to the social fabric supplied by a divisive policy promoting group identity over individual or societal welfare.

When Hispanic leaders from groups such as the League of United Latin American Citizens (LULAC) insist on "language rights"—the maintenance of the Spanish language and Latino culture at public expense—the assimilationists warn of an emerging "Tower of Babel" society.[7] When Afrocentrists such as Molefi Asante and Leon Jeffries emphasize the customs of African cultures over those of the dominant culture, their stress on African ethnicity provokes disapproval from critics such as Schlesinger, who complain that they drive "even deeper the awful wedges between races" by exaggerating ethnic differences.

The Integrative Pluralists

In 1915, Horace Kallen used the metaphor of a symphony orchestra to portray the strength through diversity of U.S. society.[8] Just as different groups of instruments each play their separate parts of the musical score but together produce beautiful music of blends and contrasts, so, too, he said, do the various populations within pluralist America. Kallen's idea of effective functional integration but limited cultural integration, however, was essentially a Eurocentric vision and reality. People of color were mentioned only incidentally and were typically not allowed to sit with, let alone join, the orchestra.

Harry Triandis not only added an interracial component to this view of integrative pluralism in 1976, but he also suggested that the majority culture is enriched by "additive multiculturalism."[9] By this he meant that one can get more out of life by understanding other languages, cultural values, and social settings. He hoped for society becoming more cohesive by finding common superordinate goals without insisting upon a loss of Black identity, Native American identity, Asian identity, or Hispanic identity. Arguing that mainstream Americans, secure in their identity, need to develop new interpersonal skills, Triandis maintained that the essence of pluralism is the development of appreciation, interdependence, and skills to interact intimately with persons from other cultures. He added,

> The majority culture can be enriched by considering the viewpoints of the several minority cultures that exist in America rather than trying to force these minorities to adopt a monocultural, impoverished, provincial viewpoint which may in the long run reduce creativity and the chances of effective adjustment in a fast-changing world. (p. 181)

This argument of cultural enrichment from diverse subcultures found another form of expression in *Beyond the Culture Wars* (1992) by Gerald Graff.[10] He suggested that exposure to differing cultural views will revitalize education by creating the dynamics of dialogue and debate. As Socrates once encouraged his students to search for truth through intellectual clashes, so, too, Graff maintained, can multicultural education help students overcome relativism and become informed about different positions.

Ronald Takaki echoed Graff's idea by recommending that the university become the meeting ground for different viewpoints.[11] American minds, he believes, need to be opened to greater cultural diversity. U.S. history, like the country itself, does not belong to one group, says Takaki, and so a change in the status quo is needed. Instead of a hierarchy of power headed by a privileged group, greater cross-cultural understanding and interconnected viewpoints are necessary.

Integrative pluralists envision a multitude of distinctive umbrellas each containing a different group, but with the umbrellas' edges attached to each other, so that, collectively, they embrace everyone. Guided equally by the many handles of the interconnected umbrellas, one can look around to see where another group is coming from within the framework of the whole.

Roses and Thorns

Cultivated for almost 5,000 years, roses were known to the Persians, Greeks, and Romans. One of our most popular flowers, the rose now comes in more than 8,000 varieties. Yet as beautiful and romantic as most people find roses to be, their thorns can hurt.

Roses seem a particularly apt analogy in any discussion about multiculturalism. Both require warmth and nurturing to bloom fully. The stronger their roots, the more they thrive. A variety of species is common to both, yet universal treatment gives vibrancy to all. Both also contain beauty and danger. Focusing only on the rose when reaching for it usually brings flesh into painful contact with a thorn; focusing narrowly on racial or cultural differences often causes the pain of isolation or conflict.

Some proponents of multiculturalism (the separatists) want to focus on only one variety of "rose" among many, whereas other advocates (the inclusionists) stress the commonality in origin that so many kinds of "roses" share. The third group of multiculturalists (the integrative pluralists) emphasizes the overall beauty of "roses" of different colors and varieties sharing the same "garden." The critics of multiculturalism, however, seem only to see its "thorns."

Completely ignoring the thorns needlessly places one at risk. If we look only at the thorns, we miss the beauty of the rose. If we pay heed to the thorns or remove them, as florists so thoughtfully do for their customers, then they cannot hurt us, and our appreciation for the rose remains unspoiled. We shall now look first at the thorns, the negative side of multiculturalism, and then at the roses, or positive side.

The "Thorns" of Multiculturalism

The "thorns" of multiculturalism are primarily those of immigration, language, culture, and race. Other thorns could undoubtedly be named, but these are the most important, for it is primarily in them that some Americans find the threat to U.S. society.

The "Immigrant Thorns"

Make no mistake about it. Continuing high immigration fuels the debate about multiculturalism, for this subject is about much more than simply preserving one's heritage. It is about power struggles among groups. It is about economics, jobs, social welfare, and tax dollars.

Concern about large numbers of immigrants arriving each year is likely to instill antipathy in many native-born White and Black Americans toward any manifestation of foreign origins through multicultural policies or programs. With more than 24 million immigrants arriving since 1971, a sizable proportion of the American public thinks there are too many immigrants in the country. Such anti-immigration sentiments have been heard in the land almost continually since large numbers of Irish Catholics began entering the United States in the early 19th century.

Public opinion polls conducted by the Roper Center in 1981 and 1982 found that two thirds of all Americans favored a decrease in immigration.[12] That heavy anti-immigration response should be understood in the context of the 1980–1982 recession and the influx of more than 200,000 Vietnamese "boat people" and 125,000 Cuban "Marielitos" within this 2-year period.

A 1992 *Business Week*/Harris Poll revealed 68% of all respondents saying the present immigration is bad for the country.[13] Forty-seven percent of Blacks and 62% of non-Blacks wanted fewer immigrants to come. In the same year, a poll of almost 3,000 Americans of Cuban, Mexican, and Puerto Rican descent, conducted by the Latino National Political Survey, found two thirds agreeing that there were too many immigrants in the United States. Obviously, anti-immigration sentiments are not confined to any one group, as more recent polls have also shown.

One multigenerational pattern about public response to immigration needs mentioning. Contemporary immigrants of any time period have almost always received negative evaluations by most native-born Americans, many themselves descendants of earlier immigrants once castigated by other native-born Americans. With the passage of time, people view these now "old" immigrant groups as making positive contributions to the cultural and socioeconomic well-being of society, as they transfer their negative perceptions to new immigrant groups.

Numerous anti-immigration organizations have emerged to lobby for restrictive laws to curtail immigration. The largest of these are the American Immigration Control Foundation, the Foundation for American Immigration Reform, and the Center for Immigration Studies.

Although these and other anti-immigrant groups vary in the intensity of their views, they all see the present immigration as a threat to the United

States. Their opposition rests on their belief that immigrants either take jobs away from Americans, often from poor people who are forced onto welfare, or else go on welfare themselves. Either way, these groups insist, the immigrants drive up social welfare costs. Other arguments include the assertion that immigrants strain law enforcement resources, contribute to an overpopulation problem through their higher birth rates, and deplete our natural resources.

Some states—such as California, Florida, Illinois, New Jersey, New York, and Texas, which are the destinations of 80% of all immigrants—clearly feel the impact of immigration more than other states. In early 1994, the New York State Senate Committee on Cities issued a report claiming that legal and illegal immigrants cost that state more than $5 billion a year in welfare, education, and criminal justice services.[14] Such reports and claims of high costs for the taxpayer provide ready ammunition for immigration critics.

If multiculturalism means favoring an immigration that places a financial hardship on the American worker and taxpayer, then many Americans oppose multiculturalism.

The "Language Thorns"

Foreigners speaking a language other than English has been a thorn in the side of many Americans for more than 200 years. In 1750, Benjamin Franklin expressed concern about the prevalence of the German language in Pennsylvania, and George Washington wrote to John Adams in 1798 against encouraging immigration because, among other things, the new arrivals "retain the language . . . which they bring with them."[15] No doubt these men spoke not only for themselves but also for a great many of their contemporaries as well.

Such complaints have reverberated down through the generations to the present day. They are now also louder and more numerous, given current migration trends. Two out of every three immigrants speak Spanish, and, as a result, more than 28 million Americans 5 years old and older speak Spanish. Another 7 million speak an Asian or Pacific Island language. Education officials expect more than 5 million children speaking more than 150 languages to enter the nation's public schools in this decade.

With the prevalence of so many non-English-speaking youngsters and adults, Americans have done more than complain. For example, Japanese-American S. I. Hayakawa, a former U.S. Senator from California and former president of San Francisco State University, founded U.S. English, an organization dedicated to making English the nation's official language;

eliminating or reducing bilingual education programs; and abolishing bilingual ballots, government documents, and road signs. By 2004, it claimed 1.8 million members. English-only laws were introduced in dozens of state legislatures in the late 1980s. Although 13 states rejected English-only legislative proposals, by 2004, 27 states had passed such legislation.

Many Americans are impatient with those unable to speak English. Their contention is that anyone living in this country should speak its language. Believing that our schools provide the "heat" for the melting pot, they are particularly irked about bilingual education programs. Critics see bilingual programs as counterproductive because they reduce assimilation and cohesiveness in U.S. society, while simultaneously isolating ethnic groups from one another. It is here that opponents use the terms "ethnic tribalism" and "classrooms of Babel" to argue that bilingual education fosters separation instead of cultural unity.[16] When LULAC leaders and others call for language and cultural maintenance programs at public expense, the monolingual adherents see red.

If multiculturalism means that English proficiency is not a priority, then many Americans oppose multiculturalism.

The "Cultural Thorns"

About 88,000 new immigrants—about 75% of them Asian or Hispanic—now arrive each month in the United States. Ethnic resiliency in language, ingroup solidarity, and subcultural patterns is both sustained and enhanced by the steadily increasing size of each new immigrant group.

Without this constant infusion of newcomers, acculturation would inexorably lessen each group's cultural isolation. Group members would gradually learn to speak English and to function more fully within the larger society. Even if such factors as limited education, poor job skills, and discrimination were present to prevent economic mainstreaming, greater cultural fusion would most likely occur over time.

Instead, we have large-scale immigration from Asian and Latin American countries revitalizing ethnic subcommunities with their language usage and cultural patterns. Differences in physical appearance, non-Western traditions and religious faiths—together with the prevalence of languages other than English, especially Spanish—suggest to some Americans that unless immigration is significantly curtailed, American culture and society are in danger of fragmenting.

What makes the cultural thorns even sharper is the new ethnic presence in our suburbs. Once the almost exclusive sanctuary of homogenized Americans, many suburbs are now the residential areas of choice for tens of thousands of first-generation Americans of non-European, mostly Asian, origin. Educated business and professional persons, seeking out desirable communities with excellent school systems, have brought racial and ethnic diversity to towns unaccustomed to such a multiethnic mix, sometimes erecting a mosque or Sikh temple, with its unique architecture, in contrast to other structures in the community.

It is not simply the presence of visibly distinct newcomers that creates tensions. These first-generation Americans live in the community but they are not of it, for they seldom interact with neighbors. Instead, they maintain an interactional network within their own group scattered throughout the area. This informal social patterning is reminiscent of other immigrants who have lived in recognized territorial subcommunities, but because these middle-class suburban ethnics live among homogenized Americans, their lack of involvement in community life encourages social distance and grates on others' sensibilities.

Besides a normal first-generation immigrant preference to associate with one's own people, some pragmatic elements deter suburban ethnic social interactions. Often the wife, filling the traditional gender role as nurturer, has limited command of English and feels insecure about conversing with neighbors. The husband is usually at work for long hours and has little free time, except to spend with the family.

Joining social organizations is a strong American orientation, as noted by Tocqueville and many others. Possessing neither time nor yet fully acculturated, few Asian Americans get involved in such typical suburban activities as parent-teacher organizations, team sports coaching, or scouting leadership. In time, this will probably change, but the present noninvolvement maintains Asian social distance from other Americans in their local communities. In response, suburbanites often view the Asians as not giving to, only taking from, the community. This reaction is especially acute when Asian American children, reflecting the high motivation and goal achievement instilled in them by their parents, appear overrepresented in garnering awards and recognition in scholarships and music.

If multiculturalism means maintenance of an alien culture and lessening community cohesiveness, then most Americans oppose multiculturalism.

The "Racial Thorns"

Except for extremist groups like the Ku Klux Klan, the National Association for the Advancement of White People, and neo-Nazis, few talk openly of race in their opposition to multiculturalism. Nevertheless, race is an important component of the multiculturalism debate.

The United States may be a less racist country than in earlier years, if civil rights legislation; public opinion polls; and the social indicators of education, occupation, income, and elected officials serve as a barometer. Yet racism still exists, perhaps less intensely in some areas than others, but it remains nonetheless. It can be found in numerous conversations, avoidance responses, subtle acts of discrimination, and myriad interaction patterns.

Institutional racism—the established laws, customs, and practices that systematically reflect and produce racial inequities in society—is a more significant factor than individuals committing overt racist actions, however. Biases remain built into the social structure, causing many individuals unknowingly to act without deliberate intent to hinder the advancement of non-Whites.

Although the Commission on Civil Rights (1981) identified areas where affirmative action could take aim at institutional racism (job seniority rules, nepotism-based recruitment or union membership, bank credit practices, culturally biased job performance tests), some of these remain problem areas. De facto housing segregation and disparities in school funding for urban and suburban schools are other examples of the multigenerational continuation of a subtle, structural racist practice. The pervasiveness of institutional racism remains both an obstacle in the path of upward mobility to many racial minority group members and a basic impediment to better interracial relations.

As successful as the United States has been in assimilating national minorities, it has been far less successful in assimilating racial minorities. African and Native Americans are still not fully integrated as mainstream Americans. Because we have never fully resolved our centuries-old twin problems of race relations and racial integration, the growing presence of people of color from developing world countries exacerbates the matter.

Racial tensions have heightened in some areas because of the influx of racially distinct, "clannish" strangers into neighborhoods unaccustomed to their presence. When this has occurred in previously homogeneous middle-class suburbs, the reactions may be more subtle, but the resentment is real and finds expression in avoidance responses, zoning regulations, and verbal complaints within one's circle of family, friends, and neighbors.

If multiculturalism means an increased racial presence and/or increased racial power that puts their own racial group to any disadvantage, then most Americans oppose multiculturalism.

The "Roses" of Multiculturalism

Roses bud, bloom, and fade away. Rosebuds give us the promise of new beauty about to arrive, and when the flowers are in full bloom, their contribution of beauty to our lives has to be experienced to be fully appreciated. Gradually, though, the roses fade and their petals gracefully fall to the ground, covering the dark earth with their pastel colors. With modest pruning, the gardener can coax other roses to appear and repeat the process again and again.

Multiculturalism is not a rose that will fade away in the United States, which has always been a land of diversity and destination for millions of immigrants. However, some "blooms" of ethnicity do fade away as, for example, we presently witness what Richard Alba calls "the twilight of ethnicity" among European Americans.[17] Moreover, what appear to some people as thorns may actually be roses instead. Let's extend our metaphor of roses onto the four types of thorns just discussed.

The "Immigrant Roses"

If a nation's strength lies in its people, then the strength of the United States clearly lies in the diversity of its people. Immigrants from all over the world have come here, and in one way or another, each group has played some role in the nation's evolution into its present superpower status.

Past immigrants built our cities, transportation systems, and labor unions, and enabled us to come of age both agriculturally and industrially. Many of today's immigrants have revitalized our cities; helped our high-tech industries remain competitive; and pumped billions of dollars annually into the national economy through their businesses, occupations, and consumerism. Combating negative stereotyping, societal ostracism, and fear about their growing size, each immigrant group then and now has worked hard to survive and put down roots. Viewed as a threat, each has proven to be an asset.

Although the immigrant roses bloom, others do not often appreciate their beauty. It is the exceptional individual who admires immigrants when they are immigrants. Only after the immigrant rose fades and its falling petals mingle with the soil that contains all our roots do we look back and cherish the bloom that is part of our heritage.

The "Language Roses"

Unlike the people of most nations who are at least bilingual, most Americans are monolingual. This limitation encourages ethnocentrism and provincialism, and places the business community at a disadvantage in the global marketplace. Mastery of a second language enhances one's mental mobility while enriching cultural insights and perspectives.

If Americans were to become proficient in a second language, encouraged to do so by the Asian and Latino population cohorts now living here, the result could easily be a society reaching greater maturity and tolerance in its intergroup relations. Most Europeans have long been at least bilingual, and their cultures and societal cohesion have not suffered. Bilingual advocates argue that bilingualism would not undermine U.S. culture either, only enrich it.

For those who do not buy into bilingualism for all citizens, the consistent findings of public opinion polls and scientific studies about English language acquisition offer comforting news. A 2003 Public Agenda study funded by the Carnegie Foundation revealed that 87% of immigrants polled said it was extremely important for immigrants to be able to speak and understand English.[18] Echoing similar newspaper polls and studies in California, Colorado, and elsewhere, a 1996 national poll showed that 80% of Hispanic parents wanted their children to be taught in English, not Spanish.[19] A few years earlier, a study by the RAND Corporation determined that 98% of Latino parents in Miami felt it was essential for their children to become competent in English. Such attitudes reach fruition according to the data, as indicated by Rodolfo de la Garza (1992), who reported that most U.S.-born Latinos and Asians use English as their primary language.[20] Teachers and other schoolchildren everywhere give corroborating testimony to this fact.

Despite all fears of Asian and Hispanic immigrants posing a threat to the English language, assimilation is still, as Nathan Glazer (1993) asserted, "the most powerful force affecting the ethnic and racial elements of the United States."[21] As the American Jewish Committee stated, "The use of additional languages to met the needs of language minorities does not pose a threat to America's true common heritage and common bond—the quest for freedom and opportunity."[22]

To allay further the anxieties of those who fear that the large Hispanic American presence is an unprecedented threat simply because of its size, we have a comparable example in our past, with the almost 4.9 million Germans who entered the United States between 1841 and 1900. Keep in mind that the U.S. population was much smaller then (23.1 million in 1850 and 62.9 million in 1890, compared to 203.3 million in 1970 and 295 million by year's end in 2004). Also, today's films, television, music, and Internet are ever-present English-learning aids that were unknown at the time of this large German presence.

In the mid- to late 19th century, so many hundreds of thousands of Germans lived in the area lying between Cincinnati, Milwaukee, and St. Louis that it became known as the "great German triangle."[23] Because so many German children attended public schools in the German triangle, the states passed laws permitting all academic subjects to be taught in German, whenever the demand was sufficient to warrant it. Ohio passed its statute in 1837; the others followed in the 1840s.

Consider the enormity of this action! In major cities, as well as in rural regions, the states of Ohio, Missouri, and Wisconsin (other states, too) authorized German as an official language for all classroom instruction! Cultural diversity, including that of language, was not only tolerated, but also encouraged.

The use of German in the public schools served a purpose other than academic instruction. It was intended to preserve the whole range of German culture, even more so after the unification of Germany in the 1870s. With an increased pride in their origins, German immigrants and their children developed a greater sense of their ethnicity than they possessed before their emigration. Because language enhanced their sense of being German, the German Americans continued to speak their language in their schools, homes, churches, and everyday business transactions.

As extensive German immigrant settlement in the region continued decade after decade, German-language instruction in all subjects continued in the public schools. Such was the case in the private schools as well. By 1910, more than 95% of German Catholic parishes had parochial schools taught in German, and more than 2,000 parishes conducted German-language services, much to the consternation of the Irish-American church hierarchy. During World War I, however, patriotic hysteria to drive the "Hun" language out of the schools prompted states such as Ohio and Nebraska to pass laws prohibiting instruction in German in all schools, public and private. A legal challenge to this action reached the U.S. Supreme Court in *Robert Meyer v. Nebraska* (1923).

Although the Court upheld the states' right to determine public school instruction in English only, its ruling on private and parochial schools was an important one with regard to language rights. Ruling that all state laws prohibiting the teaching and use of German in private or parochial schools were in violation of the Fourteenth Amendment and therefore unconstitutional, the Court declared that the rights of both parents and private/parochial schools to teach their children in a language other than English was within the liberty guaranteed by that amendment.

Despite (a) the institutionalization of academic instruction in German, (b) the steady influx of large numbers of German immigrants, and (c) more than 60 years of German language maintenance, German language usage declined. That process had already begun by 1885, as indicated by the complaints then of German American leaders that the younger generation was losing the German tongue and that parents no longer insisted on their children studying German in the schools.

As with other ethnic groups, English gradually replaced the homeland language, even among the millions of Germans so heavily concentrated in regions such as the German triangle. The German language rose once bloomed mightily in the United States, but it has faded, its petals drifting downward and blending with others that fell earlier. Perhaps the Spanish language is another such rose.

The "Cultural Roses"

The United States contains many persistent subcultures, people who steadfastly adhere to their own way of life as much as possible, resisting absorption into the dominant culture. These are usually religious groups—such as the Amish, Hutterites, Mennonites, and Hasidim—or groups whose ancestors predate the United States, such as the Native Americans and Spanish Americans in the Southwest. One could also argue that a persistent subculture exists among one fourth of the Black Americans mired in poverty for multiple generations. Until society finds an effective means to end their deprivation, these hard-core Black poor will continue to subsist within a subculture necessary for their survival.

Most racial and ethnic groups, however, are part of a convergent subculture gradually disappearing as its members become integrated into the dominant culture. For some, their "cultural roses" bloom longer than others, but at some point, the roses do fade. Besides the Germans just discussed, we have dozens of other examples of once-vibrant ethnic subcultures, ones that contemporary native-born Americans considered both persistent and a threat to the dominant culture, that converged into the mainstream.

Ethnic subcultures do not undermine the dominant culture. The United States has always had them, and at the time of their growing strength and vitality, they often contained separatist advocates. It is not uncommon for outsiders to become anxious about subgroup loyalties posing a danger to the larger society. Theodore Roosevelt's famous remark that "there is no room in this country for hyphenated Americanism" spoke to the same fears of subversion of American culture that Schlesinger has addressed as the "disuniting of America."[24]

When immigrants come to the United States, they come to join us. In forsaking their ancestral lands, they pay us the highest compliment: They want to spend the rest of their lives with us in a country where they hope to realize their dreams of a better life. They come to be a part of us, an "us" they have imagined our being after exposure to thousands of pictures, films, television shows, stories, letters, and rumors. They come to join us, not to keep separate from us. It may take some time, longer than some Americans' patience, but for most, that integration into the dominant culture occurs.

The falling petals of fading cultural roses also mingle with the soil containing all our roots. U.S. society, reflecting its multicultural past and present, keeps on being enriched with architecture, art, creative works, cuisine, music, and other cultural contributions from the diversity of its people.

The "Racial Roses"

Here we have a rare species of rose, for its bloom in a multiracial setting in the United States is difficult to produce. Too much of our past and present has been filled with racial animosity, exploitation, and violence. As I said earlier, we have never fully resolved the twin problems of race relations and racial integration in our society.

Part of our problem has been our cultural mind-set. With a simplistic "White" and "non-White" racial classification system, we have insidiously enmeshed race within our social structure. We have created and consistently reinforced an "us" and "them" mentality that manifests itself in social distance, differential treatment, deprivation, and suffering. Furthermore, our monoracial categories ignore the multiracial backgrounds of millions of African Americans, Filipinos, Latinos, Native Americans, and "Whites." We have taken a step forward in the deconstruction of race with the multiple racial census choices and in the growing recognition of the millions of biracial Americans.

As changing demographics make an increased multiracial society more evident to Americans, perhaps we shall see the removal of the weeds of racism (particularly the rooting out of institutional discrimination) and the blooming of the racial roses. Such a change will not be easy. But as the non-White segment of the U.S. population increases, so may the multiracial component of the American identity. If no longer relegated to the periphery, racial groups will be more at the center, and at the center, one finds both power and integration.

Increased racial tensions remain a distinct possibility, however, and we certainly find examples of that today. However, with the greater sharing of power that must come, that very same sharing of power could also cause greater racial acceptance.

At the risk of being accused of wearing rose-colored glasses in depicting the racial roses, I would suggest that if we can get the racial roses to bloom in this land—get to that point where each of the races displays its full beauty—then we can look past that point to the next horizon. When the racial rose petals fall and mingle with the soil common to us all, we will have moved past race as a divisive aspect of our society. This was Martin Luther King's dream, that one day his children would be judged by the content of their character instead of the color of their skin.[25]

Is Multiculturalism the Enemy?

On the battlefield of multiculturalism, pluralists and assimilationists wage war, but neither side will vanquish the other. As always, both forces will remain an integral part of U.S. society. The United States will remain a beacon of hope to immigrants everywhere, keeping the rich tradition of pluralism alive and well. Assimilationist forces, as consistently demonstrated for centuries, will remain strong, particularly on immigrant children and their descendants. Multiculturalism will no more weaken that process any more than the many past manifestations of ethnic ingroup solidarity have.

Social observers of different eras—Alexis de Tocqueville, Gunnar Myrdal, and Andrew Hacker, among others—have commented on the separate racial worlds within the United States. These separate worlds are not the result of multiculturalist teachings. Only when we break down the remaining racial barriers, eliminate institutional discrimination, and open up paths free of obstacles to a good education and job opportunities for everyone will racial integration improve. Afrocentrist schools do not undermine a cohesive society any more than Catholic schools, yeshivas, or other religious schools do. Multiculturalism is not the enemy; systemic racism is.

Notes

1. See John Leo, "The Hijacking of American History," *U.S. News & World Report* (November 14, 1994): 36.

2. See Ronald Takaki ed., *From Different Shores: Perspectives on Race and Ethnicity in America*, 2nd ed. (New York: Oxford University Press, 1994), 283–95.

3. Martin E. Spencer, "Multiculturalism, 'Political Correctness,' and the Politics of Identity," in Vincent N. Parrillo (guest ed.), "Multiculturalism and Diversity" [special issue], *Sociological Forum,* 9 (December 1994): 547–67.

4. Diane Ravitch, "Multiculturalism: E Pluribus Plures," *American Scholar,* 59 (1990): 337–54.

5. Molefi K. Asante, *The Afrocentric Idea* (Philadelphia: Temple University Press, 1987).

6. Arthur M. Schlesinger, Jr., *The Disuniting of America: Reflections on a Multicultural Society* (Knoxville, TN: Whittle Communications, 1991).

7. See Linda Chavez, "Hispanics vs. Their Leaders," *Commentary* (October 1991): 47–9.

8. Horace Kallen, "Democracy Versus the Melting Pot," *Nation* (February 18, 1915): 220.

9. Harry C. Triandis, "The Future of Pluralism," *Journal of Social Issues,* 32 (1976): 179–208.

10. Gerald Graff, *Beyond the Culture Wars: How Teaching the Conflicts Can Revitalize American Education* (New York: Norton, 1992).

11. Ronald Takaki, "Multiculturalism: Battleground or Meeting Ground?" *The Annals of the American Academy of Political and Social Science,* 530 (1993): 109–21.

12. See Rita J. Simon, "Old Minorities, New Immigrants: Aspirations, Hopes, and Fears," *The Annals of the American Academy of Political and Social Science,* 530 (1993): 62–3.

13. Michael J. Mandel and Christopher Farrell, "The Immigrants," *Business Week* (July 13, 1992): 114–22.

14. See Chris Carola, "Study: Immigrants Cost N.Y. Billions," *The Record* (January 21, 1994): 5.

15. Vincent N. Parrillo, *Strangers to These Shores,* 7th ed. (Boston: Allyn & Bacon, 2003), 142, 158.

16. Connie Leslie, "Classrooms of Babel," *Newsweek* (February 11, 1991): 56–7.

17. Richard D. Alba, *Italian Americans: Into the Twilight of Ethnicity* (Englewood Cliffs, NJ: Prentice Hall, 1985).

18. Public Agenda, "Immigrants Dispel Negative Stereotypes." Available at www.publicagenda.com/press/press_release [Accessed December 27, 2004].

19. Parrillo, *Strangers to These Shores,* 580.

20. Rodolfo de la Garza, *Latino Voices: Mexican, Puerto Rican, and Cuban Perspectives on American Politics* (Boulder, CO: Westview, 1992).

21. Nathan Glazer, "Is Assimilation Dead?" *The Annals of the American Academy of Political and Social Science,* 530 (1993): 123.

22. "English as the Official Language" (New York: American Jewish Committee, 1987).

23. Carl Wittke, *We Who Built America,* rev. ed. (Cleveland: Case Western Reserve University Press, 1967), 196–9.

24. Roosevelt's remarks come from a speech he gave in 1917 and preserved in Ralph Stout, ed., *Roosevelt in the Kansas City Star* (Boston: Houghton Mifflin, 1921), 137.

25. King's famous "I have a dream" speech was delivered on August 28, 1963, during the March on Washington for Jobs and Freedom. His actual words were, "I have a dream that my four little children will one day live in a nation where they will not be judged by the color of their skin but by the content of their character."

10

Multiculturalism After 9/11

The horrendous and tragic events of September 11, 2001, had a pronounced effect on the U.S. national psyche. Two generations of Americans had never experienced any foreign attack on their native soil, and even for an earlier generation who could recall the Japanese attack on Pearl Harbor on December 7, 1941, that action was against a military target in the mid-Pacific, not against civilian targets on the mainland. If there is one universal comment in the United States on this subject, it is this: Our lives were changed forever on that day.

Nine-eleven, as Americans call that infamous date, provoked many emotional responses, including initial shock and disbelief, followed by outrage and a desire for justice, together with a determination not to allow ourselves to be so vulnerable again. How, though, did the events of this day affect multiculturalism in the United States?

Government Response

In October 2001, the U.S. government acted decisively both within and outside its borders in reaction to 9/11. Most of the world supported its military action in an international campaign to flush out terrorist mastermind Osama bin Laden and to punish those who protected him. However, the 2003 preemptive war against Iraq, ostensibly to prevent Saddam Hussein from using the never-found "weapons of mass destruction" and to remove from power a supporter of terrorism, was far more controversial, both at home and abroad.

Other government actions in the United States, designed as protective actions in the name of national security, also generated controversy and debate about their infringement on civil rights and liberties. The USA Patriot Act—signed into law on October 26, 2001—significantly increased the surveillance and investigative powers of law enforcement agencies in the United States. The Act did not, however, provide for the system of checks and balances that traditionally safeguards civil liberties. Opponents particularly worried about its effect on the civil liberties of immigrants.[1]

In 2002, the newly created Department of Homeland Security (DHS) became the unifying core of a vast national network of organizations and institutions involved in efforts to secure the nation. This included border and transportation security, immigration, emergency preparedness and response, infrastructure protection, and the Secret Service. As the DHS took various initiatives to fulfill its mission, some of its domestic actions encountered resistance from civil libertarians and multiculturalists intent on preserving minority rights.

Here is a partial list of controversial actions that provoked criticism: (a) Arab and Muslim alien residents (noncitizens) had to register at federal offices; government officials then deported those with expired visas or faulty papers, allowing no appeal. (b) Those suspected of terrorist links were rounded up and held incommunicado, often for months. As many as 1,200 were detained for an extended period without any criminal charge lodged against them and, in most cases, without any basis in immigration law.[2] (c) Racial profiling—taking race or ethnicity into account in deciding whom to stop, question, frisk, and so on—occurred, as law enforcement officials placed Arab and/or Muslim Americans under intense scrutiny, especially at airports. (d) The Department of Homeland Security also initiated the required photographing and fingerprinting of all new arrivals from parts of the world associated with terrorism and anti-Americanism.

Public Response

How did the events of 9/11 and their aftermath affect the public's attitude about multiculturalism? A tiny minority of Americans responded with personal attacks on people assumed to be Arab and/or Muslim, as well as through verbal abuse, vandalism, and threatened boycotts of Arab-owned local businesses. At first, many first-generation Arab Americans found their loyalties questioned, especially after discovery that several of the hijackers had lived in the United States for several years as "sleeper terrorists" before 9/11. In addition, conservative and/or nativist groups called for severe immigration restrictions, but these never occurred.

More common, however, were other reactions. In areas with large concentrations of Arab Americans—such as Dearborn, Michigan, and Paterson, New Jersey—those residents put up banners in their streets denouncing the attacks and displayed U.S. flags at their homes and places of business. In local communities throughout the United States, Jews, Christians, and Muslims joined together in interfaith prayer services to demonstrate their solidarity with one another. Civic, political, and religious leaders all urged tolerance and avoidance of blaming all for the actions of a few. Letters to the editors of newspapers and calls to radio and television talk shows were overwhelmingly supportive of Arab and Muslim Americans as people "who came to join us," while denouncing the radical few "who came to hurt us." As the Arab American Institute reports, "the vast majority of Americans were disgusted by and ashamed of such acts of hatred and misdirected anger [by that] 'tiny minority.'"[3]

> Americans of all persuasions took proactive steps to come to the aid of Arab and Muslim Americans and offer their sympathy and support at a time when all Americans were dealing with the shock and trauma inflicted upon the nation.[4]

Of particular note is how local and state governments responded differently from the federal government. The city councils of New York, Los Angeles, Chicago, and Philadelphia—along with nearly 250 other municipalities and three state legislatures (Vermont, Hawaii, and Alaska)—passed resolutions denouncing provisions of the Patriot Act and called for their repeal. Whatever threat these governing bodies felt, they were closer to direct public input and expressed a more protective stance on the rights of targeted minorities caught up in a federal government effort to make the nation more secure.

Clearly, community response was not the same as the federal response. Some argued that the Bush administration trampled on civil liberties in its combative efforts to root out all internal threats. A large segment of the public—though traumatized by the terrorist acts—refused to support any broad measures against all members of these ethnic groups. This reluctance, illustrated by the actions of so many city councils (and in a national study that I will discuss in a few paragraphs), reveals an important aspect of U.S. culture: American values and attitudes are more tolerant than ever before of the "different others" in their midst, more accepting of individuals, and less willing to stereotype an entire group.

In fairness, it must also be said that President Bush and other national leaders also urged the public not to blame all Arabs and Muslims for the actions of a few "criminals." Early and forceful statements by President Bush made it clear that the federal government would not tolerate acts of violence against any Americans because of their skin color, religious affiliation, or ethnicity. The political leadership at all levels offered the voice of reason and tolerance, and it prevailed. Nevertheless, the sweeping countermeasures to combat terrorism suggested a broader "us-them" mentality than displayed by the general populace.

Several court rulings in 2004 struck down key parts of the Patriot Act as overly broad and unconstitutional. The rulings affected provisions that (a) barred giving expert advice or assistance to groups designated as international terrorist organizations, on the grounds that this part was in violation of the First and Fifth Amendments; (b) denied detainees held as "enemy combatants" the right to challenge their confinement through the U.S. courts; and (c) allowed the FBI to demand information from Internet service providers without judicial oversight or public review. This judicial curtailment of excess by the executive and legislative branches of government speaks well of the nation's ideals of protecting the rights of all minorities, even under such stressful circumstances. Embedded in U.S. culture is a respect for, and protection of, individual rights and freedom, the cornerstone of a multicultural society that even 9/11 cannot erase.

It was not that 9/11 had a negative impact on people's attitudes about multiculturalism, but rather that people's attitudes about multiculturalism had a positive impact on their responses to the diversity in their midst despite the terrorists. Americans of all races, creeds, and ethnic backgrounds united in a bond of solidarity, making sincere and sustained efforts to emphasize their commonalities. As idealistic as that statement may sound to some, this is nevertheless what happened. Evidence of this reality was shown in the largest national study ever conducted that measured Americans' acceptance of others, which coincidentally occurred soon after this national tragedy.

Measuring Social Distance After 9/11

A national study that I conducted in October to November 2001 captured the attitudes of 2,916 undergraduate and graduate students, ranging in age from 18 to 35, at 22 college and universities throughout the United States. This study, set up in spring 2001, originally was only to be a replication of social distance studies created by Emory Bogardus that had been conducted five times in the 20th century between 1926 and 1977. Because the new study was conducted in the aftermath of 9/11, it also gave insight into the initial response attitudes of this segment of the U.S. population.

Quite simply, the survey presented a list of 30 groups and asked respondents to give anonymous choices as to the degree of closeness they would allow for each group. On a 7-point scale, these choices included members of a group marrying into one's family (1.0), being part of a close social circle (2.0), a neighbor (3.0), a co-worker (4.0), a citizen (5.0), a visitor only (6.0), or excluded from entering the country (7.0). The closer a group was accepted, the less its social distance, and the lower its social distance score. Combining individual responses to get average mean scores, the results indicated how willing Americans were to accept others who were "different."

As shown in Table 10.1, the respondents—not surprisingly—relegated Muslims and Arabs to the bottom of the list, expressing greater social distance between them than for all other groups. Significantly, though, these two groups received lower (that is, more socially acceptable) mean scores than those received by 17 of the 30 groups in the previous 1977 study. What this tells us is that, although a few Americans assigned group blame to all Arabs and Muslims, and/or committed hate crimes against them, that mind-set did not extend to most respondents in this study. Their making a distinction, between the ethnicity of the terrorists and others who were Arabs and/or Muslims, resulted in such lower scores than given to past

Table 10.1

		Social Distance Rankings in 2001			
Rank	Group	Score	Rank	Group	Score
1.	Americans	1.07	16.	Filipinos	1.46
2.	Italians	1.15	17.	Chinese	1.47
3.	Canadians	1.20	18.	Puerto Ricans	1.47
4.	British	1.23	19.	Jamaicans	1.49
5.	Irish	1.23	20.	Russians	1.50
6.	French	1.28	21.	Dominicans	1.51
7.	Greeks	1.33	22.	Japanese	1.52
8.	Germans	1.33	23.	Cubans	1.53
9.	African Americans	1.33	24.	Koreans	1.54
			25.	Mexicans	1.55
10.	Dutch	1.35	26.	Indians (India)	1.60
11.	Jews	1.38	27.	Haitians	1.63
12.	Indians (American)	1.40	28.	Vietnamese	1.69
			29.	Muslims	1.88
13.	Africans	1.43	30.	Arabs	1.94
14.	Polish	1.45			
15.	Other Hispanics/ Latinos	1.45			

SOURCE: Vincent N. Parrillo and Christopher Donoghue, Updating the Bogardus Social Distance Studies: A New National Survey, *The Social Science Journal*, 42 (in press).

low-ranked groups that it is indeed an impressive finding. Americans may have felt less close to Arabs and Muslims after 9/11, but nonetheless not as distant as other generations felt to other foreigners in their midst.

No one should give too much importance to exact ranking of specific groups in the 2001 study, given the close scores, as these may be the result of sampling variability. Still, it is interesting to note the intermixing of Whites and people of color in the top two thirds of the list. This finding suggests that, in the multicultural U.S. society, a high level of social acceptance exists, regardless of color. Those from a Judeo-Christian background typically rank higher than those from non-Western religious backgrounds but, even then, the differences in social distance scores are not that pronounced.

Another interesting finding was the higher level of acceptance of Italian Americans than of other European American groups, including the English, Irish, and Germans. Statistical analyses of the data reveal that this placement occurred in part because of their high level of acceptance by Black and Hispanic Americans, as well as by White Americans, in comparison to other European American groups.[5]

Have Attitudes Changed About Immigration?

Attitudes about immigration give us a partial understanding of attitudes about multiculturalism. By comparing immigration attitudes before and after 9/11, we can get a sense of its impact on the acceptance and practice of multiculturalism.

A quick review of the polls might lead one to conclude that the answer to the above question is yes, but that would be wrong. Right after 9/11, Gallup public opinion polls found that support for reducing immigration indeed did jump sharply, from 38% in September 2000 to 58% in October 2001. This spike upwards, however, has since been declining. Opposition to immigration dropped somewhat from 2002 to 2004, as a CBS News poll found 45% expressing a desire to decrease immigration.[6] Moreover, it has been higher, as in June 1995, when another Gallup poll revealed that 66% wanted immigration decreased.[7] The point to be made here is that, just as previous chapters have shown mixed responses to multiculturalism prior to 9/11, so, too, do they appear afterwards. Nine-eleven appears not to be a causative factor in any significant change in attitudes about multiculturalism.

Furthermore, opinions differ between the mass population and the nation's elite. In a December 2002 opinion poll, the Center for Immigration Studies found that 60% of the public regarded the present level of immigration to be a "critical threat to the vital interests of the United States," compared to only 14% of the nation's leadership—a gap of 46 percentage points! Despite such public concern, federal officials have continually either advocated policies to increase the flow of immigration or else embraced policies that indicate a desire to continue immigration at its present numbers of about 1 million newcomers annually.

There are two reasons why national leaders advocated policies that so boldly contradicted the public's desire. First, they listened to opinion leaders (academics, media officials, union and corporate executives, religious and think tank leaders), and only 14% of these opinion leaders viewed current immigration levels as a problem. So, even though federal officials were not following the desires of the public, they were very much in tune with the views of the top leaders of America's institutions. Second, the public itself did not view the immigration issue as such a major concern as to mobilize to challenge current policies. When asked in 2002 to name the two or three biggest problems facing the United States, "too many immigrants ranked 13th of 65 general concerns mentioned."[8]

Throughout the country's history, American ambivalence about immigration has been common. Because of their perceived differences and threats to U.S. culture and societal cohesion, immigrants were seldom welcomed with open arms at any time. The altruistic, sometimes romantic, notions expressed by contemporaries or by those viewing the past have constantly been in contrast to people then expressing realistic concerns about the impact of immigrants on the economy or geographic areas in which they were heavily concentrated.

That ambivalence still remains, and to no greater degree now than in earlier years. Nine-eleven has less to do with these split feelings than do economic conditions and concerns about illegal immigration, not legal immigration. In short, the current views on immigration are no different now than before, suggesting that, from this perspective at least, neither have they changed about multiculturalism.

What About Tomorrow?

The world remains a dangerous place. Americans reacted on March 11, 2004, with horror and a renewed sense of vulnerability when terrorists made Madrid their new killing ground of innocent people. The continued bloodshed in Iraq is mind numbing and continues to raise concerns among Americans as to the future of that troubled country. When it comes to political and terrorist events, no one can speak with certainty about the future, but those concerns remain foremost in the minds of most Americans, and far less so is the diversity of the nation. The reelection of President Bush in 2004 revolved mainly around issues of "moral values" and public belief in his leadership against global terrorism, with little role played by the multicultural realities of U.S. society, except in the get-out-the-vote campaigns of both political parties.

The theme of this book, of course, is not about politics or terrorists. It is about diversity, about multiculturalism, and here we can make some reasonable projections about the future. Although arguments about assimilation versus pluralism continue in the land, we have also witnessed the triumph of the ideal of multiculturalism over the evil of reprehensible acts of indiscriminate killing. No curbs on immigration occurred. No assignment of group blame took place. Other than a few isolated actions immediately after 9/11, no retaliatory measures against Arab and Muslim Americans happened. Instead, Americans ignored the differences of race, religion, and place of birth to unite in recognition of a reality they sometimes forget: *e pluribus unum* (from the many, one).

We are a diverse people. We always have been, and we most likely always will be. We are an imperfect society, to be sure, and we don't always get along with one another. That's part of the growing pains of a society attempting to be all-inclusive and its people not always knowing how to achieve its ideals. Still, the U.S. Constitution and culture provide a framework wherein all individuals have equal protection under the law, as well as opportunities to attain a better life for themselves. It's the dream that still attracts so many people, and it's the cultural and structural reality that not only gives substance to the possibilities of realizing that dream, but also enables multiculturalism to flourish in the land, despite the fact that not everyone accepts it.

The issue of multiculturalism may remain controversial, but it passed an incredible test in the aftermath of 9/11. No doubt the future holds other challenges, but the reality is that, in this shrinking world of ours, a multicultural reality is the one that future generations and we must face. How we do that, how we harness that diversity into strength, is the real challenge ahead of us.

Notes

1. An excellent analysis of the USA Patriot Act and related links can be found at the Electronic Privacy Information Center. Available at http://www.epic.org/privacy/terrorism/usapatriot/#introduction [Accessed December 27, 2004].

2. For details on this subject, read the report of the Center for Constitutional Rights, "The State of Civil Liberties: One Year Later." Available at http://www.ccr-ny.org/v2/reports/docs/Civil_Liberties.pdf [Accessed April 3, 2004].

3. Arab American Institute, "Healing the Nation: The Arab American Experience After September 11." Available at http://www.aaiusa.org/PDF/healing_the_nation.pdf [Accessed December 27, 2004].

4. Ibid.

5. Vincent N. Parrillo, *Strangers to These Shores,* 7th ed. (Boston: Allyn & Bacon, 2003), 5–8; Vincent N. Parrillo, "Updating the Bogardus Social Distance Studies: A New National Survey," *The Social Science Journal,* forthcoming.

6. The CBS poll data are found at http://www.cbsnews.com/stories/2004/01/17/opinion/polls/main593849.shtml [Accessed December 27, 2004].

7. Gallup poll data can be obtained at http://www.gallup.org. An excellent detailed analysis of all polls, with graphs and data, can be found at http://www.publicagenda.org/issues/overview.cfm?issue_type=immigration [Accessed December 27, 2004].

8. A full discussion of immigration issues, as well as details of this poll, can be found at the Center for Immigration Studies at http://www.cis.org/articles/2002/back1402.html [Accessed December 27, 2004].

11

The Next Horizon

Nativists' reactions against increased U.S. diversity were often not just a response to what they perceived as a clear and present danger to the United States as they understood it. Besides their concern about the growing presence of those undesirable strangers in their midst, they also worried about their impact on the future of U.S. society.

A limerick from the early 20th century captured that worry in lines that White Anglo-Saxon Protestants (WASPs), feeling threatened by the influx of so many unlike others, did not find amusing:

In nineteen hundred and seventy-five,
Folks gathered round like bees in a hive,
To see in a tent
An American gent,
The very last Yankee alive.[1]

Numerically, WASPs have been a minority group for some time now, but they are hardly an endangered species. Still, their reduced presence and projections about their further shrinkage, along with all non-Hispanic Whites, have rekindled fears about the loss of dominance implied in the above limerick.

One final word about the limerick: "Yankee" is one of those interesting words that helps us understand the expanding mainstream category discussed in Chapter 8. It once meant a New Englander, but by the time of the Civil War, it had changed to indicate a Northerner. Since World War I, "Yankee" has simply meant any American. At the time of this limerick, however, its usage was understood to be a reference to its earlier connotation of an Anglo-American, much like Mark Twain's popular work, *A Connecticut Yankee in King Arthur's Court* (1889). Words change in their meaning, just as perceptions do about immigrants, people of color, and diversity.

The Dawning of a New Century

We recently passed through the threshold of a major calendar change, marking not only the passing of a hundred years but also of a thousand years. This combination of a new century and millennium had the futurists busy prognosticating about life in the 21st century. These predictions, as usual, ranged from the ridiculous to the sublime. Some may be accurate and others not. No one really knows what the future holds. We can only make educated guesses.

Those alive when the United States entered the 19th century could not have foretold with precision new immigration patterns, or that the nation's size would triple, or such technological advances as electric generators and lights, steam locomotives and ships, the telegraph and telephone, the reaping machine, vulcanized rubber, dynamite, radio, and moving pictures would revolutionize the way we live.

Similarly, those who were witness to the beginning of the 20th century could not accurately envision atomic energy, jet engines, radar, transistors, test tube babies, or the changing waves of immigration. How civilization will change in the 21st century or what world events will affect migration is really unknown, but that doesn't stop many from suggesting the possibilities.

Sometimes, the predictions seem uncanny. Two centuries ago, Secretary of State John Jay remarked, "The Mediterranean is the ocean of the past, the Atlantic the ocean of the present, and the Pacific the ocean of the future."[2] Given California's population, birth rates and rising standards of living in Asia, and signs of China's opening markets, Jay's prophecy seems quite accurate.

One consideration as we look to the future of multiculturalism must be the continuing economic integration occurring on this continent, as formally initiated in 1993 by Canada, Mexico, and the United States with their signing of the North American Free Trade Agreement (NAFTA), and how that will affect other aspects of intergroup relations. Furthermore, the fast-paced globalization of the world economy and its effect on living conditions in other countries will most likely influence future migration patterns. Outside social forces, as always, will play a major role in shaping the U.S. multicultural experience.

World Population Growth

The Population Reference Bureau (2004) reported that, even though fertility rates are dropping worldwide, world population growth may grow from 6.4 billion in 2004 to 7.9 billion by 2025, depending on fertility and mortality rates. As Europe shrinks by 6 million, Africa will increase by more than 438 million, Asia by 903 million, and Latin America and the Caribbean by 136 million. Developing countries will account for a greater share of the world population by 2025, representing about 84% of the total.[3] The significance of these patterns lies in their impact on immigration to the United States and this country's subsequent change in population composition. The inability of a country to support its large population has been an important push factor in emigration elsewhere. As population pressures mount in developing countries in the oncoming years, so will immigration pressures.

Current projections show continued high birth rates in most African, Asian, and Latin American countries outpacing their ability to provide a decent quality of life. In many of these nations, the fertility rate is dropping, but the population continues to rise startlingly because of the high proportion of their populations under the age of 16.

With so big a segment entering the child-bearing years, a built-in factor exists for further population expansion, because none of these countries is anywhere near zero population growth, where two adults have only two children. Mexico, for example, nearly quadrupled its population between 1950 and 2000, going from 27 million to 100 million. It might be 134 million by 2025. As our next-door neighbor and largest sending country, Mexico seems destined to send us millions more immigrants in the next few decades.

U.S. Population Predictions

The Census Bureau offers projections about the future of American diversity in its portrait of U.S. society in 2050. The government demographers base their forecast on the continuance of current trends. They assume that the birth rate will remain fairly low and life expectancy will increase slightly, whereas immigration will remain similar to the annual average now from the same sending countries.

These assumptions may be reasonable, but they are by no means certain. We can no more anticipate the actualities and ramifications of social change a half-century from now than could past Americans witnessing the advent of the 19th and 20th centuries. Actually, high, middle, and low

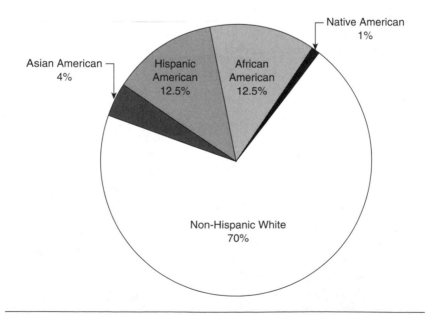

Figure 11.1   U.S. Population in 2000
SOURCE: U.S. Bureau of the Census.

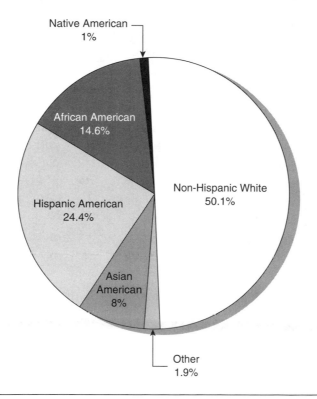

Native American 1%

African American 14.6%

Hispanic American 24.4%

Non-Hispanic White 50.1%

Asian American 8%

Other 1.9%

Figure 11.2   Projected U.S. Population in 2050
SOURCE: U.S. Bureau of the Census.

range projections exist, to give us a continuum of future possibilities. Even so, these projections rest on assumptions that may not hold true. What follows are the midrange projections from the Census Bureau.[4]

Hispanic Americans could increase their share of the population from 35.6 million, or 12.6%, in 2000 to 24.4% in 2050, when they will number about 102.5 million. This would be a population growth nearly three times their size in 2000. African Americans numbered about 35.8 million in 2000, or 12.7% of the total. By 2050, they may be approximately 61.4 million, or 14.6% of the total population. Of the almost 420 million Americans projected in 2050, about 4.4 million will be Native Americans. However, their share of the total would remain at its present 1%. In 2000, there were about 10.7 million Asian Americans, or 3.8% of all Americans. They may nearly quadruple by 2050 and reach 33.4 million, giving them an 8% share of the total population. If all of these groups are increasing proportionately within the total population, then the only group left—non-Hispanic Whites—must decrease from their present 70% portion of the population to 50.1% by 2050.

The Alarm Bells Ring

These projections have triggered alarm bells not just among nativists, who have consistently opposed liberal immigration policies, but also among some pluralists, who believe in the value of diversity. Demographer Leon F. Bouvier is one such example. In *Peaceful Invasions* (1992), he worried about projections showing the United States growing at a faster rate than other industrial nations. With about half this growth anticipated to be from immigration, Bouvier suggested that immigration restrictions were needed to strengthen America's economic stability, cultural cohesion, and quality of life.[5]

To achieve these goals, Bouvier argued for a reduction of immigration to 450,000 annually to reduce the intensity of the racial shift. A lower ceiling, he maintained, would also enhance cultural adaptation and not cultural separatism, by cutting back the source of ethnic vitality. Without the sizable continued inflow of low-level workers, he further believed that American industry would be forced to improve technologically to compete internationally in the 21st century.

Anti-immigration organizations, such as those mentioned in the previous chapter, also seize upon the Census Bureau projections to argue for lowering dramatically the number of immigrants permitted to enter. Most argue that although large-scale immigration may have been beneficial to the nation at one time, it no longer is the case, given the size and complexity of today's society.

Resetting the Alarm

Alarms keep us from oversleeping. Sometimes, though, we set them too early, or, forgetting to turn them off, they awaken us on the wrong day, causing us to lose sleep needlessly. We need to be careful that we set our alarms properly so that we do not fall victim to a false alarm.

Today's decisions affect tomorrow's outcomes, so it is important to be vigilant about the consequences of our actions, as we attempt to define what kind of society we wish to become. The problem is that too many actions often have unintended consequences. Just look at how immigration changed far differently than the sponsors of the 1965 immigration act expected! Trying to ascertain the future of immigration or population composition is no easy task.

A source of this nation's strength has always been in its people, including the positive contributions to our society and culture from tens of millions of immigrants. Millions more from around the world would like to move to the United States if they could. Yet even though immigrants are a valuable addition, this country could not possibly absorb all who want to come. Some limits are necessary, and a key part of the current debate is what those limits should be. Only a few subscribe to the radical position of open borders without any restrictions whatsoever.

Because some anti-immigration arguments are predicated on Census Bureau projections, several points need to be made that might possibly aid us in determining if the alarm has been set too early. The crux of the matter rests upon the accuracy of the predictions. Because we cannot know until the time arrives whether or not the predictions were indeed accurate, the only viable approach at this time is to identify what variables could affect even the most conservative scenario of U.S. population projections. In this way, we can understand the matter more fully and have additional insights for the formulation of public policy.

Certainly, more restrictive immigration laws would affect the projections. Anti-immigration lobbying groups, economic unrest, and public sentiment are influential variables that could influence legislation to reduce immigration totals and thereby alter the population composition.

Homeland conditions in the sending countries are a key factor in determining their emigration rates. Unless Mexico and the other developing countries boldly expand their economies, mounting population pressures will encourage a high exodus to receiving nations such as the United States. However, the world is a rapidly changing place in birth rates, technology, cultural diffusion, and global interdependence. Perhaps the social change sweeping the world will alter circumstances in less developed countries significantly enough to affect their emigration rates.

Multinational conglomerates operate not out of compassion but for profit. These developing nations offer them major opportunities for expansion and increased profits. We may expect them to open even more new factories and offices in these countries to expand their labor and consumer markets. As they do, hopefully the expanding economies will improve life opportunities in those countries.

Perhaps the next 50 years will also bring such an infusion of aid from developed countries to developing ones that their quality of life will reach satisfactory levels for their citizenry. Why should the developed nations do this? Although humanitarian reasons might be a partial motivation, they would find such aid in their own self-interests in that improved conditions in these countries would likely reduce the influx of immigrants from those countries.

If these nations develop sufficiently, the demographic transition already evident may accelerate, lowering their fertility rates sufficiently to stabilize population growth in the mid-21st century. Such a scenario would mean the lessening of causes for migration and consequently a change in the immigration patterns experienced by the United States.

The Dillingham Flaw in Reverse

In earlier discussions of the Dillingham Flaw, we spoke of using oversimplified categorizations and imposing present-day sensibilities on the past when such perceptions did not exist in those times. We can also apply the Dillingham Flaw when the same errors are committed by anyone looking into the future.

How can we be certain that today's group categories will still be valid by 2050? Right now, most White Americans bear witness to mixed European ancestry, but two generations ago, those Americans of southern, central, and eastern European backgrounds were far more likely to be of a single national lineage and religion. Group identity then was not the same as group identity today, for large-scale intermarriage has generated such a blending of peoples that "Whites" and "European Americans" have become synonymous.

In the 20th century, Italian, Polish, and Slavic Americans were once members of distinctive ethnic groups lacking economic, political, and social power. They displayed all the characteristics of a minority group in their ascribed status, endogamy, unequal treatment, and visibility. Today, most are part of the societal mainstream, displaying the traits of civic, marital, and structural assimilation. As their integration nears completion, "European American" serves as a generic term for heritage, not for everyday ethnicity, subcultural participation, or minority status.

European immigrants still arrive, and they begin the acculturation process anew, as earlier European arrivals once did. Most European Americans, however, are two or more generations removed from the ethnic experience. They are, for the most part, homogenized into a mainstream American identity, with ethnicity simply now an appreciation for their roots, occasionally marked by symbolic celebrations. Just as yesterday's categories for European ethnic Americans no longer fit today's Americans of mixed European ancestry, today's racial categories already fail to cover some of today's Americans, as we'll soon discuss. How, then, can we know with any certainty what are the right categories for tomorrow's Americans?

Using today's categories for Americans living in 2050 can easily be an unwitting application of the Dillingham Flaw in reverse. Projecting our perceptions and the existing social distance between groups onto a distant future carries a presumption that they will remain the same. Yet the only constant in life is change, and so our categories may be inadequate or irrelevant to our descendants.

Factors Influencing Change

Other demographic patterns exist to help us anticipate the future besides the fertility, mortality, and migration rates used by the Census Bureau. Some of these, particularly those dealing with marriages and children, give cause for being cautious in predicting group composition in 2050. We can detect some growing patterns that suggest different group categories in the future.

Interethnic Marriages and Children of Mixed Ancestry

Just as European nationality groups have blended together extensively through intermarriage in a multigenerational progression toward assimilation, so, too, may we expect Hispanic Americans to do the same. This process has been underway for decades and increasing steadily through the years.

Hispanics, who can be of any race, are increasingly marrying other Latinos of different national origins. More than 5.7 million married Hispanic couples now fit this category, compared to 1.9 million in 1980. Even more revealing is the outmarriage pattern. One sign of closing social distance and the final stage of assimilation is the widespread intermarriage of minority group members with those of the mainstream group. In 2003, about 1.9 million Hispanic Americans were married to a spouse of non-Hispanic origin. Although that is a small percentage of all Hispanics, it reflects a continuing upward trend.[6]

Given the past history of other groups assimilating and the current assimilationist patterns of so many second-generation Hispanic Americans, we may reasonably expect two things. First, a greater increase in Hispanic outmarriages is inevitable. Second, Hispanic achievement of social, economic, and political power—together with widespread intermarriage—will enlarge the mainstream American category once more to include them. One might even speculate that these two trends could become so universal that one day, Hispanic American will be no more a separate ethnic category than Italian, Polish, or Slavic is now.

Interracial Marriages and Biracial Children

Elimination of the racial barrier in the United States by 2050 may or may not occur, but a present-day trend suggests that the present-day simplistic racial categories are already obsolete. In recognition of this reality, the 2000 U.S. Census, for the first time in its history, allowed multiple answers in the racial category. More than 6.8 million people did so, claiming biracial status, and this number is climbing as a result of an increasing interracial marriage rate.

Since 1980, the total number of interracially married couples has more than tripled, going from 651,000 to about 2.1 million in 2003. The Black/White married couple category increased from 167,000 to 416,000, itself a doubling. Interracial couples of Whites married to a spouse other than Black (mostly Asian) grew from 450,000 to 1.5 million, while interracial couples of Blacks married to a spouse other than Whites increased from 34,000 to 132,000.[7] Although the number of Black/White intermarriages is only about one third that of other White-racial combinations, the 416,000 is significant. Such continued increases and their biracial offspring should generate pressure for the deconstruction of race as we know it and its subsequent reconstruction into more than the simplistic White/non-White classification.

Many other Americans also have a multiracial ancestry, such as virtually all Latinos and Filipinos, and many Native Americans and Native Hawaiians.[8] Among Black Americans with a multigenerational history in the United States, experts estimate that somewhere between 30% and 70% are multiracial, and so, too, are a sizable proportion of those classified as Whites.

Race always has been primarily a social construct, not one simply rooted in biological features.[9] It is defined differently in different societies, with racial boundaries blurred or distinct depending upon geographical, cultural, and political factors. In the United States, arbitrary or single-race classifications no longer apply to an increasing number of Americans. Recognizing a changing America, the Census Bureau has revised its categories several times for its decennial headcounts and, in 2000, changed its "select one only" format to allow for multiple choices, thus enabling many to identify with their mixed racial parentage.

Perhaps the day is not too far distant when the American people and their government will either broaden racial categories to include gradations between Black and White, as Brazil does, or create new official census categories like "Eurasian," "Afroindian," and "Amerlatino."

The Challenge of Racial Diversity

Despite questions about categories or the accuracy of the demographic projections, the United States is clearly becoming a more multiracial society than ever before.[10] What does this mean for race relations? U.S. society is less racist than in the past, but racism still saturates the land. Discrimination and violence sometimes give concern that race relations are deteriorating rather than improving.

Racial tensions, confrontations, and violent acts continue to occur in many geographic locales. It is a Black-White conflict in New York City or a Cambodian-Latino fight in Stockton, California. It is Blacks clashing with Korean merchants in Chicago or with Hispanics in Miami. As in Washington, DC, in 1991, it can be Hispanics rioting after a Black female police officer shot a Salvadoran immigrant. Or, as in Los Angeles in 1992, it can be a multiracial riot, with Latinos and Blacks preying on Whites, Koreans, and other Asians.

Increased racial diversity poses a crisis for U.S. society in the Chinese and Greek meaning of the word crisis. In those languages, crisis means both danger and opportunity.

The danger lies in race relations worsening. Will African Americans accept the presence and competition of Asians and Latinos? Will Asians and Latinos accept each other, when they often share urban territories? Will Whites peacefully accept the growing presence of Asians in their suburban neighborhoods? Will Whites calmly accept their diminishing status as non-White groups steadily grow numbers and strength?

The opportunity lies in a heightened awareness about the pluralist reality of U.S. society. The predominance of an Anglo-American assimilationist model worked to the disadvantage of those considered different or unassimilable. Understanding the American tradition of racial diversity could lead to an appreciation of its existence and ultimately to greater societal cohesion. Such a possibility would make the United States as powerful a world model for intergroup harmony as its political system has served as a government model for more than 200 years.

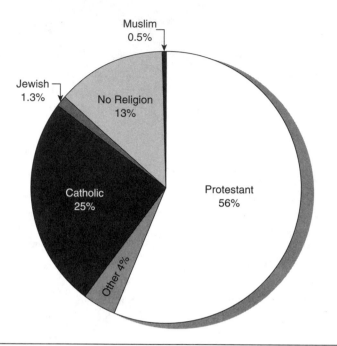

Figure 11.3   U.S. Religious Membership in 2000

SOURCE: Egon Mayer, Barry A. Kosmin, and Ariela Keysar, *American Religious Identification Survey, 2001.* Available at http://www.gc.cuny.edu/studies/aris_index.htm.

Among the range of race relations possibilities, then, lie increased tensions and violence at one end of the continuum and interracial harmony at the other. Obviously, we should strive to attain the latter and avoid the former. America's real future may fall short of the ideal, but that is not reason enough to stop trying to fulfill the dream of Martin Luther King, Jr.

Increased Religious Diversity

Earlier immigrant waves changed the United States from an almost exclusively Protestant nation into a country of three major faiths: Protestant, Catholic, and Jewish. Because religion is so closely intertwined with ethnicity, current migration patterns offer clues about the religious preference of future Americans, if present trends continue.

Protestants now account for about 56% of the total population, and Catholics for about 25%. Jews comprise about 1%, Muslims slightly less, and about 4% profess other religious faiths. Thirteen percent express no religious preference.

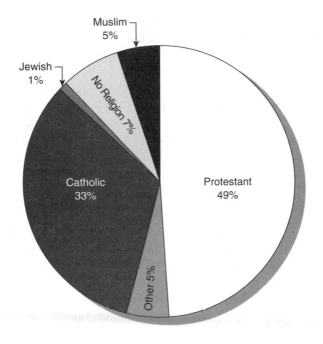

Figure 11.4   Projected U.S. Religious Membership in 2050

SOURCE: U.S. Bureau of the Census, *Current Population Reports*, Series P25-1092 (Washington, DC: Government Printing Office, 1992); *Statistical Abstract of the United States 1994* (Washington, DC: Government Printing Office, 1994).

Because Latin America and Asia are the major sending regions for about 75% of all immigrants to the United States, we can identify the prevailing religions in those countries and project them onto those entering the country. Realizing also that immigrants tend to have a higher birth rate than native-born Americans, and that some religions are more zealous in seeking religious converts, demographers can factor in those variables as well when projecting the future of religious affiliations.

Latin America and the Philippines are mostly Catholic, and as major sources of new immigrants accounting for more than half the total, they will help Roman Catholics increase dramatically in size. By 2050, Catholics may increase from one fourth of the American people to one third. They might also constitute the majority of residents in such heavily populated states as California, Florida, Texas, and New York.

Another rapidly growing religious group is the Muslims. Appealing to many African, Middle Eastern, and Asian Americans, Islam is becoming a more noticeable presence as mosques now pepper the American landscape.

Within a few years, Muslims will surpass Jews to become the third largest religious denomination in the United States. By the middle of this century, Muslims may account for 5% of the U.S. population, whereas Jews decrease to about a 1% share of the population.

Other Eastern religions—particularly Buddhists, Hindus, and Sikhs—should continue to grow substantially in the United States. By 2050, they may comprise 1% to 2% of U.S. society. In contrast, Protestants will likely drop below 50%. Mainstream denominations seem destined to decline the most, as fundamentalist denominations continue to gain new converts.

One should not assume cultural homogeneity will prevail among the two rapidly growing Catholic and Muslim faiths. Both will be composed of many unassimilated minorities. Catholics will be found among multi-generational Americans of European and African ancestry, and among such newer groups as Haitians, Filipinos, Indochinese, Latinos, and others. Muslims will include native-born African, Arab, and Asian Americans, as well as immigrants from those regions.

Religious diversity is becoming ever more pronounced throughout the land. If Census Bureau projections hold true and American Protestants fall below 50%, then no major religious faith will be dominant in the United States. We shall be a land where all faiths are minorities. When no religion was dominant at the time of the nation's founding, we benefited from the separation of church and state doctrine. Perhaps a future of all minority religions foretells a time of even greater ecumenism and tolerance.

The Mainstreaming of Women

U.S. society has embarked on an irreversible path toward gender equality. Great strides forward have been achieved since the 1960s, but much remains to be accomplished before parity with men is a reality. When women achieve social, economic, and political power equal to men, they will then be fully integrated into the society, or mainstreamed.

All the indicators point toward further progress. By 2013, the U.S. Department of Education projects the number of women enrolled in under-graduate degree programs will increase to 8.9 million, up from 8.1 million in 2005.[11] The U.S. Department of Labor projects the female labor force participation rate to rise from its present 59% to 62% by 2012.[12] An increasing number of women continue to choose college majors and careers that were mostly male domains previously. More women are becoming lawyers and judges, seeking elected political office, and moving into positions of power and influence.

As these trends continue and as women's higher expectations go onward, we may anticipate the experiences of women to be as different from now in 2050, as today's women find their opportunities in contrast to those in 1950. Furthermore, the glass ceiling of limited upward mobility that women experienced in 20th-century work settings may well disappear if present-day trends and challenges continue.

The Ever-Changing Mosaic

The metaphor of a mosaic to describe U.S. society is helpful in many ways. When we examine a mosaic up close, it is easy to see the individual tiles with their different colors. It is also easy to see the flaws—those individual tiles that are chipped, cracked, or spotted. We cannot help but notice the mortar between the tiles that separates (joins?) them.

Up close, we see everything and we see nothing. It is another version of failing to see the forest for the trees. We are able to focus on the individual differences of the tiles, but until we step back, we are unable to grasp the beauty of the big picture that the tiles collectively present to us. When we do step back, the borders between the tiles fade as they blend into one another. The flaws we were so critical about are meaningless now in appreciating the beauty of colors and design that the artist has provided for our enrichment and enjoyment. The whole is the sum of its parts, to coin a phrase.

In a very real sense, the United States is a mosaic of men and women of different colors, religions, and national origins. We are a microcosm of the world itself. We have become what Ben Wattenberg calls the "first universal nation."[13]

And yet, one aspect of the mosaic metaphor does not fit us at all. A mosaic is something fixed, static, and unchanging, and we have never been that. Tens of millions of people from all around the world have come to this country, made it their home, and invigorated it with their energy and determination. From its colonial diversity to its present-day diversity, the United States each year has experienced new arrivals and new changes to its population mix.

If we are a mosaic, then we are an ever-changing one. Some might prefer to call us a kaleidoscope to allow for continually changing patterns, but I prefer the idea of an ever-changing mosaic. Looking in a kaleidoscope is an individual experience, but gazing at a mosaic can be a shared one, and shared experiences are what the metaphor is partly about. Moreover, the mosaic metaphor extends the analogy further, enabling us to use its close-up flaws as comparable to the criticisms often directed against nonmainstream groups.

Whether one uses the metaphor of an ever-changing mosaic or a kaleidoscope to describe its people, the United States continues to manifest a dynamic cultural pluralism that has always marked its existence, even in colonial times. Although it has a greater mix of races and nationalities today, we have examined how, in some ways, the United States is actually less multicultural than in its past. What we are experiencing today in large-scale immigration and minority group (including female) challenges to the status quo is part of the continuing dynamics of a nation evolving to make its reality resemble more its ideals.

Despite fears about divisiveness, the mainstream group is larger than ever before. Despite male apprehension about the feminist movement, women are becoming a more integral part of the mainstream and dispelling many myths as they do. Despite concerns about language retention, today's immigrants want to learn English and do so no slower than past immigrants, and perhaps even more quickly because of the mass media. Despite nativist anxieties about non-Westerners not blending in, Asians are demonstrating their desire to integrate by having the highest naturalization rates among all of the largest sending countries.

Multiculturalism is neither new nor a threat to the stabilization and integration of U.S. society. Extremists come and go, but the core culture remains strong, the American Dream prevails, and men and women seek to be part of it, bringing with them the diversity that *is* America. Multiculturalism, then, is an old, continuing presence that strengthens not weakens, enriches not diminishes, and nourishes not drains—a civilization whose character and temperament have long reflected the diversity of its people.

Notes

1. J. M. Flagg, *Life* (January 12, 1922).
2. In Leon F. Bouvier, *Peaceful Invasions: Immigration and Changing America* (Lanham, MD: University Press of America, 1992), 149.
3. *2004 World Population Data Sheet* (Washington, DC: Population Reference Bureau, 2004).

4. U.S. Bureau of the Census, *U.S. Interim Projections by Age, Sex, Race, and Hispanic Origin*. Available at http://www.census.gov/ipc/www/usinterimproj/natprojtab01a.pdf [Accessed December 27, 2004].

5. Bouvier, *Peaceful Invasions*.

6. U.S. Bureau of the Census, *Statistical Abstract of the United States: 2004-2005* (Washington, DC: U.S. Government Printing Office, 2004.), Table 52, p. 48.

7. Ibid.

8. See T. P. Wilson, "People of Mixed Race Descent," in *American Mosaic: Selected Readings on America's Multicultural Heritage*, eds. Y. I. Song and E. C. Kim (Englewood Cliffs, NJ: Prentice Hall, 1991).

9. See Paul R. Spickard, "The Illogic of American Racial Categories," in *Racially Mixed People in America*, ed. M. P. P. Root (London: Sage, 1992), 12–23.

10. See, for example, Juanita Tamayo Lott, "Do United States Racial/Ethnic Categories Still Fit?" *Population Today*, 21 (January 1993): 6–7.

11. National Center for Education Statistics, *The Condition of Education 2003* (Washington, DC: U.S. Government Printing Office, 2004). Table 5.1, p. 101.

12. U.S. Bureau of Labor Statistics in U.S. Bureau of the Census, *Statistical Abstract of the United States: 2004-2005,* Table 570, p. 371.

13. Ben Wattenberg, *The Birth Dearth,* 2nd ed. (New York: Pharos, 1989).

Index

Acculturation, 132, 145, 155, 184
Adams, John, 73
Addams, Jane, 6
Additive multiculturalism, 151
Affirmative action, 115, 157
African Americans. *See also* Black
   Americans
  in Age of Expansion, 88–90
  census of 1790 data, 68
  churches, 65–66
  in colonial America, 48–50, 55
  Crèvecoeur's omission of, 9–10
  in early national period, 68
  in Industrial Age, 98–100
  interracial marriages, 186
  literacy laws against, 99
  middle class status of, 100
  migration of, 99–100
  musical culture among, 89
  in Northern states,
    89–90, 99–100
  population growth of, 181
  population rate for, 138–139
  in post-Revolutionary War
    America, 65–66
  racism against, 99
  religion among, 89
  religious institutions for, 65–66
  segregation laws against, 99
  in Southern states, 88–89, 99–100
  Tocqueville's writings about, 79
African immigrants, 121
African Methodist Episcopalian
   Church, 66
African Methodist Episcopal
   Zion Church, 66
African slaves. *See also* Slaves
  cultural diversity among, 48–50

  language diversity among, 50
  in Revolutionary Army, 55–56
Age of Enlightenment, 40, 53
Age of Expansion
  African Americans in, 88–90
  Chinese immigrants in, 90–91
  French immigrants in, 72, 80–82
  immigration in, 77–78
  Irish immigrants in, 82–83
  Mexican immigrants in, 91–92
  Native Americans in, 85–88
  Tocqueville's writings, 78–79
Alba, Richard D., 12, 18,
   57, 158, 164
Alien Act, 73–74
America
  Age of Expansion in. *See* Age
    of Expansion
  colonial. *See* Colonial America
  cultural identity of, 143–144
  early national period in. *See* Early
    National Period
  German triangle in, 160–161
  Industrial Age in.
    See Industrial Age
  Information Age in.
    See Information Age
  linguistic independence of, 62
  mosaic of, 191–192
  multiracial composition of, 162
  national identity of, after
    Revolutionary War, 61–63
  population in, 180–184
  race in, 137–139
  racial tensions in, 162–163
  religious diversity in, 188–190
  rural society in, 66
  subcultures in, 161

territory expansion, 69–70
in 21st century, 178–179
American Dictionary of the English Language, An, 62
American Dream, 1–2
American Jewish Committee, 159
American Notes, 80–81
American Protective Association, 107
American Revolution
  consequences of, 56
  Revolutionary Army, 55–56
  Revolutionary War, 43
American Spelling Book, 62
Anglicans, 52, 62, 65
Anti-immigration organizations, 153–154, 182
Arab Americans, 168–169, 171, 175
Arab immigrants, 103, 124
Asante, Molefi K., 150, 164
Asian Americans. *See also* Chinese immigrants; Japanese Americans
  in Industrial Age, 100–101
  in Information Age, 116–119
  population growth of, 181
  population rate for, 138–139
  social isolation in community, 156
Asian Indian immigrants, 117
Assimilation
  description of, 4, 159
  ethnic intermarriages and, 12
  history of, 7
  of Italian immigrants, 106
  of minority groups, 145
  of Native Americans, 85–86
  pluralism vs., 7
  of racial minorities, 157
Assimilation in American Life, 7
Assimilationists, 149–150, 163

Balkanization, 2, 150
Baptists, in colonial America, 52
Battle of Tippecanoe Creek, 70
Beals, Carleton, 94
Berger, Peter, 5, 18, 145
Berkhofer, Robert F., Jr., 37
Beyond the Culture Wars, 151

Bias
  cultural, 130
  economic competition, 131
  racial, 130
  religious, 130
Bilingual education programs, 155
Bilingualism, 159
Billigmeier, Robert H., 94
bin Laden, Osama, 168
Biology, as ideology, 16
"Birds of passage," 106–107
Black Americans. *See also* African Americans
  in Industrial Age, 119–121
  interracial marriages, 186
  population rate for, 138
  subculture among, 161
Black Hawk, 87
Blaine, James G., 101
Blauner, Robert, 97–98, 109
Bogardus, Emery, 142, 146, 171
Bonacich, Edna, 109
Boorstin, Daniel J., 54, 57
Boundary flaw, 16–17
Bouvier, Leon F., 182, 192
Bremer, Frederika, 79–80
Bridenbaugh, Carl, 57
Briggs, Vernon, 131
Brimelow, Peter, 2, 17
British immigrants
  differences among, 41
  in Information Age, 116
Buddhists, 190
Burt, Jesse, 37
Bush, George W., 170, 174

Calvinists, 84
Cambodian immigrants, 119
Campbell, Mildred, 40, 56
Carola, Chris, 164
Carroll, J.B., 37
Carroll, John, 62
Catholics
  in colonial America, 52
  discrimination against, 107
  French, 81
  growth of, 189–190

Irish, 83
    population percentages, 188–189
    in post-Revolutionary War
        America, 62–63
Catton, Bruce, 41, 57
Catton, William B., 41, 57
Census of 1790
    African American population, 68
    description of, 66
    ethnic populations, 67–68
    Native American population, 68
    White population statistics, 66–67
Central European Americans,
    105–107
Chavez, Linda, 164
Child labor, 97
Chinchilla, Norma Stoltz, 127
Chinese Exclusion Act, 144
Chinese immigrants
    in Age of Expansion, 90–91
    in Industrial Age, 101
    in Information Age, 116–117
Christianity, 85
Christians, 125
Civil Rights Act of 1964, 114
Civil War, 93
Clark, William, 23, 70
Clay, Henry, 60
Clothing diversity, among Native
    Americans
    description of, 26
    Northeastern Native
        Americans, 28–29
    Northern Plains Native
        Americans, 27–28
    Northwestern Native
        Americans, 27
    Southeastern Native Americans, 28
    Southwestern Native
        Americans, 27
Cole, Donald B., 57
Colonial America
    African slaves in, 48–50, 55
    Anglicans in, 52
    assimilation in, 41
    Baptist Church origins in, 52
    beginnings of, 43–45

Catholics in, 52
colonies in, 44–45
cultural homogenization in, 56
cultural norms in, 40
cultural pluralism in, 43
Dillingham Flaw in, 42
diversity in, 44–45
Dutch in, 46–47
English Americans in, 54
ethnic communities in, 42
ethnic settlements in, 43–45
European influences on, 40
geographical variances in, 45–51
Great Awakening in, 53–54
immigration in, 41
Middle Colonies, 45–48, 50, 54
minority acculturation in, 56
minority separatism in, 55
Native Americans in, 48, 55
New Amsterdam, 44
New England Colonies, 45
racial diversity in, 55
regional cultures in, 50–51
religious diversity in, 51–54
religious groupings in, 47–48
religious intolerance in, 52–53
Revolutionary Army, 55–56
settlements in, 43–45
slaves in, 48–50
social organization in, 51
Southern Colonies, 48, 50, 54
women in, 51, 56
Commission on Civil Rights, 157
Congregational Church, 64
Contrast, The, 61
Crèvecoeur, Michel Guillaume
    Jean de, 8–9, 18, 137
Cuban immigrants, 122
Cult of ethnicity, 150
Cultural bias, 130
Cultural enrichment, 151
Cultural homogeneity myth, 5–6, 66
Cultural homogenization
    census of 1790 and, 66–67
    in colonial America, 56
    in early national period, 60, 71, 74
    in Industrial Age, 108

Cultural identity, 143–144
Cultural pluralism
    assimilation vs., 7
    in colonial America, 43
    description of, 4
    early advocates of, 6–7
    in early national period, 64
    inclusionist multiculturalists'
        view of, 149
    in Industrial Age, 98
    in Information Age, 114
    multiculturalism and, 8, 148,
        161–162
    in Native Americans, 22
    in present-day America, 145
    reassertion of, 7–8
    Triandis' writings about, 151
Culture
    ethnic group relations
        affected by, 121
    language and, 23
    multiculturalism and, 155–156
Culture and Democracy in the
    United States, 7

Daniels, Roger, 101, 110, 127
de Kalb, Baron, 55
de Lafayette, Marquis, 55
de la Garza, Rodolfo, 164
Democracy in America, 78
Demographics
    intermarriage effects on, 185–186
    interracial marriage effects
        on, 186–187
Department of Homeland
    Security, 168
Dewey, John, 6
Dickens, Charles, 80–81, 94
Dillingham, William P., 12–13
Dillingham Commission, 12–14
Dillingham Flaw
    avoidance of, 14, 145
    chain reaction, 15
    in colonial America, 42
    concept of, 14–15
    definition of, 12, 14
    dispelling of, 138

example of, 14
    misconceptions secondary to, 15
    in reverse, 184–185
Discrimination
    against Catholics, 107
    structural, 137
Disease, Native American tribes
    affected by, 36
Disuniting of America, The, 150
Diversity
    clothing, 26–29
    history of, 5
    housing, 29–32
    language, 22–24
    misconceptions about, 5–6
    racial, 187–188
    religious. See Religious diversity
    sociohistorical reality of, 17
Division of labor, among Native
    Americans, 24–25
Dolan, Jay P., 94
Dominican Republic
    immigrants, 122
Donoghue, Christopher, 172
Douglass, Frederick, 89
Driver, Harold E., 37
DuBois, W.E.B., 109
Dutch immigrants, 105

Early National Period
    African Americans in, 68
    antiforeign responses in, 73–74
    arts and letters in, 61–62
    census of 1790. See Census of
        1790
    common culture in, 71–74
    cultural differences during, 59
    cultural homogenization in,
        60, 71, 74
    cultural pluralism in, 64
    ethnically diverse population in,
        67–68
    foreign languages in, 72–73
    French influences in, 72
    gender roles during, 60
    global turmoil during, 60
    immigration in, 70–71, 73–74

linguistic independence during, 62
national identity during, 61–63
Native American battles during,
    69–70
political democracy in, 71–72
politics in, 64–65
population growth in, 71
property owners in, 63
religious independence during,
    62–65
religious institutions during, 65–66
rural society in, 66
social class in, 63–64
social structure in, 63–64
territory expansion, 69–70
White population data, 66–67
women in, 60, 64
Eastern European Americans,
    105–107
Economic competition, 131
Ecumenicism, 14
Education
    bilingual programs, 155
    of Black Americans, 119–120
    of women, 115
Edwards, Jonathan, 53
Elkins, Stanley, 75
Emerson, Ralph Waldo, 10, 18
England, emigration from, 70–71
English language
    as primary language of America,
        154–155
    Hispanic Americans' use of, 159
    public opinion regarding, 159
Episcopalian Church, 65
Ethnic communities, 80
Ethnic families, 96–97
Ethnic groups. See also specific
        ethnic group
    conflicts among, 92, 107–108
    nonparticipation in community
        activities, 156
    public opinion toward,
        after 9/11, 172
    in suburbs, 155–156
Ethnic intermarriages.
    See Intermarriages

Ethnicity
    African, 150
    cult of, 150
Ethnic Myth, The, 8
Ethnic subcultures, 161
Ethnic tribalism, 8
Ethnocentrism, 158–159
Ethnogenesis, 50
European Americans
    acculturation of, 184–185
    Central, 105–107
    Eastern, 105–107
    Northern, 104–105
    Southern, 105–107
    Western, 104–105
European immigration
    during Industrial Age, 97–98
    during Information Age, 116
European patriarchal values, 40

Farb, Peter, 37
Farley, Reynolds, 12, 19
Farrell, Christopher, 164
Federalists, 72–73
Feminism, 126–127
Ferguson, Robert B., 37
Filipino Americans, 117
Fillmore, Millard, 92
Fishman, Joshua, 78, 94
Fitzpatrick, John C., 57
"Five Civilized Tribes," 86
Flagg, J.M., 192
Flanders, 80–81
Florida, 70
Foreign-born population
    native-born population vs., 145
    perception of, 144
    statistics regarding, 135–137
Foreign language, 154–155
Fourteenth Amendment, 137
France
    cultural influences on America, 80
    Flanders, 80–81
    immigrants from. See French
        immigrants
Franklin, Benjamin, 47, 65, 154
Fredrickson, George M., 99

French Canadian immigrants, 105
French immigrants
    cultural separateness of, 140
    in early national period, 72
    influences of, 72, 80–82
    in Information Age, 116
    statistics regarding, 81–82
French Revolution, 60, 73
*Frontier in American
    History, The*, 11
Fuchs, Lawrence H., 41–42, 57

Gaustad, Edwin S., 57
Gender roles. *See also* Women
    during Early National
        Period, 60
    in Industrial Age, 96–97
    in Native Americans, 24–26
    in slave families, 88–89
Genovese, Eugene D., 94
German Americans
    in Industrial Age, 104–105
    power of, 142
    violence against, 108
German immigrants
    academic instruction of, 160
    in Age of Expansion, 72, 83–85
    cultural separateness of, 140
    decline in, 93
    diversity of, 84–85
    in early national period, 65
    education of, 160
    in Industrial Age, 104–105
    influence of, 84
    in Information Age, 116
    in Milwaukee, 84
    statistics regarding, 83–84,
        93, 159–160
    subculture of, 159–161
German Lutheran Ministerium of
    Pennsylvania, 62
German triangle, 160–161
Ghost Dance Religion, 102
Glazer, Nathan, 6, 18, 159, 164
Gordon, Milton, 7, 18
Graff, Gerald, 151, 164
Grant, Madison, 107, 110

Great Awakening, 53–54
Gullah, 50

Haitian Americans, 120
Hamilton, Nora, 127
Hayakawa, S.I., 154
Henretta, James A., 18, 57,
    75, 94, 109
Herrnstein, Richard, 13
Higgs, Robert, 100, 109
Higham, John, 145
Hindus, 190
Hispanic Americans.
    See also Mexican Americans
    definition of, 121
    English language usage by, 159
    in Industrial Age, 101–102
    in Information Age, 121–124
    interethnic marriages among,
        185–186
    population growth of, 181
    population increases, 159
History of New York, A, 61
Homes of the New World, The,
    79–80
Homestead Act of 1862, 87
Housing
    among Native Americans, 29–32
    communal structures, 29, 31–32
    single-family dwellings, 32
Hoxie, Frederick E., 110
Hughes, Charles Evans, 101
Hui kuan, 90–91
Hupa, 35
Hussein, Saddam, 168
Hutchinson, Anne, 51–52

Illegal aliens, 144
Ill Soo Kim, 127
Immigrants. *See also specific
    immigrant group*
    acculturation of, 132
    American Dream of, 1–2
    antipathy toward, 153
    assimilation of, 131–132
    backlash against, 2
    bias against, 130–133

British, 41
contributions by, 158
in early national period,
    70–71, 73–74
economic benefits of, 135
Emerson's view of, 10
in late 19th century, 93
legislative acts against, 73–74
Martineau's defense of, 79–80
nativist perceptions of, 2–3
negative reactions toward, 2
perceptions regarding, 144
public image of, 144, 153
societal contributions by, 158
Immigration
    in Age of Expansion, 77–78
    between 1790 and 1820, 70–71
    anti-immigration organizations,
        153–154, 182
    biases against, 130
    Civil War's effect on, 93
    in early national period, 70–71
    in 18th century, 40–41
    English legislation effects on,
        70–71
    European, during Industrial Age,
        97–98
    future of, 182–183
    in Industrial Age, 96
    multiculturalism and,
        153–154, 158
    National Origins Quota Act of
        1921 effect on, 108
    national quota restrictions on, 7
    9/11 effects on attitudes toward,
        173–174
    organizations against, 153–154
    public opinions regarding,
        153, 173–174
    reasons for, 1, 183
    recent increases in, 144–145
    restrictions on, 182
    states impacted by, 154
Immigration law, 134
Immigration rate
    caveats, 134–135
    changes in, 133–134

computation of, 133
limits on, 133
Inclusionists, 149
Indians. See Native Americans
Industrial Age
    African Americans in, 98–100
    Asian Americans in, 100–101
    Central European Americans in,
        105–107
    changes during, 95–96
    child labor in, 97
    cultural homogenization in, 108
    cultural pluralism in, 98
    Eastern European Americans in,
        105–107
    exploitation of labor during, 96
    German immigrants in, 104–105
    Hispanic Americans in, 101–102
    immigration in, 96
    intergroup conflicts in, 107–108
    Irish immigrants in, 105
    labor force changes during, 95
    Middle Eastern Americans in,
        103–104
    minority family economics
        in, 96–97
    Native Americans in, 102–103
    Northern European
        Americans in, 104–105
    onset of, 93
    Pacific Islanders in, 100–101
    population diversity in, 97–98
    sojourners in, 106–107
    Southern European Americans in,
        105–107
    Western European Americans in,
        104–105
    women's role in, 96–97
Information Age
    African immigrants in, 121
    Asian Americans in, 116–119
    Asian Indian immigrants in, 117
    Black Americans in, 119–121
    Chinese Americans in, 116–117
    Civil Rights Act of 1964, 114
    cultural pluralism in, 114
    economic differences in, 113–114

European Americans in, 116
Filipino Americans in, 117
Haitian Americans in, 120
Hispanic Americans in, 121–124
Jamaican Americans in, 120–121
Japanese Americans in, 117–118
Korean Americans in, 118
Latin America immigrants in, 113
Mexican Americans in, 122–123
Middle Eastern immigrants in, 124
minority rights in, 114–115
National Origins Quota Act of
    1921 repeal in, 111–112
Native Americans in, 124–125
North African immigrants in, 124
religious diversity in, 125–126
technological advances in,
    111–112
Vietnamese Americans in,
    118–119
women in, 115
Institutional racism, 157
Integrative pluralists, 150–152
Intergroup conflicts
in Age of Expansion, 92, 107–108
in Industrial Age, 107–108
Intermarriages
among Hispanic
    Americans, 185–186
Crèvecoueur's writings about, 9
melting pot theory and, 9, 12
studies on, 12
Interracial marriages, 186–187
Iranian Americans, 124
Irish immigrants
agriculture by, 82
catholicism among, 83
decline of, 93
in Industrial Age, 105
in Information Age, 116
labor by, 82–83
living conditions for, 82
religion of, 83
statistics regarding, 77–78, 82, 93
women, 83
Iroquois, 24, 30, 87
Iroquois Confederation, 31, 34–35

Irving, Washington, 61
Islam, 189
Italian immigrants, 106, 116

Jackson, Andrew, 86–87
Jamaican Americans, 120–121
James, William, 108
Japanese Americans
in Industrial Age, 101
in Information Age, 117–118
Jay, John, 179
Jefferson, Thomas, 62, 65, 70
Jeffries, Leon, 150
Jensen, Arthur, 13
Jews, 188
Jim Crow laws, 99
Johnson, Lyndon B., 112
Jones, Woodrow, Jr., 127
Josephy, Alvin M., Jr., 37
Journey Through Texas, A, 80

Kallen, Horace, 6–7, 18, 150, 164
Kammen, Michael, 54, 57
Kantrowitz, Barbara, 127
Karok, 35
Kayal, Joseph M., 110
Kayal, Philip M., 110
Kennedy, John F., 112
Kestler-Harris, Alice, 109
King, Rufus, 65, 130
Kinzner, Donald J., 110
Kitano, Harry H. L., 127
Korean Americans, 118
Kosciuszko, Thaddeus, 55
Ku Klux Klan, 107–108, 156

Language
among African slaves, 50
among Native Americans, 22–24
culture and, 23
diversity of, 22–24, 50
in early national period, 72–73
English as primary,
    154–155, 159
foreign, 154–155
geographical isolation
    effects on, 72

multiculturalism and, 154–155,
    158–161
perceptions affected by, 23
public opinions regarding,
    154–155
social isolation effects on, 72
Laotian immigrants, 119
Latin America immigrants, 113
Laurenti, Luigi, 131, 146
League of the Five Nations, 34
League of United Latin American
    Citizens, 2, 150, 155
Lenni Lenape, 32
Leo, John, 163
Leslie, Connie, 164
*Letters from an American
    Farmer*, 8
Lewis, Meriwether, 23, 70
Lieberson, Stanley, 12, 19
Lincoln, C. Eric, 94
Lindner, Eileen W., 128
Lodge, Henry Cabot, 101
Lorber, Judith, 16, 19
Lott, Juanita Tamayo, 193
Louisiana Purchase, 70
LULAC. *See* League of United
    Latin American Citizens
Lurie, Nancy O., 37
Lyman, Stanford M., 94

Main, Jackson T., 75
Mainstream Americans
    ancestry group of, 141–142
    caveats, 141–142
    concept of, 139–140
    expanding identity of, 143, 145
    historical changes in, 140–141
    immigration changes, 140
Mamiya, Lawrence H., 94
Mandel, Michael J., 164
Mandelbaum, David G., 37
Martin, Philip, 146
Martineau, Harriet, 79–80, 94
Matrilineal society, 24
Matrilocal society, 24
Maxwell, James A., 37
McKitrick, Eric, 75

Melting pot
    Crèvecoeur's writings
        about, 8–10
    definition of, 9
    Emerson's writings about, 10
    history of, 8–9
    "mainstream American" ingroup
        affected by, 140
    Turner's writings about, 10–11
    Zangwill's writings about, 11–12
Menominee, 32
Mexican Americans. *See also*
    Hispanic Americans
    in Age of Expansion, 91–92
    in Industrial age, 101–102
    in Information Age, 122–123
Mexico, 180, 183
Middle Colonies, of colonial
    America, 45–48, 50, 54
Middle Eastern Americans, 103–104,
    124
Midgley, Elizabeth, 146
Miller, John C., 75
Minorities
    acculturation of, in colonial
        America, 56
    actions by, 2–3
    interethnic marriages among,
        185–186
    parallel religious institutions
        created by, 65–66
    racial, 157, 187
    rights of, in Information Age,
        114–115
Minority nationalism, 149
Monroe, James, 65, 74
Multiculturalism
    additive, 151
    benefits of, 192
    cultural pluralism and, 8, 148
    cultural "roses" of, 161–162
    cultural "thorns" of, 155–156
    debate regarding, 147–148
    description of, 3–4, 147, 192
    factors that affect reaction
        toward, 148
    history of, 6–8

immigrant "roses" of, 158
immigrant "thorns" of, 153–154
inclusionists view of, 149
integrative pluralists' view of,
    150–152
language "roses" of, 158–161
language "thorns" of, 154–155
media influences on, 148
in Native Americans, 21–22
after 9/11. *See* 9/11
public opinion of, 170–171
racial "roses" of, 162–163
racial "thorns" of, 156–157
resentment about, 148
"roses" analogy of, 158–163
separatists view of, 149–150
"thorns" analogy of, 152–157
viewpoints on, 148–152
Murray, Charles, 13
Muslim Americans, 168–169,
    171, 175, 188–190

NAFTA. *See* North American Free
    Trade Agreement
Nash, Gary B., 43, 57, 63, 75
Natchez, 34, 36
National Association for the
    Advancement of White
    People, 156
National identity, 61–63
National Origins Quota
Act of 1921
    description of, 108
    repeal of, 112–113
Native Americans.
    See also specific tribe
    in Age of Expansion, 85–88
    alcohol use among, 103
    assimilation of, 85–86
    battles with, 69–70
    census of 1790 data, 68
    Christianity conversion by, 85
    clothing diversity among, 26–29
    in colonial America, 48, 55
    Crèvecoueur's omission of, 9–10
    democratic style of, 32–33
    division of labor among, 24–25

in early national period,
    60–61, 69–70
economic disintegration of, 36
European diseases' effect on, 36
expulsion of, 86–87
forced relocation of, 86–88
gender roles among, 24–26
Ghost Dance Religion, 102
housing diversity among, 29–32
in Industrial Age, 102–103
in Information Age, 124–125
language diversity among, 22–24
multiculturalism among, 21–22
Northeastern, 28–29
Northern Plains, 27–28
Northwestern, 27, 33, 36
Oklahoma Territory relocation
    of, 87
pluralism among, 22
population rate for, 138–139
religious values and beliefs, 35–36
reservations for, 87, 102–103
during Revolutionary War, 60–61
social organization diversity
    among, 32–35
social status variations
    among, 33
Southeastern, 28, 34
Southwestern, 27
status and influence
    among, 25–26
stereotypical generalizations about,
    21–22, 37
Tocqueville's writings
    about, 79, 86
tribal governance, 24
tribal locations of, 30
values-related diversity among,
    35–36
Whites' views of, 22
women's role among, 24–26
Naturalization Act, 73
Neidert, Lisa, 12, 19
Neo-Nazis, 156
New Orleans, 80–81, 88
Nigerian immigrants, 121
Nightingale, Florence, 74

9/11
  civil liberties after, 168, 170
  controversial actions after,
      168–169
  description of, 167
  emotional reactions to, 168
  federal government response to,
      168–169
  immigration and, 173–174
  legislation passed after, 168
  local government responses to,
      169–170
  public response to, 169–171
  retaliation after, 170, 175
  social distance after, 171–173
  state government responses to,
      169–170
Nopales, 123
North African immigrants, 124
North American Free Trade
    Agreement, 179
Northeastern Native Americans,
    28–29
Northern European Americans,
    104–105
Northern Plains Native Americans,
    27–28
Northwestern Native Americans
  clothing styles of, 27
  religious diversity among, 36
  slavery among, 33

Ohio River Valley, 60
Olmsted, Frederick Law, 80, 94
Olson, James S., 109, 146
Olson, James Stuart, 54, 57
Oregon, 87
Outgroup
  definition of, 14
  religion effects on prejudice and
      avoidance of, 14–15

Pacific Islanders, 100–101
Panama Canal, 96
Park, Robert E., 7, 18
Parrillo, Vincent N., 75, 145,
    164, 172, 175

Passel, Jeffrey S., 146
Passing of the Great Race, The, 107
Patriot Act, 168, 170
Peaceful Invasions, 182
Perceptions
  description of, 4–5
  factors that affect, 144
  language's influences on, 23
  past, 132
Pietists, 84
Plains Indians, 102–103
Pluralism
  cultural. See Cultural pluralism
  religious, 54
Pluralists, 150–152, 163
Polish immigrants, 116
Politics, in early national period,
    64–65
Population
  foreign-born, 135–137, 144
  immigrants' effect on, 134–135
  U.S., 180–184
  world, 179–180
Populist Party, 98
Prejudice, 143
Protestant Episcopalian Church
    of America, 62
Protestants, 62–63, 188, 190
Pueblo, 31–32, 35
Pueblo Bonito, 29, 31–32
Puerto Ricans, 102, 123
Pulaski, Casimer, 55

Quinn, Arthur H., 75

Race, 186–187
Race and Culture, 7
Racial bias, 130
Racial diversity, 187–188
Racial minorities, 157
Racial profiling, 168–169
Racial tensions, 187
Racism
  description of, 99, 119, 137
  institutional, 157
  multiculturalism and, 156–157,
      162–163

Randolph, John, 47
Ravitch, Diane, 3, 18, 149, 164
Religion. *See also specific*
    religious group
  of African Americans, 89
  democratization of, 53
  in early national period, 62–66
  Great Awakening, 53–54
  outgroup prejudice and avoidance
      because of, 14–15
  in post-Revolutionary War
      America, 62–63
  of slaves, 89
Religious bias, 130
Religious diversity
  in colonial America, 51–54
  future increases in, 188–190
  in Information Age, 125–126
  societal effects of, 126
Religious intolerance, 52–53
Religious pluralism, 54
Religious tolerance, 9, 54, 126
Religious values and beliefs
  among Native Americans, 35–36
  in colonial America, 51
  of Irish immigrants, 83
Reservations, 87, 102–103
Revolutionary Army, 55–56
Revolutionary War
  description of, 43
  early national period after.
      See Early National Period
  Native American alliance with
      British, 60–61
Robert Meyer v. Nebraska, 160
Roosevelt, Theodore, 13–14, 161
Rose, Peter, 6–7, 18
Rourke, Mary, 128
Russell, Howard S., 37

Saltzman, Amy, 127
Sapir, Edward, 23, 37
Schlesinger, Arthur M., Jr.,
    2, 17, 150, 164
Sedition Act, 73–74
Sellers, Maxine, 42, 57
Seminole, 87

Separate pluralism, 149–150
Separation of church and state,
    64–65
Separatist multiculturalists, 149–150
September 11, 2001. *See* 9/11
Shaman, 36
Sherman, William Tecumseh, 74
Shockley, William, 13
Shoshoni, 35
Sikhs, 190
Simon, Rita J., 132, 146, 164
Slavery
  African, 48–50
  in Age of Expansion, 88
  Native American, 33
  statistics regarding, 88
  Tocqueville's writings
      about, 79
Slaves
  cultural diversity among, 48–50
  family structure of, 88–89
  language diversity among, 50
  living conditions for, 88
  musical culture among, 89
  religion among, 89
  in Revolutionary
      Army, 55–56
Smith, James M., 146
Social barriers, 143–144
Social class, in early national
    period, 63–64
Social isolation, 72, 155–156
Social organization
  among Native Americans, 32–35
  in colonial America, 51
Social organizations, 156
Social reality, 23–24
Social stratification, 142
Social structure
  of Chinese immigrants, 90
  in early national period, 63–64
  racial bias in, 157
Society in America, 79
Sojourners, 106–107
Southeastern Native Americans
  caste systems among, 34
  clothing styles of, 28

Southern Colonies, of colonial
America, 48, 50, 54
Southern European Americans,
105–107
Southern states
African Americans in, 88–89
cultural variations in, 88
Southwestern Native Americans, 27
Spencer, Martin E., 146, 164
Spickard, Paul R., 193
Steinberg, Stephen, 8, 18, 40–42, 57
Stoddard, Ellyn R. J., 94
Strand, Paul J., 127
Structural discrimination, 137
Subcultures, 161
Suburbs, 155–156
Syrians, 104

Takaki, Ronald, 151, 163–164
Tecumseh, 61, 70
Terrorism, 174. See also 9/11
"Test Act," 65
Thai immigrants, 119
Tipis, 32
Tipping point, 131
Tocqueville, Alexis de,
78–79, 86, 94, 156
Tongs, 90–91
Treaty of Guadalupe Hidalgo, 91
Triandis, Harry C., 151, 164
Turkish Americans, 124
Turner, Frederick Jackson,
10–11, 18
Twain, Mark, 178
Tyler, Royall, 61

Ulrich, Laurel, 57
United States. See America
Universal cycle theory, 7

Values
among Native Americans, 35–36
diversity of, 35–36
Van Buren, Martin, 46–47
Van Every, Dale, 94
Veltman, Calvin, 78, 94
Vietnamese Americans, 118–119

Virginia, 65
von Steuben, Baron Friedrich
Wilhelm, 55

Wadsworth, Benjamin, 52
War Hawks, 60
War of 1812, 61
Washburn, Wilcomb F., 38
Washington, George, 154
WASP. See White-Anglo-
Saxon-Protestant
Waters, Mary C., 12, 19
Wattenberg, Ben, 191, 193
Wayne, "Mad Anthony," 70
Weatherford, Jack, 38
Webster, Noah, 62, 73, 75
Western European Americans,
104–105
Western Indian Confederacy, 70
White Americans
interracial marriages, 186
population rate for, 138
race relations, 137
White-Anglo-Saxon-Protestants,
66, 177–178
White ethnics
cultural differences among, 142
description of, 7
religious differences among, 142
Whitefield, George, 53
White supremacy, 99
Whorf, Benjamin, 23, 37
Wilkinson, Eliza, 60
Williams, Roger, 52
Wilson, T.P., 193
Winthrop, John, 51
Wittke, Carl, 94, 164
Woloch, Nancy, 57
Women. See also Gender roles
in colonial America, 51, 56
in early national period, 60, 64
educational opportunities for, 115
equality for, 190–191
in Industrial Age, 96–97
in Information Age, 115
Irish immigrants, 83
labor force equality for, 190–191

mainstreaming of, 190–191
in Native American
    culture, 24–26
after Revolutionary War, 60
World population, 179–180
Wounded Knee, 102

"Yankee," 178
Yurok, 35

Zangwill, Israel, 11–12, 18
Zuni, 35